CONTENTS

Scholastic Children's Books,
Commonwealth House, 1–19 New Oxford Street,
London, WC1A 1NU, UK
A division of Scholastic Ltd
London ~ New York ~ Toronto ~ Sydney ~ Auckland

Claudia and Mean Janine
Boy-Crazy Stacey
The Ghost at Dawn's House
First published in the US by Scholastic Inc., 1987, 1988
First published in the UK by Scholastic Ltd, 1990
First published in this edition by Scholastic Ltd, 1998

ISBN 0 590 19879 3

Typeset by Rowland Phototypesetting Ltd,
Bury St Edmunds, Suffolk
Printed by Cox & Wyman Ltd, Reading, Berks.

1 2 3 4 5 6 7 8 9 10

The Babysitters Club

CLAUDIA AND MEAN JANINE

1st CHAPTER

"Coffee's ready!"

"Where's my sweater?"

"Mum! I ironed my blouse last night and now it's wrinkled! How did that happen?"

"I need two dollars!"

"I *said*, the *coffee* is *ready*!"

It was a pretty typical morning at my house. Summer or winter, my parents and sister and I are always rushing off in different directions. Since it was July and school was out, my sister Janine was off to advanced summer courses at Stoneybrook University, I was off to a drawing class, and Mum and Dad were just off to work as usual. The only one who wasn't off to any place was Mimi, my grandmother.

On school mornings, I wake up slowly. Mimi has to prod me to get out of bed, prod me to get dressed, prod me to eat breakfast, and prod me to go out the front door. This is because I don't like school.

In the summer, no one has to prod me. I like holidays and I *love* art classes. I love drawing and painting and crafts.

I am thirteen years old, which means I am now officially a teenager. Mum says that doesn't mean much, because I've always been a teenager. By that, I think she means that I can be difficult to live with. I'm smart, but I don't like school or homework. My family is conservative, but I'm wild. I like loud clothes. I like to dance. I can be a real pain sometimes.

On the other hand, Janine, who is sixteen, has never been a teenager, according to my mother. Janine is clever and likes school. Actually, that's not quite right. She's super-intelligent (a genius), and she doesn't just go to school. She goes, as I mentioned, to college. Well, she takes college courses, but she's still a high school student. She'll be a junior at Stoneybrook High this fall. Anyway, she never gives anybody a bit of trouble. She studies, studies, studies. My parents think she's wonderful. They brag to our relatives about how she's only sixteen and can handle college work. They expect her to become something really important like a physicist.

Janine wears clothes that are pretty boring. When she outgrows them and passes them along to me, I pass them right along to Kristy Thomas or Mary Anne Spier, who live across the street. They don't care too much about clothes, but I wouldn't be caught dead in Janine's things. I'd rather have to pay for all new clothes with the money I earn baby-sitting than wear Janine's free but yucky button-down shirts, grey kilts, and crew-neck sweaters.

Do you get the feeling that Janine and I are different from each other?

To be frank, my sister and I have next to nothing in common. I'm outgoing and have a lot of friends; Janine sticks to herself and has almost no friends. (That's what happens when your parents want you to be a physicist.) I've already had two semi-boyfriends; Janine, quite possibly, doesn't know what boys are. I have lots of interests: reading mysteries, baby-sitting, painting, and drawing; all Janine cares about is her computer.

I can hardly even talk to Janine. She uses such big words, it's like talking to a *dictionary*. Sometimes she teases me about not being as clever as she is. Mum says she does that because underneath, she wishes she were a little like me, with friends and interests and stuff, and feels left out of our family. Mum also says that I'm not fair to Janine sometimes—that inside, Janine is sensitive and loving, and creative in her own way, but that I don't see those things because I won't look beyond the big words. Also, I wouldn't admit this to just anybody, but I have a feeling I'm a big disappointment to my parents. Brains are important to them, and I want to be an artist, not a scientist. I've tried to tell them you have to be clever to be a good artist, but they're not convinced. So, okay, I'm a teeny weeny bit jealous of my sister. She can *always* make our parents happy.

Anyway, on that busy Wednesday morning, I finished dressing in my favourite art class outfit—black jeans, a giant bright blue T-shirt, and a snake bracelet that I wore above my elbow—and ran downstairs. I was the second one into the kitchen.

Mimi greeted me in her gentle way. "Good morning, my Claudia," she said softly. I hardly notice Mimi's accent any more, but she does have one. Our family is Japanese, and Mimi, who is Mum's mother, didn't come to the United States until she was in her thirties. I'm surprised she speaks English as well as she does, I mean, considering that for half her life she spoke only Japanese.

"Morning, Mimi!" I replied.

Mimi was fixing breakfast. (She was not, however, the person who'd been yelling about the coffee earlier. That was my father. Every morning, he comes downstairs as soon as he stumbles out of bed, and gets the coffee going pronto for himself and Mum. They practically can't see without a little caffeine in their bodies. Mimi and I drink herbal tea.)

I sat down at my place at the kitchen table. A few moments later, Mum joined me, then Janine, and then my father. Mimi served up the scrambled eggs she'd made, and sat down next to me.

"This is lovely, Mother," said my mum to Mimi. "Honestly, I don't know what we'd do without you."

"Me, neither!" I added.

"And I do not know what I would do if I did not have you to take care of," said Mimi earnestly.

Mimi has been living with us since before I was born. My grandfather, Mimi's husband, died not long after my mum and dad got married.

"And what is everybody going to do today?" asked Mimi.

"The usual," replied my father cheerfully. "Oh, but I'll be a little late tonight," he added. "We have a five-thirty meeting this afternoon. It may go on for a while." Dad is a partner in an investment business in Stamford, Connecticut, which is not far from Stoneybrook.

"The usual for me, too," said Mum. Mum is the head librarian at the local public library. This has been a big boon to Janine, who needs books the way most people need food and water. It has not been much help to me, since the only books I read are mysteries. My favourites are Nancy Drews, which the library doesn't have, and which I have to hide from my parents. They think Nancy Drews aren't worthwhile.

"I," said Janine, "have one class this morning and two this afternoon. I believe I'll spend the day on campus. I can work at the computer library between classes."

"What a thrill," I murmured. Janine tried to make everything she did sound important and wonderful.

"Claudia," warned my mother.

Janine looked hurt. "Well, what are *you* going to do today?" she asked me. "Re-invent the wheel?"

"Ha, ha." Janine can't even make a joke. "No," I said. "I'm going to drawing class this morning. After lunch I'm going to baby-sit for Jamie Newton for a couple of hours. Then Stacey and I are going shopping, and then I have a meeting of the Babysitters Club."

"Oh," said Janine in a small voice. She looked a little wistful.

The Babysitters Club is something Kristy Thomas (from across the street) thought up. She and I and three other girls have this club that is really a business. Kristy is our chairman. We earn money baby-sitting for the families in our neighbourhood. Three afternoons a week we hold half-hour meetings in my bedroom. (I have a phone.) Our clients call us during those times to tell us when they need baby-sitters. Then Mary Anne Spier checks the calendar in our

Babysitters Club Record Book to see who's available, and we call the parent back to say which one of us will be sitting. The parents like this arrangement because they only have to make one phone call to reach five girls, so they're pretty much guaranteed a sitter. It saves them time.

I'm the vice-chairman of the club.

Mary Anne is the secretary. She's in charge of our record book, where we keep track of our clients, their addresses and phone numbers, our appointments and stuff like that. Mary Anne is perfect for the job. She's well organized and clever, and she has the neatest handwriting of anyone in the club. I've lived across the street from Mary Anne for as long as I can remember, and although I like her, I still feel I don't know her very well. Mary Anne's on the shy side, and she and Kristy have always been best friends.

Our club treasurer is Stacey McGill. She keeps track of the money we make. Stacey moved to Stoneybrook about a year ago, and she and I got to be really good friends. We're very much alike. Stacey's from New York, where it's okay to be wild. I don't think anyone from New York could ever be boring.

Then there's Dawn Schafer. Dawn joined the Babysitters Club a few months after Kristy, Mary Anne, Stacey and I started it. She's also a newcomer to Connecticut. She and her mum and brother moved here from California after her parents got divorced. (Her mum grew up in Stoneybrook.) Dawn and Mary Anne quickly became good friends, and Mary Anne was the one who got Dawn into the club.

For ages, Dawn wasn't an officer of the club because the rest of us were filling the four main posts. Then Kristy made her the official alternate officer, which means that she can take over for anyone who has to miss a meeting.

At first, Kristy was pretty jealous of the friendship between Mary Anne and Dawn, but she likes Dawn now. Besides, Kristy's had plenty to think about. Our club chairman was just in a wedding—her own mother's! Kristy's parents got divorced several years ago, and Kristy and her mum, her two big brothers Sam and Charlie, and her little brother David Michael had done okay on their own. But when Mrs Thomas met this man, Watson Brewer, the two of them fell in love and finally got married. Kristy was the bridesmaid.

I went to the wedding. It was wonderful. Kristy wore a long dress, and shoes with heels, and flowers in her hair. It was very romantic. The one bad thing about the marriage is that the Thomases have to move. They're not going far—just into Watson's house, which is across town—but it will cause some problems for the

Babysitters Club. For instance, Kristy has to travel three miles to get to our meetings. We're hoping her brother Charlie will be able to drive her, even if we have to pay him.

I was shaken out of my daydreaming by the sound of dishes clattering in the sink. Breakfast was over. Mum and Dad were clearing the table. Janine was swallowing the last of her orange juice. Quickly, I finished my scrambled eggs.

"So," said Janine, out of the blue, "may I ask how your agency plans to function once your founder is residing in a different district?"

"You may," I replied, stalling. I had no idea what she was talking about.

"Oh, I understand," said Janine. "You want to play games. Well, I'll comply. All right, how *does* your agency plan to function once your founder is residing in a different district?"

"Huh?"

"I *said*—"

"Janine, talk in English, will you?"

"I *am*!" Janine looked hurt again. "I can't help it if this is the manner in which I speak."

"And I can't help it if I don't understand you."

"Oh, never mind," said Janine. She sighed. It might have been a sad sigh, it might have been an exasperated one. I couldn't tell. "I was simply trying to uphold my end of a meaningful conversation with my sibling."

"You were trying to *what*?"

"*Talk to you*!" exploded Janine.

"Well, why didn't you just say so?"

"I *did*." Janine stood up. "Very well. Have fun drawing and baby-sitting and shopping." How did Janine always manage to make me feel that I couldn't do anything worthwhile?

"And you have fun talking to machines!" I yelled after her as she left the kitchen.

Janine mumbled something that sounded like, "At least they communicate with me." Now what was that supposed to mean?

It was another happy morning at the Kishis'.

As I left the house a little while later, Mimi put her arms around me and said, "Have fun today, my Claudia."

"I will," I replied, giving her a kiss.

Janine watched us from the front garden. Then she looked away. When her ride came along, she got into the car without even waving to us.

2nd CHAPTER

I'm the first to admit it—I'm a junk food addict. I like sweets. I like biscuits. I like all sorts of things that are bad for you. I stock up on the stuff I like and stash it around my room. Since my Nancy Drew books are also hidden, I have to know a lot of good hiding places. If anyone were to search my room, they'd find cakes in the desk drawer, liquorice in my pencil case, *The Clue of the Tapping Heels* and *The Message in the Hollow Oak* under my mattress, M&M's in my jewellery box, and *The Clue in the Crossword Cipher* at the bottom of a box of art supplies.

To get ready for our Babysitters Club meeting that day, I got out the M&M's. I also got a box of twiglets from the kitchen. They were for Stacey and Dawn. Stacey's diabetic and can't eat sweets, and Dawn's into health food. I don't think twiglets are particularly healthy, but I suppose they're better than M&M's. I also set out our record book, and another book that Kristy insists we keep up-to-date—our Babysitters Club Notebook, which is a sort of diary. We're supposed to record every single baby-sitting job in it, and then read it about once a week so we know what's going on at the homes where the other club members have baby-sat.

At five-fifteen, my friends started to show up. Stacey was first. She walked proudly into my room, looking smug.

"I didn't know you were going to get your hair cut!" I exclaimed when I saw her.

"I decided not to say anything," Stacey replied. "I wasn't sure how I'd look. Do you like it?"

"I love it! Did you get it permed again?"

"Yup. But after this I might let the perm grow out."

Stacey sat on my bed. Her blonde hair, which had been long and fluffy, was now cut to just above her shoulders. It made her look older.

"Gosh," I said, "maybe I should get my hair cut."

"Oh, don't!" cried Stacey. "Your hair is amazing. How long did it take you to grow it to that length?"

"Years," I admitted.

"It's so beautiful. Don't you dare touch it!"

"Touch what?" asked a voice. Dawn was

standing in my doorway.

"Speaking of long hair . . ." said Stacey.

"Hi, you guys." Dawn came in and eased herself onto the floor. She had to swing her hair out before she sat down. That's how long *her* hair is. And it's white-blonde.

When Dawn and I stand next to each other, we look kind of like a photograph and its negative.

"Her hair," Stacey said, answering Dawn's question. "Just because I got mine cut, Claudia—"

"Aughh!" shrieked Dawn. "I didn't even notice. Oh, Stace, it looks fantastic!"

"Thanks," said Stacey, grinning.

A few moments later, Kristy and Mary Anne showed up. Mary Anne joined Dawn on the floor. We'd all been leaving my director's chair for Kristy. She likes to sit in it and take charge. Sometimes she wears a visor, or sticks a pencil over one ear. Anything to make her stand out as our chairman.

"Okay, baby-sitters," said Kristy, after she and Mary Anne had oohed and aahed over Stacey's haircut. "Business first. Stacey, what's in the treasury?"

Stacey had brought a rumpled manila envelope along with her. "Give me your subs first, you guys," she said.

We each forked out a dollar.

Stacey put the money on the bed and emptied the contents of the envelope over it. "Nineteen dollars exactly," she announced.

She said this after one pretty quick glance at the bills and change, which is why she's our treasurer.

"Not bad," said Kristy. "Well, I have two interesting pieces of news, speaking of the money. One is that Charlie passed his driving test today."

"Yea!" cheered the rest of us.

"The other is that I asked him about driving me to the meetings and to sitting jobs in this neighbourhood after we move to Watson's."

"Yes?" I said eagerly. The whole future of the club depended on whether Kristy could get to the meetings.

"I offered to pay him a dollar for each trip he had to make—that means two dollars for every meeting."

Mary Anne, Stacey, Dawn and I were practically biting our nails. We had discussed the amount of Kristy's offer endlessly. Would Charlie laugh at a dollar? Would he even want the job of driving Kristy all over town? It was important to us because we had decided to pay Charlie out of the clubs subs. We didn't think it was right to ask the chairman of her own club to pay for car rides when no one else had to.

"And," Kristy went on, "he said a dollar is too"—I groaned—"much!" she cried. "He said fifty cents each way is plenty!"

"All right!"

"So we don't have to worry. The problem

is solved. And cheaply!"

The phone rang then, and I picked it up. "Hello, Babysitters Club."

"Hello, this is Dr Johanssen."

"Oh, hi," I said. "It's Claudia."

"Oh, Claudia. I need a sitter for Friday evening next week. Mr Johanssen and I are going to a cocktail party. We'll need someone from six until about eight."

"Okay, I'll call you right back."

I got off the phone. "That was Charlotte's mother," I told the members of the club. "She needs someone from six to eight, a week from Friday."

Mary Anne checked the calendar in the record book. "You and Stacey are free," she announced.

I looked at Stacey. "You go," I said. "Charlotte really likes you. You're her favourite sitter."

"Thanks," said Stacey. "That's great. I haven't seen her in a while."

I called Dr Johanssen back to tell her that Stacey would be sitting. Then we took a few more phone calls.

When the phone finally stopped ringing, Kristy said, "You guys, I have an idea."

I raised my eyebrow. Kristy has more ideas than anyone I know.

"Yeah?" said Stacey, sounding slightly suspicious.

"See, I thought last week went pretty well," Kristy began.

Kristy was referring to the days before her mother's wedding when, believe it or not, the members of the Babysitters Club had taken care of fourteen children. What had happened was that all these friends and relatives of Kristy's mother and Watson Brewer had shown up to help them get ready for the wedding. Only they brought their kids along, since they were coming from out of town and were planning to stay until the wedding was over. Mrs Thomas knew the kids would just be in the way while the adults were trying to cook and stuff, so the club members sat for all of them for five days at Kristy's house. It really had gone well. We were very proud of ourselves.

"*I* think we did a good job," I agreed cautiously.

"Well, I got to thinking," Kristy went on. "Here it is, the summer holidays. We're out of school, the children we sit for are out of school, and at least until next month when two of us are going away, there isn't much to do around here. In other words, there are a lot of kids at loose ends."

"Yeah?" said Stacey for the second time. We all wanted Kristy to get to the point.

"So how about a play group?"

"A what?" asked Dawn.

"A play group," Kristy repeated. "We could easily run one this month. It'd be great for the kids."

"But when would we baby-sit?" asked Mary Anne.

"Oh, in the afternoons and evenings. And weekends," Kristy added. "We'd just hold the play group a few mornings a week. It could be outdoors, in somebody's garden, just like last week at my house. We could tell all our regular customers about it, and they could send their kids over any time they wanted. We could charge, say, three dollars per kid per morning. That's a bargain for our clients, and even divided five ways, the money should be good for us, since chances are there wouldn't be enough jobs for every single one of us to be sitting if we *weren't* holding the play group."

"It *would* be kind of fun," I said. "Just think, all the kids we sit for would get to know each other."

"Yes!" said Mary Anne. "We can ask Jamie Newton, the Pikes, Jenny Prezzioso . . ."

"The Barrett kids," added Dawn.

"Nina and Eleanor Marshall," I suggested.

"Charlotte," Stacey offered.

Kristy's eyes were gleaming. She was glad we liked her idea. "As soon as we get it all worked out, we'll call our clients," she said excitedly.

"We can entertain the kids just the way we did last week," I pointed out. "Art projects, stories, games."

"Their parents will like that," said Kristy thoughtfully.

"Hey!" I exclaimed. "Remember when Jamie Newton had to spend one morning with all the kids last week? His mother said she thought it would be good for him because it would help him learn to get along with other children. Maybe other parents will like that, too."

"Good point," said Kristy. "Hey, Mary Anne, maybe you'd better take notes. We might want to remember this stuff."

Mary Anne began scribbling in the notebook.

"Where should we hold the play group?" Kristy asked. "We can't have it at my house. We'll be moving soon. We better not have it at your house, either, Mary Anne, since your dad works. I think the parents would want to know that an adult was around."

"Good point," said Dawn. "I guess I'm out, then. Mum's still looking for a job. She could find one any day."

"I'd love to have it here," I said, "but I don't know. Mimi has seemed awfully tired lately."

"Is she all right?" asked Mary Anne quickly.

"Fine. She just lies down a lot."

"My house would be okay, I think," said Stacey. "And Mum is usually around. I'll have to check with her, but I'm sure it'll be all right."

"Stacey's house?" Kristy asked the rest of us.

We nodded.

Our newest business had a home.

3rd CHAPTER

As soon as Mrs McGill gave Stacey permission to use their house, my friends and I decided to spend one afternoon talking to our clients about the play group in person. We thought the door-to-door approach would be nicer than just a flier stuck in a letterbox, and nicer even than a phone call. So after lunch one day, the five of us set off.

We *did* have fliers with us. We had spent a long time writing the flier, making sure it included all the information parents would need to know. We planned to hand them out in person, though, and then stay around to answer questions.

This is what our flier looked like:

SUMMER PLAY GROUP

Give your kids a treat!
Art projects, stories, games!
Come to the Babysitters Club
Summer Play Group!

Place: Stacey McGill's backyard
612 Fawcett Avenue
Time: 9:00–12:30—Mondays,
Wednesdays, Fridays during July
Cost: $3 per child per morning

For further details, call:
THE BABYSITTERS CLUB
KL 5–3231
Mondays, Wednesdays, Fridays,
5.30–6.00

SUMMER PLAY GROUP:
the unique alternative to baby-sitting.

Our first stop was Jamie Newton's house. We found four-year-old Jamie, his mum, and his baby sister, Lucy, in the front yard.

"Hi-hi!" called Jamie when he saw us.

"Are you here to baby-sit me?"

"No," I said, laughing. "Five baby-sitters! What would you do with five baby-sitters, Jamie?"

"Have *lots* of fun," he replied cheerfully.

"Hi, Mrs Newton," said Kristy. "Hiya, Lucy."

Lucy is only about seven months old. She's adorable. She can sit up, and she knows how to crawl. Not very fast yet, but she's getting there. She gave us a big grin, and we could see that a couple of new teeth were coming in.

Lucy was sitting on a blanket next to Mrs Newton, teething on a biscuit and playing with a colourful set of plastic rings.

"Hello, girls," said Mrs Newton. "Goodness, it's the whole club. What's going on?"

"This," replied Kristy, and she handed Jamie's mother one of our fliers.

Mrs Newton read it carefully. "What a wonderful idea!" she said when she was finished. "You certainly are ambitious, girls."

"We thought it would be fun," said Kristy.

"And a good experience for the children," added Dawn, trying to sound adult.

"I couldn't agree with you more," replied Mrs Newton. "Jamie starts nursery school in September. This will be perfect for him. He's not around kids his own age much, and

I'm afraid school will be sort of a shock for him. If he can at least get used to sharing before he goes to school, that'll be a step in the right direction."

"Great!" I said. "So we can count on Jamie? I mean, he doesn't have to come every time. You don't even have to let us know whether you'll bring him or not. But you're interested?"

"Definitely. He'll be there."

The other club members and I managed to wait until we were safely out of sight of the Newton's house before we let out little shrieks of excitement.

"Let's go to the Pikes' next," suggested Mary Anne. "Then we can go to the Prezziosos' and the Barretts'. They're all in that neighbourhood."

We quickened our pace.

"I bet the Pikes will want to send Claire and Margo," said Stacey as we walked along, "and maybe Vanessa and Nicky. Mallory and the triplets are probably too old." (There are eight Pike kids.)

"I'm sure Mrs Barrett will want to send Buddy and Suzi," said Dawn thoughtfully, "but I don't know about Marnie. I'd love to have her, but she's not even two years old. That's kind of little."

What nobody was saying (or at least what no one except Mary Anne was saying) was that we hoped Mrs Prezzioso wouldn't want to send four-year-old Jenny, either. Mary

Anne's the only one who likes her. If you ask me, Jenny is a big fat brat. With a capital B.

Kristy rang the Pikes' doorbell, and Mallory answered it. Mallory, the oldest Pike, just had a birthday, and is eleven. She's very good with her younger brother and sisters. I bet she'll be a baby-sitter herself one day.

"Hi, Mal," said Kristy. "Is your mum here?"

"Yeah, she's out the back. Hold on a sec." Mallory yelled for her mother, then let us into the living room. "What's up?" she asked. "How come you're all here?—Did one of the triplets do something?"

I giggled. "No. Why?"

"Oh, I don't know. Usually, one of the triplets *has* done something. And when you open the door and see a whole posse of baby-sitters, you think . . ." Mallory shrugged.

"You think trouble?" asked Kristy.

"Yup."

My friends and I talked to Mrs Pike and left one of our fliers with her. Mallory seemed interested in the play group, but before we had left, she walked off glumly.

We looked questioningly at Mrs Pike. "Is Mallory okay?" asked Mary Anne.

Mrs Pike nodded. "She's at a funny age, though. She thinks she's too old for some things and too young for most others. I'm sure she'd like to come to the play group, but feels she's too grown up for it."

"Maybe," said Kristy, "she could come for free and be our helper. I don't think we can afford to pay her. But if she wanted to be a sort of baby-sitter-in-training, we'd love to have her. She's always a help."

"That's a lovely idea!" said Mrs Pike. "I'll talk to her about it. I know she'll be delighted. And," she added as the members of the club were leaving, "I'll probably be sending Claire, Margo and maybe Nicky to the play group every now and then."

"Great!" we said. "Thanks, Mrs Pike."

The next stop was the Barretts', but they weren't home, so we left a flier in their mailbox. The three Barretts are Buddy (eight, and a good friend of Nicky Pike), Suzi (four), and Marnie (one, but closer to two). Their parents are separated and Mr Barrett has moved out, so the kids are having a rough time. Sometimes they can be a handful, but basically they're nice.

We went on to the Prezziosos'. I'm sure Kristy, Stacey and Dawn were praying that no one would be home there, either. I know I was. But when Mary Anne rang the bell, Mrs Prezzioso answered it.

She was all dressed up, which wasn't unusual. She likes her family to look as if they're getting ready to pose for a fashion magazine.

"Hello, girls. What may I do for you?" asked Mrs P. primly. And then, before one of us could answer, she dropped her voice and whispered, "Our little angel is asleep, so we must keep our voices down." (The little angel is Jenny.)

Mary Anne stepped forward. We had asked her to do all the talking at Jenny's house. "We wanted to let you know," she whispered, "that we're starting a play group."

"A what?" Mrs P. leaned over, cupping a hand around one ear.

"A play group. And we think it would be perfect for Jenny."

"You think what?"

"We think it would be perfect for Jenny. Here, take a flier."

"A what?"

"A flier." Mary Anne handed her one.

Mrs P. skimmed it. "I suppose the art projects would be a bit messy, wouldn't they?" Mrs P. was holding the flier by one corner as if it were a wet painting that was going to leap onto her white suit and smudge it.

"Well, some might be," I admitted, since I was in charge of art projects. "But . . . um—"

"But we provide smocks," Kristy broke in.

"That's right—smocks," I repeated.

"It sounds nice. I'll have to think about it," Mrs P. said.

We couldn't wait to get out of there.

"Okay, call us if you have questions," said Kristy.

We went to a few more houses, and then we gathered in my room.

"You know," said Kristy, "I hadn't thought about things like smocks. I wonder if we're forgetting anything else."

"Let's see," said Mary Anne, flipping through the notes she'd been making. "Two picnic tables will be set up in Stacey's yard. We'll each bring our own Kid-Kit with us, so we'll have books and games and puzzles and stuff. Claudia, what kinds of art supplies do you have? Maybe we should buy some things."

"It might be a good idea," I said. "I don't want to use up *all* my materials. And I don't have any paper or crayons right now.

"Well," Stacey spoke up, "there's money in the treasury, and I guess that's what it's for."

"Right," agreed Kristy. "So if we buy some art supplies, Mary Anne, what shape are we in?"

"I think we're all set," she said.

And I couldn't help adding, "Ready to roll!"

Our play group would begin in just a few days.

4th CHAPTER

On Sunday evening, the night before the first session of tne Babysitters Club's play group, my parents went out to dinner. They left Mimi and Janine and me on our own which we don't mind at all. Mimi usually makes a special meal—not a Japanese meal, but one that we like and don't get to eat very often.

As soon as Mum and Dad had left, Mimi and I went into the kitchen.

"What shall I make tonight, my Claudia?" Mimi asked.

"Mmm," I said thoughtfully. "We could have spaghetti and meatballs, or we could have breakfast-at-dinner, or—"

"Or I could prepare tiny pizzas."

I laughed. "Mini-pizzas, Mimi," I said. "They're called mini-pizzas."

"That I will never be able to say," replied Mimi, "for Minnie is the mouse. It does not make sense."

"Mouse pizzas!" I exclaimed.

It was Mimi's turn to laugh. "I have an idea," she said. "Would you like a special breakfast-at-dinner? I could prepare waffles in the waffle iron."

(Mimi pronounces *iron* the way it's spelled: eye-ron.)

"Oh, yum! We haven't done that in months! Do we have toppings?" I asked.

"We have butter and syrup and whipped cream and fresh strawberries."

"Oh, boy!"

"Would you please ask your sister if she wants waffles, my Claudia?"

"Okay," I replied. I knew Janine would want waffles. She always goes along with whatever the rest of us have decided.

I found Janine in her room. She was in front of her computer, naturally. A future physicist has to work hard.

"Do you want waffles for dinner?" I asked her abruptly. "That's what Mimi and I chose."

Janine looked up from the keyboard. "You already chose waffles?" she repeated. (I'd just said so, hadn't I?) "Sure. Waffles are fine. How come you didn't ask me what I wanted?"

"I'm asking you now."

"They're fine," Janine said again. Sighing, she turned back to the computer.

I stuck my tongue out at her and ran downstairs.

"Waffles are fine!" I told Mimi.

"Very good. Would you set the kitchen table, please? I will start making the batter."

We went to work. I love to help Mimi in the kitchen. I don't know why Janine doesn't. Of course, we hardly ever remember to ask her.

Soon the table was set. I poured glasses of orange juice and spooned out little bowls of leftover fruit salad. Then I called Janine to the table.

Mimi had put the waffle eye-ron by her plate. She would make the waffles right at the table. The eye-ron was big and old-fashioned. I loved to watch Mimi work it. She would turn it on, then test it with water to see if it was hot enough. If the drops of water bounced off the skillet, it was ready. Then Mimi would brush it with butter, pour on some batter, and close the lid. *Hissss*! Somehow she always knew just when to lift the lid for a perfect golden-brown waffle.

Mimi started cooking and we started eating. When we'd each eaten one waffle, Mimi began again.

"Boy," I said, as the eye-ron hissed, "I have a big day tomorrow."

Janine looked up with interest. "What are you going to do?"

"First of all," I said, "our play group starts in the morning."

"I trust you are prepared for it, both financially and phy—"

"We're all set," I said, cutting Janine off.

"Tell us again how your play group will work, my Claudia," said Mimi.

"Well," I said, "it's kind of like a nursery school. It will run from nine till twelve-thirty on Monday, Wednesday and Friday mornings. Anyone who wants to bring their kids by for the morning is welcome to. We won't have an attendance list or anything. We just plan to keep things . . . um . . ."

"Flexible?" suggested Janine.

"Loose," I said, frowning at her.

"Oh."

"Anyway," I went on, "we've told the Newtons, the Pikes, the Barretts and all our regular customers about the play group. And we'll have arts and crafts and story-time and stuff. I think everyone will have fun."

"And Janine, what do you plan to do tomorrow?" asked Mimi.

Janine took a large bite of waffle. "The usual," she replied. "School."

"You are enjoying your computer studies?"

"Oh, immensely," said Janine. "Programming is so logical. And once you master the basics, it can be . . . um . . ."

"Boring?" I suggested.

"Thrilling." Janine gave me a dirty look.

"What are you doing tomorrow, Mimi?" I asked.

"I am not certain, my Claudia. I was invited to a tea, but I have been a little tired. I will see how I feel tomorrow."

"Mimi, you should rest more," I said.

"Yes, you should," added Janine. "You work awfully hard. And you *look* tired."

"Do not worry about me," said Mimi. "Who would like another waffle?"

"Me!" I replied.

"*I*," said Janine.

"Well, it's not like she didn't know what I meant," I said. "Me, I, what's the difference?"

"The difference is that in the case of an indirect—"

"Girls, that is enough for now," said Mimi gently. "What would you like to do after our breakfast-at-dinner?"

"Watch TV," I said.

"Well, I was going to do some more work," said Janine, "but maybe—I mean, if you both want to, we could play Trivial Pursuits."

"You are willing to play with us?" Mimi asked Janine, looking as surprised as I felt.

"Yes," she said. "If you *want* to," she repeated hesitantly.

"I would like to play," said Mimi. "How about you, my Claudia?"

I absolutely hate Trivial Pursuits. I'm no

good at it, and Janine knows it, which may be why she asked us to play. I'm not a good student, and I don't care about history or geography or science. What I like are my mysteries and art. There are questions in Trivial Pursuits about art and literature—about paintings and books and stuff—but they're really difficult. I bet hardly any of them are about Nancy Drew.

However, I knew Mimi would want me to play, so I agreed to.

We cleaned up the mess from our breakfast-at-dinner and set up the game on the kitchen table. Janine chose a blue playing piece, Mimi chose yellow, and I chose red. We rolled the dice. I got to go first.

I managed to land on a space for a literature question.

Janine pulled a card from the box. "The McWhirter twins originated the idea for what book?" she asked. "Hey, you know this one, Claudia! It's easy."

"It is not. And I do not. Know it, I mean."

"Yes, you do. You have this book in your room. You really like it."

Well, now I was feeling stupid. See why I hate this game?

"*The Phantom of Pine Hill*," I said sarcastically.

"No!" cried Janine. "Be serious. Come on!"

"Janine, tell Claudia the answer, please," said Mimi. "She does not know it."

"It's *The Guinness Book of World Records*, silly."

"It's *The Guinness Book of World Records*, silly." I mimicked her.

Janine ignored me. "My turn!" She rolled the dice and landed on a geography space.

Mimi read her a question. "The equator passes through what three South American countries?"

"Ecuador, Brazil, and Colombia," replied Janine without even thinking. And also managing to say them with a perfect Spanish accent.

What did she do—memorize all five thousand game questions?

Janine rolled again. And again and again and again. She answered one question after another and was halfway to winning before it was Mimi's turn.

Mimi got three right in a row.

My turn again. Unfortunately, I landed on a history spot. That's my worst subject of all.

"Who was known as The Little Corporal?" asked Janine.

I hadn't the vaguest idea. "Kermit the Frog," I replied.

Janine made a face at me. "No. Napoleon Bonaparte." She didn't even check the answer on the back of the card.

"You're making that up!" I accused her. "Show me the card!"

Janine showed me. "See? It *was* Napoleon Bonaparte."

(Who was Napoleon Bone-apart?)

Janine's turn. She went around and around the board, and then managed to land in the special space for her final question.

"Goody. We get to choose the category," I said to Mimi. "Let's give her sports."

"All right," said Mimi, smiling.

I pulled out the next card. "What was Babe Ruth's actual name?"

"Oh, easy," said Janine. "It was George Herman. That's it. I won!"

"Cheater!" I cried. "You looked! You must have looked!"

"I did not," Janine retorted. "I just knew it."

"Nerd!"

Janine slammed the board shut and walked off in a huff.

"Claudia," said Mimi, "that was not nice. It was not called for."

"But Mimi!" I couldn't think of anything to say. Mimi was right. Janine hadn't cheated and I knew it. Janine would never cheat. "Mimi . . . Oh, you just take Janine's side because she's cleverer than I am. Mum and Dad love her more because she's more clever, and I bet you do, too!"

Mimi closed her eyes. "I am very tired, Claudia. I think I will go to bed now."

"But it's only eight o'clock," I said.

"Good-night, Claudia."

Mimi rose and walked slowly towards her bedroom. She closed her door.

5th CHAPTER

I felt terrible. I sat at the kitchen table and stared at the folded-up game board and the scattered playing pieces. Mimi was hardly ever cross with me.

After a while, Janine came back. "Where's Mimi?" she asked.

"She's gone to bed."

"Oh. Well, I wanted to say that in case you're wondering, I won't tell Mum and Dad about *The Phantom of Pine Hill*."

"Huh?"

"You made a mistake earlier."

"While we were playing the game? Yeah, you're right. I made lots of them."

"What I mean is that when I asked you about the book the McWhirter twins originated, and said that you have a copy of it in your room, you answered the question with, '*The Phantom of Pine Hill*'. Now, you know that Mum and Dad don't permit you the

Nancy Drew serial, so you are probably regretting the fact that you accidentally admitted that a book from that serial is in your room. I just wanted to assure you that I will not report this to Mum and Dad. I'm also assuming that Mimi knows about Nancy Drew and has agreed to a pact of silence. Is that correct?"

I wasn't entirely sure what Janine was saying. I had a lot of food hidden in my room, but no cereal. And until Janine brought it up, I hadn't even realized what I'd said about Nancy Drew. However, I decided that "thanks" might be a safe answer.

"Thanks," I said.

"You're welcome. Am I right about Mimi? She knows about Nancy Drew?"

I sighed. "You're right. But you're wrong about the cereal."

Janine looked confused. Then she sat down across from me and shook her head. "Goodness," she said.

"What?"

"I—sometimes I wish I were as close to Mimi as you are."

"Well, maybe if you'd leave your computer alone for fifteen minutes, you'd be closer to all of us. You act like you're married to that thing. Does it make a nice husband?"

Janine rolled her eyes. "That's ridiculous!"

"Oh, so now I'm stupid *and* ridiculous!" I shouted.

Janine opened her mouth, but before she could say anything, we heard a heavy thud. It sounded as if it had come from the first floor, not too far away. Over at Kristy's, the thud could have been her collie, Louie, letting himself inside, or one of her brothers fooling around. But we don't have any pets, and the only person at home was Mimi.

My eyes met Janine's.

Without a word, as if we were acting as one person, we leapt up from the table and dashed out of the kitchen and through the dining room and living room to Mimi's closed door.

Janine knocked on it.

Right up until that moment, I didn't think anything was *really* wrong. I was sure we would hear Mimi answer, "Come in," maybe sounding a little cross.

But there was no answer.

"Maybe she's already asleep," I suggested.

"Maybe." Janine opened the door a crack, just wide enough for us to see that Mimi's light was on.

"Mimi?" Janine said.

Still no answer.

Janine opened the door all the way.

I screamed.

Janine gasped.

Mimi was lying on the floor in a heap.

Before she fell, she must have been getting undressed to go to bed, because she was wearing only her blouse, her slip, and her stockings. Her shoes were lined up neatly next to the wardrobe door.

"She's been murdered!" I shrieked.

"No she hasn't," said Janine. "But I think she's had a heart attack or something."

"Is she dead?" I asked.

We both knelt next to Mimi. She looked so little, all crumpled on the floor. Her eyes were shut, and she was as white as a sheet.

Janine took her wrist in one hand. "I can feel her pulse! Claudia, call nine-nine-nine."

There was a phone on Mimi's nightstand. I lunged for it and called the emergency number. "My grandmother has had a heart attack!" I blurted out as soon as someone picked up the phone.

"Tell them she's unconscious," said Janine.

"She's unconscious," I said. "Please hurry." I gave the person our name, address, and phone number, and hung up.

"What should we do?" I wailed.

Janine bit her lip. She was still holding Mimi's hand, patting it gently. "I don't think we're supposed to move her," she said, "but we should keep her warm. Let's cover her with her bathrobe and try to put her slippers on. Then I'll stay in here, and you go and wait outside so you can show the ambulance where to come."

"Okay," I replied. I got Mimi's robe and fuzzy slippers out of her wardrobe. Janine put the slippers on while I covered Mimi. Then I ran outside and stood impatiently on our front step.

I heard the siren long before I saw the ambulance. At last the ambulance screeched into our drive, and the attendants hopped out and wheeled a stretcher up the path in what seemed like two seconds.

"Hurry!" I said. "She's inside. I'll show you where."

I banged through the front door with the attendants at my heels.

"Thank goodness," said Janine when she saw us, but she stayed where she was, sitting with Mimi, until the attendants lifted Mimi onto the stretcher.

"What happened?" one asked me.

"I'm not sure," I replied. "She said she was tired and wanted to go to bed early. So she came in here, and a little while later we heard a thump. My sister and I ran in and found her lying on the floor. We didn't move her," I added, "and we tried to keep her warm."

"You did just fine," said the man.

"What do you think is wrong?" Janine asked him. She glanced worriedly at Mimi's small, still form on the stretcher as the attendants checked her vital signs. "I guessed a heart attack, but perhaps she fell. Or it's possible that she has a head injury."

"I don't think so. There's no sign of trauma to the head," the attendant said. "But don't worry. She's breathing fine, which is a good sign. We'll find out soon enough what's wrong."

While we'd been talking, the attendants had been wheeling the stretcher towards the front door, and we'd been trailing along behind. They whisked Mimi outside and down the front path.

"One of you want to come with us?" asked the attendant. "By the way, where are your parents?"

"They've gone out for the evening," Janine replied. "They should be home soon. Claudia, perhaps I should ride with Mimi and you should remain behind to wait for Mum and Dad. You could also try phoning them at *Chez Maurice*." She turned to the attendant. "When they reach the hospital, should they go to the emergency room?"

"Yes," he replied. "If she's not there any longer, the receptionist will know where she's been taken."

"All right, Claudia?" Janine asked me. "Try the emergency room first." She acted like I was three years old or deaf or something.

"Okay, okay."

The next thing I knew, the ambulance was gone. I felt like sitting down right on the front path and crying. Instead, I went inside, looked up the number for the *Chez Maurice* restaurant, and dialled it. I must have dialled too fast, though, because the voice that answered said, "Hello, the Arnolds' residence." I hung up and tried again. This time, a perky voice said, "*Bon soir, Chez Maurice.*"

"H-hello?" I said. "My name is Claudia Kishi and my parents are having dinner there—I mean, at your restaurant. There's an emergency and I have to talk to them."

"I am *trés* sorry, but zey have just left."

"Are you sure?" I asked. "The Kishis? I mean, the Kishi party?"

"*Certainement.*"

I hoped that was French for certainly.

"Okay. Thanks," I said.

"*Bon nuit.*"

I walked all around our house, thinking. I decided that it would take Mum and Dad only about fifteen minutes to get home, unless they decided to go somewhere else first. I wandered into Mimi's room, and hung up her skirt and put her shoes in the wardrobe. It occurred to me that she would probably have to stay in the hospital at least overnight, so I found her smallest suitcase and opened it on her bed.

Suddenly I had something to do. I moved quickly, tossing in her nightgown, toothbrush, toothpaste, a Japanese book she was reading, her glasses and a few other things. To remind her of home, I added the special haiku poem written in Japanese that hangs over her bed.

Then I locked the house and sat down on the front step with Mimi's suitcase in my lap. I looked across the street. Both Kristy and Mary Anne's houses were dark. I knew that if they'd been home, they would have come over as soon as the ambulance had driven up.

I waited and waited. All I could think about was my argument with Mimi. I had been mean to her and then she'd had a heart attack. I wondered if you really could give a person a heart attack.

At last I spotted my parents' car down the street. I raced to the end of our drive and waved frantically to them. When Dad slowed down, I flew into the car, explaining what had happened. Mum grew silent. She didn't say a word as Dad sped through the streets of Stoneybrook.

We reached the hospital in record time. The nurse in the emergency room directed us to the intensive care unit. We took the slowest lift in the entire world to the fourth floor. When we stepped out, we found Janine in the hall. She was pacing back and forth, wringing her hands, and she'd been crying.

"They won't tell me a thing!" she

exclaimed as my parents rushed up to her.

Dad found a nurse and talked quietly with her. Then the four of us sat in a lounge at the end of the hall. My mother couldn't speak. Every time she started to say something, tears filled her eyes and she choked up. Dad held her hand and kept trying to tell her that everything would be okay.

"I've never seen Mum so upset," I whispered nervously to Janine.

"Well, Mimi's her mother," she replied. "We'd be pretty upset if Mum had to be rushed to the hospital."

I nodded. At times like this, Janine didn't seem so bad after all.

A little while later, a doctor came to the lounge. "It was a stroke," he told us. "A serious one. She's in a critical but stable condition. At the moment, she's not able to move or speak, but I've seen people make remarkable recoveries following strokes. We won't know much more for the next twenty-four to forty-eight hours. She's not awake now, and there's nothing you can do for her, so I suggest that you go home, try to get some rest, and come back in the morning."

With heavy hearts, we turned around and went home.

6th CHAPTER

Monday

Today was a good news–bad news day for us baby-sitters. The good news was that ten children came to the first session of our play group and it went really well. The only real problem was Jenny Prezzioso. I should have known. She's a pain. Buddy Barrett, Nicky Pike, and David Michael are kind of wild when they get together, but they're manageable. We're going to have to do something about Jenny, though. Got any ideas, Mary Anne?

The bad news was about Claudia's grandmother, Mimi. It turns out that she had a stroke last night and is in the hospital. The news kind of upset us, but we were able to put our worries aside and run the play group okay, which I guess proves that we're professionals.

Well, as Dawn said, the play group got off to a great start. The baby-sitters gathered at Stacey's house at eight-thirty. I felt really guilty going, since Mum and Dad were leaving for the hospital to be with Mimi, but Mum had called intensive care to find out how she was doing and the nurse said she was still unconscious. So my parents didn't see any reason for Janine or me to go with them.

Because of all the upset at my house, I was the last one to arrive at Stacey's. I decided I should tell the club members the bad news right away. There was no point in holding it back, and they had a right to know.

When I walked into Stacey's garden, a boxful of art supplies under one arm, I found everybody busy. Stacey, wearing a pair of knee-length lime-green shorts, matching green high-topped trainers, and a large white T-shirt with a gigantic taxicab on the front, was setting up benches at the two picnic tables. Mary Anne and Kristy, much more casual dressers, were each wearing blue jean shorts, running shoes and T-shirts. Mary Anne's shirt, though, was pretty, with a scoop neck and lace edging on the sleeves, while Kristy was wearing an old grey thing that had probably once belonged to Sam or Charlie. It said BOHREN'S MOVERS in faded black letters across the back. Dawn, in a surprisingly New York kind of outfit (she usually goes for California casual), was wearing striped trousers with braces over a red shirt. The three of them were going through the contents of their Kid-Kits, pulling out story-books and board games.

"Hi, you guys," I said.

Mary Anne, the most sensitive of all of us, must have been able to tell I was upset just be looking at me, because she immediately said, "What's wrong, Claud? Are you all right?"

"Can you guys come here for a sec?" I replied. "I have to tell you something."

My friends all know Mimi well, since the meetings of the Babysitters Club are held at my house. Kristy and Mary Anne know her really well, just because the three of us have grown up together, but Mary Anne is especially close to her because her own mother died years ago. The news was going to upset them all.

Everyone dropped what they were doing and ran to me.

"What is it?" asked Stacey.

"I have bad news," I said, "and I thought you should know right away. Mimi had a stroke last night."

Mary Anne gasped, and Dawn gripped her hand.

"She's okay," I said quickly. "I mean, she can't move, but she's breathing, and the doctor said it's possible she can make a good recovery. We just have to wait and see."

Everyone except Mary Anne relaxed a little. "Can we visit her in the hospital?" she asked, her voice quavering.

I shook my head. "Not yet, anyway. She's in intensive care. Maybe when she's moved to her own room in a different wing."

Mary Anne's lower lip began to tremble.

"Hey!" I said. "I just had an idea. The kids could make get-well cards for Mimi today. Most of them have at least met her."

"That's a great idea!" Kristy chimed in. "We'll combine an art project with . . . with . . ."

"With learning to care about others," said Dawn. "Perfect. The parents will love it. And more important, Mimi will love the cards."

We felt cheered, and rushed around getting the last things in order. Just before nine o'clock, Kristy gathered us together and said, "I thought we should have a schedule for the day—a loose one. Since it's the first day, we'll just sort of see how things go. Anyway, if this is okay with you guys, I thought we'd start off with an hour and a half when the kids can do whatever they want. Then we'll have music for about twenty minutes, then our snack"—we'd bought canned juice and crisps—"then stories—maybe one for the older kids and another for the younger ones—and then a group thing, like a game of hide-and-seek or something. If there's any time left before twelve-thirty, they can just play on their own again."

That was Kristy, always in charge. We agreed that her plan sounded good.

"And," continued Kristy, "I think I know who our first kid is going to be."

"Who?" we asked.

"David Michael."

"David Michael!" I exclaimed. "That's great but why is he coming over? He's got your brothers and your mum, and besides I thought he'd had enough of kids after the week with your cousins over at your house."

"He had," said Kristy, "but Sam and Charlie have summer jobs, and Mum's trying to get the house packed up. Besides, there may be some boys his age here. Nicky Pike or someone."

"Well, fine," I said. And at that moment, David Michael walked uncertainly into the McGills' garden, clutching three dollars in one fist.

Shortly after David Michael arrived, Charlotte Johanssen came over. Then Mrs Newton walked Jamie over.

And *then* Mallory Pike showed up with her brother Nicky and her three sisters, Claire, Margo, and Vanessa, plus Suzi and Buddy Barrett and Jenny Prezzioso.

"Mum told me I could help you," Mallory said proudly. "So I started by walking the kids over. I told them about crossing streets and stuff."

"That's wonderful," said Kristy.

"What should I do now?" asked Mallory.

Kristy explained the schedule to her. "Why don't you just kind of keep an eye on the kids while they're playing? You know, stop any fights, or suggest things to them if they seem bored."

"Okay."

Now before I tell you about the trouble that Jenny caused, I should mention how the kids were dressed that morning. Most of them were dressed kind of like Kristy and Mary Anne—in T-shirts and shorts or blue jeans. Suzi Barrett was wearing a faded sundress and Claire was wearing short overalls over a striped shirt. Every last one of them was wearing trainers.

Except for Jenny Prezzioso.

Jenny was wearing a pale pink, spotlessly clean party dress with puffed sleeves and white smocking across the front. On her feet were lacy white socks and pink shoes.

The very first thing that happened that morning was that Jenny skidded and fell on her knees. I have to admit that for just a second I was more worried about the grass stain on the hem of her dress than I was about her knees.

"*Wahh*!" wailed Jenny, not even crying real tears.

"Why don't you take your shoes and

socks off?" I suggested. "It's a nice warm day. You won't slip so much in bare feet."

"No," said Jenny stubbornly. "I want to look pretty."

"But when you fell down you got dirt on your dress. See?" I pointed to the grass stain.

Jenny looked at it, considering. Then she looked at her shoes.

"I don't want *to take off* MY PINK SHOES!" she screeched, her voice growing louder with every word.

"Okay, okay, okay."

But that was just the beginning. Jenny didn't know how to share. She wouldn't cooperate with the other children. She said she wanted to play by herself, but when the other kids left her alone, she complained bitterly.

"Nobody likes me," she wailed. She was sitting at a picnic table making a get-well card. She lowered her head onto her arm, the picture of despair.

A blue crayon rolled across the table, heading for her lap.

I dived for it and caught it before it landed on her dress.

"But Jenny, you said you didn't want to play with them," I pointed out.

"*Well, I do now*!"

"So go and play."

"I can't. I'll get my dress dirty."

I rolled my eyes. Jenny was what Mimi

would call "a trial". But apart from Jenny, the kids had fun at the play group that morning. And they made a total of nineteen cards for Mimi.

That afternoon I baby-sat for Jamie Newton and his baby sister, Lucy, while Mrs Newton ran errands and went to a club meeting. I was glad I had so many things to do. Being busy kept my mind off Mimi.

I loved taking care of Jamie and Lucy. The Newtons had been practically the first clients of the Babysitters Club. But Jamie was the only little Newton at the time. Then Lucy was born. All of us club members had wondered how Jamie would react to a new baby in the house. We were sure he'd be jealous. And he was a little bit, but only sometimes.

Now the Newtons were planning a big party for Lucy's christening. The party was coming up soon.

"Look at this stuff. Look at all this stuff," Jamie said to me after his mother had left. He led me into the dining room. "Mummy is getting ready to give a party, a big one. And it's all for *her*." Jamie nodded his head toward the first floor, where Lucy was taking her afternoon nap.

The Newtons did seem to be getting ready for a very large party. The dining room table was covered with boxes of crackers, cans of peanuts, tins of sweets, stacks of napkins; plus glasses, silverware, plates, a punch bowl and cups, serving spoons, and more.

"You know what?" I asked. "When you were Lucy's age, your parents gave a great big party after your christening."

"They did?" Jamie brightened. Then he frowned. "But I don't remember it!" he said loudly.

"Shh." I put a finger to my lips. "The baby—"

"I know," said Jamie sullenly. "The baby is sleeping."

Uh-oh, I thought. This doesn't look good.

But when Lucy woke up a little later, Jamie was the first to hear her crying. He leapt up from the floor, where we were playing a game of snap, and ran to her room. I followed. When I caught up with him, I found him standing by her crib, one arm between the slats, patting her on the back and saying softly, "Claudy's here. Claudy's here. You can stop crying now, Lucy. Claudy's here."

It was a nice scene. I filed it away in my memory.

I got Lucy dressed and gave her some juice, and then I suggested that we take a walk. Jamie wanted to go over to my house. He likes my art supplies, but he also likes Mimi, and I think what he really wanted was to see for himself that she was actually gone. I wasn't sure how much "in the hospital" meant to him.

So I put Lucy in her pram, and we walked to my house.

"Is Mimi here?" asked Jamie as I was unlocking the front door.

"Nope. Remember—I said she's in the hospital. She's sick."

Jamie mulled that over and went on to a different subject. "Is anybody here?"

"Just us," I told him. "Want to look at my paints?"

Jamie shook his head. "Let's play outside."

I sat on the lawn and played with Lucy while Jamie turned somersaults in the grass. Presently a car pulled up and Janine got out.

" 'Bye!" she called to her driver. "See you tomorrow!"

Jamie ran over to me as the car drove away. "Who's that?" he whispered.

"That's Janine, my sister. You know her."

Jamie decided she was safe. "Hi-hi," he said to Janine.

"Hello, Jamie," she replied. She looked at Lucy and me. "Hi, Claudia . . . Oh, look at you, Lucy. You're so big!"

"How was school?" I asked.

Janine sat down and began playing pat-a-cake with Lucy. "It was very exciting," she replied. "Physics and astronomy are a fascinating combination of science—"

"J*anine*," I exclaimed, irritated.

"What?" She let go of Lucy's hands.

"I don't believe you!" I exploded.

"*What*?" Janine said again. She stood up.

I stood, too, and we faced each other.

Jamie looked on with interest.

"You didn't even ask about Mimi," I accused her. "Or about Mum."

"You didn't give me a chance. You inquired how school was. Besides, I know how both of them are. I phoned Mum from the campus this afternoon. There's no appreciable difference in Mimi. And Mum's . . . well, she's all right."

"Why didn't you tell me?

"I repeat—you did not give me a chance."

"Janine, you are so mean!"

Janine glared at me. Then, to everybody's surprise, I actually raised my hand as if to hit her, but I dropped it quickly. (Jamie was now wide-eyed with fascination. He was looking back and forth between Janine and me.)

Janine shook her head. Then she stomped into the house.

"Mean Janine," I muttered. "Come on, Jamie. Let's go."

Janine had spoiled my whole afternoon.

7th CHAPTER

When I finished at the Newtons', I ran home and just made it in time for the meeting of the Babysitters Club. I found Kristy and Mary Anne waiting on the front step, their chins in their hands.

"Why aren't you guys inside?" I asked. "You know you can always go to my room if I'm late."

"We didn't think anyone was here," said Kristy gloomily.

"Well, you're almost right," I said. "The only one here is Janine."

"No Mimi," said Mary Anne.

"Nope. No Mimi," I said.

The Monday afternoon meeting of the Babysitters Club was sort of glum.

"What are we going to do about Jenny?" I asked when everyone had arrived. I searched my hiding places and found a bag of winegums which I passed around.

"She does cause problems," agreed Mary Anne.

"She starts fights with the other kids," Stacey pointed out. "Sometimes she doesn't even mean to, but she does anyway. By not sharing or something. I saw Claire Pike ask Jenny for a red crayon that she wasn't using. When Jenny wouldn't give it to her, Claire got mad, turned around, and whacked Suzi Barrett."

"If we could at least get her mother to dress her in play clothes, it would be helpful," said Kristy. "One of us should talk to Mrs Prezzioso."

"Yes, *one* of us should," I said pointedly. We all looked at Mary Anne.

"*Me*?" she squeaked.

"You're the only one who likes her," Kristy said bluntly.

Mary Anne made a face. "But she doesn't *have* any real play clothes. I know that for a fact. Maybe we should just make her wear one of the painting smocks all morning."

The phone began to ring then, and we stopped to set up some appointments. By the time we'd finished, we'd half forgotten about Jenny.

"You know what would usually happen right about now during a meeting?" Mary Anne asked. She went on without waiting for an answer. "Mimi would come in for some reason—to ask us if we needed anything, or to remind us not to eat too much before dinner."

"Yeah," I said. "I think I'll call Mum at work and see if anything's going on." Kristy has this rule about not making personal calls during club meetings, but I knew she'd let me break it. I didn't even bother to ask if it was okay.

I picked up the phone and dialled my mother's office at the library.

"Hello!" called a voice.

"Mum?" I asked.

"Claudia?"

"Mum?"

"Hey, dope, your mum's *home*!" Kristy said, nudging me in the ribs and grinning.

I dropped the phone. "Mum?" I could hear her coming up the stairs.

My mother appeared in the doorway. "Hi, girls," she said. She looked awfully tired.

"How's Mimi?" I asked right away.

"Good news. She just woke up. She can't move or speak yet, but she's awake."

"Wonderful!" exclaimed Kristy.

"Can I see her?"

"Yes. Family members may see her one at a time for about ten minutes each. We'll go back to the hospital after supper. Speaking of which, Claudia, I'll need your help with supper tonight. I'm afraid we've all got awfully used to having Mimi take care of us." Mum began to sound sort of teary again.

The meeting broke up soon after that, and I joined my mother in the kitchen. "Where's Janine?" I asked. "Can't she help, too?"

"Oh, I didn't even bother to ask her," replied Mum distractedly. "I'm sure she's busy with her schoolwork."

And what did my mother think the Babysitters Club was, I wondered. A game? But I didn't say anything. I looked through the freezer. "Here are some frozen chips. And here are some beefburgers. We could heat these up."

"Fine," said Mum. "Help me make a salad, honey. Then we'll be ready."

After our makeshift dinner, Mum and Dad and Janine and I drove to the hospital. The closer I got to Mimi, the more worried I became. All I could think about was the mean way I had behaved. I clutched the nineteen get-well cards in my hands and kept hearing my ugly words over and over again, and Mimi's quiet voice telling me good-night. She hadn't called me "my Claudia", so she really must have been hurt. What would I say when I saw her?

"Mum, can Mimi hear us?" I asked.

"Well, that's a silly question," said Janine.

Dad glanced at her in the rearview mirror. "I'd be interested in your answer,

Dr Kishi," he said.

"The answer," said Janine, "is, of course she can hear us."

"According to the neurologist, the answer is, we think she can hear us, but we're not sure how well."

"Oh," said Janine quietly.

"Why did you want to know, Claudia?" Dad asked.

"I . . . I just wanted to be sure she could hear me when I—when we talk to her."

We drove on in silence.

At the hospital, Mum and Dad led Janine and me to Mimi's room.

Mum went in first, looking as nervous as a cat.

"Can I please go in next?" I begged, when she came out.

"*May* I," Janine corrected me, glancing warily into the room.

I ignored her. I don't think she was even aware that she'd said it.

"Sure," Mum answered me. "Watch the clock on the wall, honey, and stick to the ten-minute time limit. The nurses are strict about that. And don't be frightened. There's a lot of equipment in the room. Just remember that it's there to help Mimi."

I crept into the room. It was dim and quiet except for the hum of machinery. Mimi was hooked up to a couple of things with TV screens on the fronts. There were no pictures on the screens, though. Just lighted dots that kept zigzagging from one side to the other. Next to her bed was a stand with a plastic sack of clear liquid at the top. A tube ran from the sack down into a needle that was stuck into Mimi's wrist. I shuddered.

Mimi looked like a little doll lying in the metal bed with the scary machines around her.

I tiptoed over to her bed. "Mimi?" I whispered.

Mimi's eyes were open, but she wasn't quite looking at me.

"Mimi?" I whispered again.

Nothing. The same dull stare. It was spooky.

Too spooky. I couldn't stand her eyes. So I backed away. I backed all the way out of the room, knocking into the wastebasket as I went.

"Claudia?" said my mother. "Are you all right?"

"You go, Janine," I said, ignoring Mum's question.

I stood by the doorway holding the nineteen get-well cards, and watched Janine. Mum stood right behind me with her hand on my shoulder.

I saw Janine's face as she took in the machines. I saw her eyes widen as she took in Mimi's blank stare. But Janine stayed where she was. She began talking to Mimi just as if they were sitting across from each other over cups of tea. She talked quietly to her for the full ten minutes. I wish I could have heard what she was saying.

When Janine came out, Mum looked at me, wordlessly asking if I wanted to go in again.

I shook my head. Then, tears welling up in my eyes, I fled down the hall to the lounge and sat in front of the drink machines until it was time to go home.

The next evening, we went back. I'd spent all day talking to myself, saying things like, "Don't be selfish" or "Don't be a baby. Mimi needs you."

So the second time I went into her room, once again bringing the get-well cards, I was prepared. I tried to ignore the dim light and the humming machines. And I tried to remember Mimi the way she was before the stroke.

I looked around the room.

In a corner was a wooden armchair with vinyl cushions. I pulled it next to the bed and leaned over. I forced myself to look into Mimi's eyes.

"Hi, Mimi," I said.

She blinked her eyes, but that was all. Had she heard me? How awful not to be able to wave or smile or anything.

"Mimi, I'm only allowed to stay for ten minutes," I told her. "So I'll tell you what's been going on." I paused. "Well, we had our first play group. Do you remember what that was?"

Mimi blinked her eyes, but I noticed that they were focused somewhere on the ceiling.

"Well, you probably do. Anyway, it went fine. And guess what the art project was. The kids made get-well cards for you. They were all very sorry to hear that you're in the hospital. A lot of the kids made two or three cards. I brought them with me. This one is from David Michael. See?" I held it up. "It says, 'Get will soon Mini.' And this is from Margo Pike. She's just learning to write, so the letters spell 'HGDOMYLSP,' but she translated for me, and they mean, 'Please feel better. I hope you can come home soon. Love, Margo.' She drew a picture of a fireman for you. And Buddy Barrett made this one: 'Der Claudi's granmohter plese fell better verry soon and com back becase we want you to plese fell better verry soon. Yours truly, Hamilton Barrett, Junior.' It took him twenty minutes to write that. I showed Mimi the rest of the cards. Then I said, "I think we'll put them over here on the windowsill. They'll kind of cheer up the room."

I lined the cards up. It was hard to keep thinking of things to tell Mimi. I wasn't used to one-sided conversations. Kristy wasn't used to one-sided conversations. Kristy would have done fine, since she could talk the ear off a donkey, and Janine had done okay the night before, but I'm not a big talker. If I knew for sure that Mimi could hear me it would have been a little easier, but she wasn't giving any signs. The only movement I'd seen was when she blinked her eyes.

Her eyes! I had an idea.

I stood up. "Hey, Mimi," I said, leaning way over and looking right into her eyes. "If you can hear me, blink your eyes."

Mimi blinked.

I gasped. But maybe it was just an accident. She'd been blinking a lot already.

I tried something else. "Mimi, if my name is Claudia, blink *two* times."

Mimi blinked twice.

"You *can* hear!" I exclaimed. "Oh, wow! Now we can talk! Mimi, this will be our code. One blink means yes. Two blinks mean no, okay?"

Mimi blinked once.

"Do you like your get-well cards?" I asked.

One blink.

"Do you know you're in the hospital?"

One blink.

"Mimi, my ten minutes are almost up, but I have to tell you something really, really important. I . . . I'm sorry I yelled at you the other night. I didn't mean what I said. I love you very much, and I'm sorry. Do you understand?"

One blink.

"Oh, I wish I could hug you," I said tearfully, "but I don't see how. Too many machines and tubes. Okay?"

One blink.

Mum was signalling to me from the hallway. I had to leave. I rushed out and told everyone about the blinks. Dad got hold of a doctor, and Mum ran in to "talk" with Mimi. It was exciting.

Still, when we returned home that evening, we were silent and sad. It was awful that Mimi had to talk by blinking her eyes. And the doctors still didn't know how much better she would get.

I wandered around my room for a while, and then decided I wanted some company. Mum and Dad were on the phone with relatives, so I peered into Janine's room. She was at her computer. The keys were clackety-clacking away a mile a minute. The funny thing was, she looked like she was crying a little, but when I called to her, she didn't answer. I guess she couldn't hear me over the noise.

8th CHAPTER

Wednesday

Well, Karen Brewer strikes again. Leave it to Karen. When she's around, things are never dull. Today was the second session of our play group and Andrew and Karen came to it. Watson's ex-wife needed a last-minute sitter for them, so she called Watson and he decided to drop them off at Stacey's.

In the past, Karen has scared other kids with stories about witches, ghosts, and martians. Today, she had a new one — a monster tale. But it was a monster tale with a twist, as you guys know. I'm not sure there's anything we can do about Karen. The thing is, she usually doesn't mean to scare people. She just has a wild imagination.

But, oh boy, when Karen and Jenny got together . . . .

I'm sure glad Kristy likes Karen Brewer so much, since they're stepsisters now. And I like Karen myself, but she's a handful! She's not the unpleasant kind of handful that Jenny is, but she's still a lot to manage.

Anyway, as Kristy said, Karen and Andrew needed last-minute looking-after, so Watson dropped them off at Stacey's. They were a little late, and were the last ones to arrive at the play group.

We had almost the same group of kids as we'd had on Monday. Mallory came over with Claire, Margo and Nicky (but not Vanessa); Jenny; and Buddy Barrett (but not Suzi). David Michael, Charlotte, and Jamie all showed up. And so did Nina and Eleanor Marshall, two little girls the club sits for sometimes. Nina is four and Eleanor's two. Eleanor was the baby of the group, but she seemed to have fun.

When Karen and Andrew arrived, the kids (except for Jenny) were playing happily. Charlotte, Claire and Margo were making collages by gluing foil stars and coloured tissue paper onto pieces of cardboard. Nina was looking at a book with Eleanor. Buddy, Nicky and David Michael were roaring around, playing something Nicky had invented called Blast into Superspace. And Jamie was building with his Lego, which he'd brought over.

Mallory was helping out at the art table, but what were the five of us baby-sitters doing? We were gathered around Jenny, trying to convince her to put on a smock. The smock was a shirt that had belonged to Stacey's father. It was old but clean, and in perfectly good condition. Jenny refused to wear it.

The day before, Mary Anne had somehow found the courage to phone Mrs Prezzioso and suggest that she dress Jenny in play clothes. And today Jenny had shown up in Mrs P's idea of play clothes, a brand new white sundress with ruffles around the bottom, trimmed with pale pink ribbon and white lace, and brand new white sandals. The sandals were the fancy kind, more like shoes with holes punched on top in a pretty design.

We baby-sitters were horrified.

"All in white!" Stacey had moaned. She clapped a hand to her forehead.

"And the dress is freshly ironed," added Dawn, awestruck.

"These are play clothes?" cried Kristy. "Look at the other kids: shorts, shorts, shorts, blue jeans, shorts, shorts, overalls"—that was Eleanor—" shorts, jeans, very old sundress"—that was Margo. "And all of us and Mallory are in, well, *fairly* old clothes." (Some of us looked nicer than others.)

"Come on, Jenny," I said. "Just put the smock on."

"No."

"Why not?"

"This is my new dress. I want everyone to see it."

"We've all seen it. It's beautiful," I told her. "And if you put the smock on, you can keep your dress beautiful—all nice and clean like it is now." I held the smock out to her.

"*No.*"

"Look, this can be *your* smock," Stacey suggested. "Your special smock. Nobody else will have one like it. Claudia could even put your name on it."

This is what was going on when Karen and Andrew showed up.

Karen marched jauntily into the garden, with Andrew several steps behind her.

I was relieved to see that both were wearing shorts. And trainers.

"Here we are!" Karen announced gaily. (Watson had phoned Kristy earlier to say that they'd be coming.)

"Hiya, Karen. Hi, Andrew," said Kristy. She turned away from Jenny to give them each a hug. When Kristy stood up Karen peered around her and spotted Jenny.

"Who's that?" she asked, frowning.

"That's Jenny Prezzioso," Kristy told her.

"How come she's all dressed up? Is she going to a birthday party?"

"This is my new dress," Jenny said proudly. She whirled around, making the ruffles fan out. "Isn't it pretty?"

"I don't know," replied Karen. She narrowed her eyes. "You'll have to keep it awfully clean."

"So what?" said Jenny.

"So what?" Karen mimicked her.

It was time to step in. "Karen," I said, "David Michael's over there." I pointed him out. "Why don't you go play with him and his friends?"

Karen glanced at Jenny again. It was instant hatred, I could tell. I've seen it happen before. It was like that with me and Beverley McManiman in fourth grade. We were enemies the entire year.

"Okay," said Karen. She started to walk away. But as she left she called over her shoulder—*very* casually—to Jenny, "Watch out for the monster." Then she kept on walking.

"What monster?" Jenny cried.

"Karen," Kristy said warningly.

Karen kept on walking, as if she hadn't heard them.

"What monster?" Jenny shrieked. She ran after Karen.

"Hey, come back!" I called. "Your smock!"

Now Jenny was pretending not to hear.

Since Karen was older than Jenny and had longer legs, she reached David Michael quickly.

I looked at the other club members as Jenny hurried to catch up with Karen.

"Now what?" I said.

"Oh, let them go," replied Dawn.

"But Jenny's dress—"

"Maybe we should just let it get dirty," said Mary Anne unexpectedly.

We looked at her in surprise. That was a very un-Mary-Anne-like thing to say.

"Well, what does Mrs P. think goes on at a play group?" she asked.

"Yeah," I said. "And what does Jenny *do* all day when she's at home? Doesn't she ever get dirty?"

"We have our reputations to think about," said our chairman nervously. "If Jenny goes home with a ruined dress, Mrs P. might be really upset. She might tell Mrs Pike and Mrs Pike might—"

"*Eeee*!"

"What was that?" I asked.

Before we could find out who had shrieked—and why—David Michael ran up to us and said breathlessly, "What's big and red and eats rocks? A big, red rock-eater, that's what!"

We looked at the group in the corner of the garden. They seemed fine. David Michael had run back to them, and the three boys and Karen were talking earnestly, probably telling jokes (although we couldn't be sure). Jenny listened from a few feet away.

"We can't worry about Jenny all day," I pointed out. "We'd better get to work."

Kristy joined Jamie with his lego, Mary

Anne sat down with Nina and Eleanor, and Dawn and Stacey wandered over to the kids at the art table.

I decided to keep an eye on the entire group. That was when I noticed Andrew. He was still standing at the entrance to Stacey's garden.

"Hey, Andrew," I said, approaching him.

Andrew looked at his feet and dug the toe of one trainer into the grass. He's very shy.

"Andrew, does anyone ever call you Andy?" I asked.

"Mummy calls me Andy-Pandy," he said.

"Would it be all right if I called you Andy?"

He nodded.

"Good," I said. "Let's go and see what your sister's doing." I took Andrew by the hand and led him towards the group of kids. I thought that all of them looked kind of frightened.

"What's going on, you guys?" I asked brightly.

The kids looked up. They saw Andrew and me, and they all began screaming. Then they ran away.

"What on earth?" I exclaimed.

"Monster!" shrieked Jenny.

Andrew and I ran to her.

Jenny let out another shriek. "Get that boy away from me!" she cried, pointing to

Andrew. "He's a monster!"

"Oh, Jenny," I said, "A *mon*ster? Where did you get that idea? He's just Andrew."

"No, no! He turns into a monster! She said so." Now Jenny was pointing to Karen.

"Oh, brother," I said. "Karen, come here right this minute."

Karen crept over. She stopped about fifteen feet away from me.

"Come *here*," I repeated.

Karen shook her head. Then, "What time is it?" she asked.

"Almost ten o'clock. Why?"

"Because," replied Karen, trembling, "Morbidda Destiny put a spell on Andrew last weekend. At ten o'clock today he's going to turn into a monster."

Andrew looked up at me and smiled. "Grrrrrr," he said.

"Aughhh!" screamed Karen, Jenny, David Michael and most of the kids in the garden. They'd all been listening. They didn't know that Morbidda Destiny was a weird old neighbour of Karen's whom Karen thought was a witch. But they believed that Andrew was going to turn into a monster.

Kristy glanced at me and shrugged.

"All right," I said, looking at my watch. "In a few seconds it will be ten o'clock. Let's count down together, and you'll see that Andrew is just Andrew."

"Ten," I said, "nine, eight"—the kids joined in nervously—"seven, six, five, four, three, two . . . *one*!"

"*Aughh*!" The kids had all covered their eyes and were screaming.

"Hey, Kristy. Whistle," I told her.

Kristy put her fingers in her mouth and let loose with an ear-blasting whistle. Everyone stopped screaming. They looked at Andrew.

"*Don't growl*," I whispered fiercely to him. Andrew obeyed.

Slowly, things returned to normal. Jenny, however, seemed quite subdued. Later, Andrew saw us sitters fussing with Jenny about her smock again. "Put it on," he told her impatiently.

Jenny's eyes grew wide. She grabbed for the smock.

I grinned. "Andy," I whispered, "tell her to wear it every time she comes to Stacey's."

"Grrr," said Andrew. "You wear that . . . wear that every day."

"Okay," said Jenny. "Okay."

Across the garden, I saw Karen cover her mouth with her hands and giggle.

9th CHAPTER

One evening, when Mum and Dad came home from work, Mum was grinning. She looked like somebody who knew a secret.

"Hi, honey," she said. "Oh, you started supper! Thank you. That's wonderful."

"You've been acting very responsibly lately," Dad added.

Responsibility is sort of a touchy subject with my parents and me. For as long as I can remember, I've heard, "If you'd just do your homework when it's assigned . . ." or, "If you'd be on time for once . . ." or, "If you'd just think ahead the way Janine does . . ."

And now Dad was telling me I was acting responsibly. Well, it was true that I'd started dinner several times recently, and I'd spent a lot of time with Mimi in the hospital. On the other hand, I'd given Mimi the stroke in the first place. I'd lost my temper and been rude to her. That certainly wasn't very responsible.

"Hey, Mum, how come you're smiling?" I asked. "Something happened, didn't it?"

"I'll say," she replied. "Where's your sister?"

"Guess."

"Working at her computer."

"Well, close. She's upstairs studying, or at least she was earlier. Do you want me to get her?"

"Please. Dad and I will finish getting dinner ready."

I ran upstairs. Janine's door was closed, so I knocked on it.

"Come in!" she called.

"Thanks for helping me with dinner," I greeted her sarcastically.

Janine frowned. "You didn't tell me you were starting dinner. I would have helped if I'd known."

"Well, you have a watch, don't you? It's six o'clock. Couldn't you have guessed?" But I felt bad. It was true. I hadn't asked Janine for help, and I didn't make dinner every night, so why should she have known?

"Have you come into my bedroom merely to torment me?" asked Janine. "Or do you have some other purpose?"

"Some other purpose," I mumbled.

Janine was seated at her desk. Three fat textbooks were open in front of her. A half-filled sheet of lined paper was in her hand.

At her feet were several balls of crumpled paper. She glanced at the paper in her hand, as if she couldn't bear to keep her eyes off it for very long.

"Well?" said Janine.

"Mum said she had good news. She wants us to come downstairs right away."

"Very well."

Janine placed bookmarks in her texts and slid the paper into a folder. Then she followed me to the kitchen.

Mum and Dad were just dishing up the supper I'd started, which was frozen carrots (I mean, formerly frozen carrots), a lettuce salad, and baked chicken.

"Claudia says you have some news," Janine said, slipping into her chair.

"Yes, we do," replied Mum. She waited until the four of us were seated. Then she went on. "As you know, at first Mimi couldn't move at all, though she has been able to move her left side a little bit recently. Well, today, using her left hand, she actually fed herself part of her lunch, *and* she tried to speak. Several times."

"Oh, boy!" I cried. "That's great! Isn't it?"

"It was good enough to get her out of intensive care," said Dad, smiling.

"Where is she now?" asked Janine. She was smiling, too. In fact, we were all smiling. We probably looked sort of goofy.

"She's in a normal room," Dad replied.

"A private one."
"Can we visit her tonight?" I asked.
"*May* we?" Janine, Mum, and Dad all corrected me at once.
"*Sheesh*," I said. "*May* we visit her?"
"We certainly may," said Mum.
With that, dinner was eaten in a jiffy. Janine had looked busy before, but we didn't hear a peep from her about having to finish any work. She helped me pick a bouquet of flowers from our back garden for Mimi, and then the four of us were off to the hospital.
Mum and Dad showed Janine and me to a different wing on the same floor as the intensive care unit where Mimi had been. This time, we could all go in to see her at once.
Mimi looked much better. There was no needle stuck in her wrist, and most of the machines were gone. Also, she was sort of sitting up (actually, the folding bed was making her sit up), and someone had washed and fixed her hair.
When we filed into the room, Mimi tried to smile and got about halfway there. Then she raised her left hand in greeting.
"Hi, Mimi!" I cried. "You can wave! That's great!" I rushed to one side of the bed and kissed her cheek.
Janine stood on the other side of the bed, while Mum and Dad sat in chairs.
"Are you feeling better?" I asked Mimi.

She blinked her eyes once.

"Good," I said.

"Mum said that you are partially able to feed yourself," Janine spoke up.

In answer, Mimi raised her left hand again and wiggled the fingers.

I glanced at Mum and Dad, wondering whether it would be all right to say anything about the fact that Mimi had tried to speak. I wanted to tell her how great that was, but before I could say anything, Mimi made a gurgling sound in her throat.

Janine and I both leaned forward quickly.

"What did you say?" I asked.

More gurglings. Then a sort of "mmm" sound.

I looked helplessly at Mum, who got to her feet and came over to the side of the bed.

"I'm sorry, Mother," said Mum. "We couldn't quite catch that."

"Maybe she could write it down," I suggested.

"I don't know," said Mum. "She's not left-handed."

"I think we ought to attempt it," said Janine. "Perhaps it would work."

"All right," said Mum. She looked at Mimi. "Mother, do you think you could write down what you want to say?"

Mimi frowned slightly, then blinked once.

"Here," said my father, standing up. "I've got a pad and pencil."

"I think she'll need something bigger," I said.

Everyone looked at me. "Why do you think that?" asked Dad curiously.

"I just—just do." I've had enough trouble in school to know what will be easy, and what will be difficult.

"I'll see what I can find," said Dad.

He headed for the nurses' office and returned with a couple of pieces of notebook paper. Janine propped Mimi's arm up on the little table that slid across the bed. She put Dad's pencil in her hand and the paper on the table, holding it in place for Mimi.

Mimi appeared to be concentrating very hard. After several moments she began to write. It took forever. When she finally stopped, this is what was on her paper:

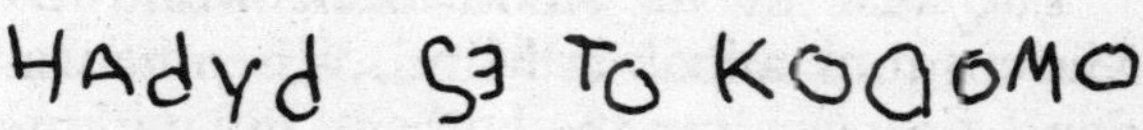

We all stared at it.

"Mum," I whispered, pulling her away from the bed, "something's wrong. I know Mimi's right-handed, but why is everything all mixed around and upside down?"

Mum shook her head slightly and put a finger on my lips. She turned back to Mimi. Dad and Janine were still puzzling over the message.

"I think the first word is *happy*," Janine was saying.

"If I'm not mistaken," Mum broke in,

"she's saying she's happy to see you girls. *Kodomo* is Japanese for *child* or *children*."

"Why didn't she just say *children*? Or use our names?" I asked.

"I don't know, honey," replied Mum.

"Well, what's going on in here?" came a hearty voice.

Standing in the doorway to Mimi's room was one of her doctors.

"Girls, you remember Dr Marcus, don't you?" asked Mum. "Dr Marcus, this is Janine, and this is Claudia."

Dr Marcus stepped into the room and shook hands with Janine and me. Then he went to Mimi's side. "I hear you've been making lots of progress today," he said.

Mimi blinked once and waved her left hand.

The rest of us stood back while Dr Marcus took a look at Mimi. When he was done, he went into the hall and my parents joined him for a brief conference. They took Mimi's note with them. Janine and I stayed behind, talking to Mimi. I told her I was turning into a cook, but that I wasn't nearly as good as she was.

When we were home that evening, Dad told us what the doctor had said.

"Mimi is making average progress."

"Just average?" I asked in disappointment.

"Average is fine."

Not when it's a C in school, I thought.

"She's going to start having therapy," added Mum.

"What sort of therapy?" Janine wanted to know.

"All sorts," replied Mum. "Physical, speech, and occupational. Occupational will help her relearn basic skills such as eating, dressing and brushing her teeth. When she's well enough, they'll help her with cooking or sewing or whatever. But they'll start small—with anything that's giving her trouble. Right now her brain is just sort of mixed up. The doctor thinks she'll make plenty of improvement, but it will take time."

"But—but it's like she's a little kid!" I sputtered.

"In a way, that's right," replied Dad. "Only it won't, for instance, take her five or six years to be able to read and write again. Her brain already knows how. It's just having trouble sending the proper messages to the rest of her body."

"The hospital is going to provide her with some therapy every day," said Mum. "But Dr Marcus said that the more stimulation she gets, the faster she'll improve. Your father and I realized that if we each took a couple of hours off from work every afternoon, one or the other of us would be here from about two o'clock, when she'll return from therapy, until six."

"Well . . ." Janine said slowly.

But I interrupted her. "I'll spend the mornings with her! I can switch to Saturday art classes." It was the least I could do, considering I'd nearly killed her.

"Oh, that would be *wonderful*," said Mum enthusiastically. "Just what she needs."

Janine looked a little disappointed. "Oh," she said, "I suppose it *would* be an exercise in futility to attempt to rearrange my course schedule. But what about your club's play group, Claudia?"

I paused. Good question. Then I put my nose in the air. "What's a silly old play group compared to Mimi?" I said loftily. But for some reason, I didn't feel nearly as good about my decision as I sounded.

10th CHAPTER

Wednesday

Today's play group was over hours ago and I'm still laughing about what went on. Now this is an example of something great that probably could never have happened in New York City. It started when David Michael brought Louie to the play group. Just to set things off on the wrong foot, it turns out that Jenny is afraid (and I mean terrified) of dogs. Remember that for the future, you guys. Then David Michael decided we needed to give Louie a bath. That's when the trouble really began. When the morning was over, Louie was the only one who was both clean and dry. Thank goodness Jenny was wearing her smock.

Claudia — we miss you!

It was nice of Stacey to say that. I missed the play group, too. But Mimi was more important. Luckily, the other club members agreed with me. They'd been disappointed when I'd said I'd have to drop out of the play group. But they'd understand. They all wanted Mimi to get well as much as I did.

Anyway, Stacey called to tell me about the Louie-washing. When she got to certain points in the story, she would start laughing again, and laugh so hard she could barely speak.

The reason Louie went to the McGills' was that Mrs Thomas made him go. The Thomases were moving the next day, and Louie was in the way. Anyway, Mrs Thomas sent David Michael to the play group with Louie in tow. And she sent over three dollars for each of them. The money was accompanied by a note that said:

Dear Kristy,
Please, please, PLEASE watch Louie this morning and don't send him home before 12.30. He nosed through the rubbish right after you left, and strewed spaghetti all over the kitchen floor. Thank you.
Love, Your Old Mum

When David Michael came over, it was about nine-thirty, and Jenny, Mallory, Claire, Margo and Nicky, Suzi and Buddy, Nina and Eleanor and Jamie had already arrived. Louie was kind of wound up, so he gallumphed into Stacey's back garden, barking happily.

"Ohhhhhaughhhhh!" shrieked Jenny, as Louie bounded over to the art table and stuck his wet nose in her face.

"Uh-oh," said Stacey. "David Michael, move him away from the art stuff, okay?"

"Okay," said David Michael. "Here," he added, handing Kristy the money and note from their mother. Then he tugged on Louie's collar and hauled him to another part of the garden.

"What's wrong?" Stacey asked Jenny, picking her up.

Jenny was wearing her smock. She had barely taken it off, even at home, since the time Andrew the monster had told her to wear it every day. Apparently, her mother was somewhat upset about that, because with the smock on, she could hardly show off Jenny's gorgeous wardrobe.

"I don't like him," Jenny wailed.

"Louie won't hurt you. He's a nice old dog—a collie. See all his fluffy fur? Isn't he pretty?"

"No," said Jenny, shaking her head and wrinkling her nose. She buried her face against Stacey.

Stacey had to admit that Louie wasn't looking his best. He needed to be brushed, and he had spaghetti sauce on his nose and feet.

"Well," she said lamely, "he's nice, anyway." She sat Jenny back on the bench at the picnic table.

Jenny raised her head and looked around nervously. "Where's that dog now?" she asked.

"Over there. See? Jamie's petting him. Jamie doesn't mind old Louie."

"He's dirty," said Jenny. "He's a messy-face."

"Well, you're protected. You've got your smock on."

"Monster smock," whispered Jenny.

Stacey sighed. She left Jenny with Mallory and wandered over to Jamie and David Michael. Kristy joined them.

"How do you think Louie's going to like his new neighbourhood?" Stacey asked Kristy.

"Oh, I think he'll like it all right. It's too bad he's not a pedigree Shih Tzu or Pomeranian, though. Or a pedigree anything. He'd fit in better with all those rich, snobby dogs. I bet those dogs don't even have dog kennels in their gardens. I bet they have little dog mansions."

Stacey laughed. Then she said, "I thought Louie was a pedigree collie."

"Nope," replied Kristy. "One of his grandfathers was a sheep dog."

"How would anyone ever know that?" asked Stacey.

"Rich people find out all sorts of things

you wish they didn't know," said Kristy.

"Will they know he got into the spaghetti this morning?" asked David Michael.

"Anyone would know that," Stacey replied. "He looks, smells and feels like spaghetti sauce."

"Well, then," said David Michael, "do you have a bath?"

"A bath?" asked Stacey. "What for?"

"We'll have to give him a bath."

Stacey looked at Kristy.

Kristy began to smile. "It's not a bad idea," she said.

"And," added David Michael, "we have to fix him up."

"Huh?" said Kristy.

"You know, fluff his fur, put some ribbons on him, find his lead. I don't want any of those rich people or rich dogs making fun of him tomorrow," David Michael said fiercely.

Stacey began to giggle. "We'll beautify him," she said. "What do you think, Kristy? We do have a bath in the garage. It might be fun."

Kristy looked around the McGills' garden, smiling. "The garden is fenced in. Everyone's in old clothes. Jenny's got her smock on. If we just tell the kids to take their shoes off . . ."

Ten minutes later, Mallory, the four members of the Babysitters Club, and the ten kids had taken their shoes off and lined them up on the benches at the picnic tables. Even Jenny had consented to remove her shoes, but only after Kristy told her that Andrew would want it that way. Stacey had found the bath and told her mother what they were going to do. Now the bath was being filled by the hose while David Michael removed Louie's collar.

"What kind of soap do you use?" Stacey asked.

"Johnson's Baby Shampoo," replied David Michael.

"It makes his fur shiny and fluffy," added Kristy.

"I don't think we have any baby shampoo," said Stacey. "I'm not sure my mum will let me use up shampoo on a dog, anyway."

In the end, they used an ordinary bar of soap.

When the bath was filled and the soap was floating in the water, Kristy called out, "Oh, Lou-ie!"

Louie looked around, saw the bath of water, and fled to a corner of the garden.

"Oh, Lou-ie!" cried David Michael.

"Oh, Lou-ie!" cried most of the rest of the kids.

David Michael, Buddy and Charlotte began stalking Louie around the yard.

"You shouldn't have taken his collar off so soon," Charlotte pointed out.

"I know," said David Michael, "but we'll get him."

And they did. The three of them ambushed him from behind a fir tree. Then they surrounded him, joined by Suzi and Margo, and hustled him over to the tub.

"Okay, in you go, boy," said Kristy. She and David Michael heaved him into the water. They looked as if they were used to doing it.

SP-LASH! A sort of tidal wave washed over one side, soaking Jamie and Claire, who laughed delightedly.

Four kids pounced on poor Louie and began wetting him down. Nina dived for the soap and fell in the bath. After Dawn fished her out, the kids crowded around, each wanting a turn to soap Louie. During all of this, the only sound Louie made was a pitiful whine when Kristy and David Michael tossed him in the water.

When Louie was good and soapy, Mary Anne asked, "Is it time for the hose?"

"I think so," said Kristy. She helped Louie out of the bath. He stood, dripping on the lawn, waiting for what was to come.

"He shrank!" cried Nina. "What happened? Oh, he *shrank*!"

"No, he didn't," said Dawn patiently. "He's just wet. You'll see."

Mary Anne approached with the hose.

"Shouldn't someone hold him?" asked Dawn.

"Nah," said David Michael. "He knows the only way to get the soap off is to let us rinse him."

And at that moment, Louie streaked across the yard in a soapy flash. Eight children ran after him. (Jenny was cowering on a lawn chair, and little Eleanor was playing with her toes, unaware of what was going on.)

"Tackle him!" yelled Buddy.

Nicky leaped for him, but Louie slipped out of his grasp. He was running around the McGills' garden in a big circle.

"Go that way!" cried Charlotte, pointing.

Half the kids turned around and ran in the other direction. Louie saw them coming. *He* turned around and ran into the rest of the kids.

"Gotcha!" said Margo. She, Nicky, Suzi and Jamie fell on Louie in a slippery heap.

"Hold him!" shouted David Michael. "Here comes the water!" David Michael twisted the nozzle and a spray of water shot out. It scored a direct hit on Louie and the children.

By the time Louie was rinsed off, dried off, and calmed down, he looked beautiful. ("He's fat again," said Nina, with relief.) But the kids were soaked, and so were their clothes.

"Thank goodness it's a warm day," said Stacey. "They can dry off in the sun while they beautify Louie."

When the morning was over, Louie was a canine masterpiece. Stacey had plaited his fur. Charlotte had tied a ribbon at the end of each plait. Margo and Mallory had painted red nail polish on his claws. David Michael had run home long enough to find his collar.

The children inspected him critically.

"Does he have any clothes?" asked Nicky. "A sweater or something?"

"No," said Kristy, "But I think he's dressed up enough. Now if he can just stay this way until tomorrow . . ."

The children began to go home. David Michael was the last to leave. He led Louie proudly out of McGills' yard on the lead.

It was then that Kristy turned to the other club members. "You don't think Louie looks too much like a girl, do you?" she whispered.

Nobody said a word.

"Oh, well," Kristy went on. "If anybody asks tomorrow, I'll just say his name is Louella. They'll never know."

11th CHAPTER

Mimi's therapy really helped her. Every day she learnt more things. And just like a child, she learnt the physical things—like sitting up, standing up, trying to walk—pretty quickly, but her speech was coming along slowly. She reminded me a lot of Lucy Newton. Lucy could sit up, crawl and pull herself into a standing position. She could wave bye-bye and feed herself a bottle or a biscuit. But she couldn't talk.

She and Mimi were both trying hard, though. Lucy was learning to imitate sounds, and Mimi was trying to remember words. That was the funny thing about Mimi. After she was able to talk again, she sometimes mixed up her words, and often couldn't think of ones she wanted to use.

The speech therapist had given me flash cards to help Mimi's vocabulary and memory. I would hold up a picture, and

Mimi would try to say the name of the object. Sometimes she could say it right away. Other times she would struggle.

Once I held up a picture of a bird. "It—it skies in the fly. No, it flies in the sky," said Mimi, sounding frustrated. "It has wings. It catches worms. It builds nests. But I . . . oh, you know what it is, my Claudia."

Other times, she would say the Japanese word for the picture instead.

I asked the doctor about it, and he said Mimi had something called aphasia. "It will get better," he assured me.

Unlike Lucy, however, Mimi had one big problem: She still had very little use of her right hand. And when she tried to walk, she limped badly on her right leg. The doctors now seemed to think that she might never get back the full use of the right side of her body although they did think she'd get somewhat better. Just in case, however, the occupational therapist was teaching Mimi how to write and do other things left-handed.

One morning I was at the hospital with Mimi. She was sitting in an armchair and had insisted on getting dressed. We were waiting for her speech therapist to come, and I was quizzing her.

I sat cross-legged on her hospital bed. "What colour is this?" I asked, holding up a corner of the white sheet.

Mimi frowned. "*Shiroku . . .*"

"English, Mimi. In English."

"It's . . . not black," she said finally.

"White," I reminded her.

"Oh, yes. I—I can know this." (As I said, she would mix up her words sometimes.)

I held up one of her flash cards. "What's this?"

"*Hitsuji* . . . no . . . sheep!" said Mimi.

"That's right! hey, Mimi, you're doing great!"

"She certainly is," said a voice.

Dr Marcus had appeared in the doorway.

I greeted him happily. I liked Dr Marcus a lot. So did Mimi (even though she had said so in Japanese and Mum had had to translate).

"In fact, she's doing well enough to go home tomorrow."

"Home?" I cried. "Tomorrow? Oh, that's terrific!"

Mimi smiled. "Mmm," she said, nodding, and I knew she couldn't think of whatever words she wanted to use. But her smile said everything.

That night, Mum and Dad and I held a meeting about Mimi. My parents had spent the afternoon talking to Dr Marcus and the nurses and therapists.

"She'll have to go to the hospital every day for therapy," said Dad. "Mum and I will arrange to do that. She's supposed to be at the hospital from about two to five."

"But what will she do all morning?" I asked.

"She can look at magazines or watch TV," replied Mum. "But mostly she ought to practice what she's learning in therapy. She can't be left alone—"

"I'll stay with her," I volunteered immediately. "You will?" asked Mum. "Are you sure? It would be wonderful if you could. We don't want to interrupt Janine's classes."

(I was sure that would be a relief to Janine. All she had done the past week was bury her nose in one book after another. She said she had exams coming up, but it seemed to me that she just didn't care much about Mimi.)

"We'll pay you, of course," Mum went on.

"Pay me!" I said. "You don't have to pay me. This is Mimi. I *want* to take care of her. I'm part of her family."

"Yes, but you'll be missing out on the play group. And you'll have to work with Mimi at least part of the time. You won't be simply keeping her company. She'll need help. It'll be a lot of work."

"We-ell . . ." I said.

"I think we ought to pay you your regular baby-sitting wages," said my father.

"I agree," said Mum.

"Okay," I gave in. "But only if you don't

tell Mimi. I wouldn't want her to know I'm getting paid to help her. I think it would hurt her feelings. Deal?"

"Deal," replied my parents.

So Mimi came home from the hospital the next afternoon, and the following morning was the beginning of my first day taking care of her. Of course, I had plenty of help during breakfast, but by eight-thirty when everyone had left, Mimi and I were on our own. I knew I could call our neighbours, the Goldmans, or Stacey's mother, if we had any trouble. And all the emergency numbers in the entire country were posted by the phone in the kitchen. It felt weird, though, not to have the Thomases around for help. Kristy had moved. Her home was right across town now.

Mimi sat in the kitchen with me while I cleaned up our breakfast dishes. Every so often I'd ask her a question.

"What am I doing now, Mimi?"

"You are . . . are . . . washing the . . . the things we eat from."

"What are those things called?"

"They are . . . plants. No, plates. And the round things we drink from."

"And what are those called?" I knew Mimi must be frustrated, but I wouldn't give up.

Questions, questions, questions. That's what the first two hours of the morning were. We walked from room to room. I asked her about everything. When she had trouble, I'd give her a memory trick to help her. (That's how my third-grade teacher helped me with my terrible spelling.)

"The next time you need to remember the name of this," I said, pointing to a chair, "picture a cherry growing bigger and bigger until it explodes, spraying out cherry juice. And when you think of *cherry*, remember the word *chair*."

"Oh, no," said Mimi, smiling. "I am sure I will call that a cherry from now on, my Claudia."

But she didn't. When I pointed to the chair about ten minutes later, Mimi frowned, then smiled. I knew she was picturing the exploding cherry. "That," said Mimi triumphantly, "is a chair."

Later, I got out Mimi's writing book and she practised writing with her left hand. When she had had a rest, she helped me make beds, doing a pretty good one-handed job.

We had just finished lunch out on the back porch, when the doorbell rang. "I'll get it!" I said. "You stay here."

I ran through the house and opened the front door. There were Stacey, Mary Anne, Kristy and Dawn, all holding papers and packages.

"Hi, you guys!" I greeted them happily.

"Hi!" said everyone.

"We just finished the play group," added Stacey. "We thought we'd come and visit Mimi."

"Oh, that's great," I said. "She's out on the back porch."

My friends followed me to the porch. When they saw Mimi, they zoomed in on her like a bunch of bees who had spotted a flower.

They all began talking at once, and dropping presents in her lap.

Immediately, Mimi forgot her words. I heard her mumble, something about *kodomo*. Aside from that, she resorted to, "Mmm," and smiling. But when the girls sat down and Mimi felt less flustered, she perked up.

"I am . . . happy to see you," she said slowly.

"Oh, boy, are we ever happy to see *you*," replied Mary Anne emphatically.

"Look," said Stacey, "Charlotte made you that flower." She pointed out what must have been the day's art project: a section of an egg carton stuck on a pipe cleaner and painted brilliant colours.

"And David Michael doesn't go to the play group any more," said Kristy, "so he sends you a joke instead. His joke is, How many elephants can you fit in a sports car?"

"How many?" asked Mimi.

"Six. Three in front and three in back!"

"Oh . . ." Mimi smiled, but looked mystified.

"The Thomases have moved, Mimi," I told her. "Remember? They were getting all packed up and everything."

"Oh . . . oh, yes," said Mimi, and I knew she really had remembered. "Do you like nor yew house?"

Nobody laughed. They knew what Mimi meant.

"The house is fine," said Kristy. "I'm not sure about the neighbourhood, though. There aren't many kids around. Watson said most of them got sent to camp for the summer."

My friends stayed a while longer. When they left, it was time to help Mimi get ready to go to the hospital. Dad showed up at one-forty-five to drive her there, and then I had to go to the Newtons' to baby-sit.

Lucy was just getting ready for a nap when I arrived. Mrs Newton seemed to be in a rush. "Can you finish with her?" she asked me. "I've got a meeting in fifteen minutes, and Lucy is in a mess from lunch. She needs her nappy changed, too."

"Sure," I replied. "Where's Jamie?"

"On his way in. He was playing in the garden."

"Hi-hi," said Jamie, appearing in the doorway to Lucy's room.

"Honey, I'm going to leave now," Mrs

Newton told Jamie. "You have fun with Claudia."

" 'Bye, Mummy," said Jamie casually.

Mrs Newton dashed downstairs.

Jamie crossed the room to Lucy, who was lying on her changing table. "Hi-hi, Lucy-Goosey," he said, making a silly face at her.

Lucy smiled at him.

Jamie picked up a toy squirrel and zoomed it around Lucy while I tried to change her. Her smile became a grin, and she waved her arms in the air.

Jamie looked critically at Lucy. "Your face is messy," he said.

"I know it is," I told him. "I'm going to clean her up in a minute."

"I'll clean her up," said Jamie.

"No, I'd better do it," I said. "It's a big job. She's got baby food in her hair, and I need to change her vest, too."

"I can do it."

"Maybe," I said, "but let me do it anyway. It'll go faster."

"Boy," said Jamie crossly. Then he stood on his tiptoes and shouted into his sister's face, "Stupid baby! Why did we ever get you?"

Lucy burst into tears at the sudden noise, and Jamie stomped down the hall, muttering something about, "Won't even let me help." Then he sulked for a while. By the time Lucy woke up from her nap, though, he was his old cheerful self. He tickled Lucy and played pat-a-cake with her. And when I let him help me dress her, I thought he would burst with pride.

We had a fun afternoon, but when I left the Newtons', I was exhausted. It had been a long day. And I had the nagging feeling that Jamie and Lucy reminded me of Janine and me, but I wasn't sure why.

12th CHAPTER

Thursday

This morning I didn't baby-sit— I Mimi-sat. Claudia was sitting for Nina and Eleanor all day, so Mrs. Kishi asked if I could stay with Mimi. I was happy to, of course, but I wasn't expecting Mimi to be so different. She can't even remember the simplest things sometimes. In case any of you stays with Mimi while she's getting better, you should know that she gets upset easily. Frustrated, I guess. She yelled at me and Mimi has never, ever yelled at me. In fact, as far as I know, she has never yelled at all. So be careful.

Now, the funny thing is, although Mimi yelled at Mary Anne, she never yelled at me or Mum or Dad or Janine the entire time she was sick. Maybe it's because we're her family. I guess it's one thing for me to trail around after her, pestering her with questions, but something else for a friend of the family to do it. I bet she was embarrassed. She was probably embarrassed just for needing a sitter in the first place. After all, she was a grown woman, not a baby like Lucy Newton. Anyway, I felt terrible for Mary Anne. She's shy and sensitive, and things like this really upset her.

The reason Mary Anne was staying with Mimi was that I had told the Marshalls over a month ago that I would sit for Nina and Eleanor. Mr and Mrs Marshall had a very important all-day event to attend in Stamford, so they had called way in advance for a sitter. I didn't want to back out of the job, Mum and Dad didn't want to take any more time off from work than they already had, and they didn't want to ask Janine to miss a class.

So we asked Mary Anne to stay with Mimi. Of course she said yes immediately.

I didn't have to be at the Marshalls' until ten o'clock, but I told Mary Anne to come to my house at nine-thirty. That gave me plenty of time to show her Mimi's exercise book and flash cards, and to explain what things Mimi could and couldn't do, what to fix for lunch, when Dad was coming home, etc.

Mary Anne listened patiently and asked me a few questions. She knew where I'd be if she needed help. I told myself I could always bring Nina and Eleanor back to my house, if necessary.

At ten minutes to ten, I had to leave. "Okay, Mimi," I said. "I'll be over at the Marshalls'. I have to baby-sit. But Mary Anne will stay with you. Dad'll be here a little before two."

"This is fine, my Claudia," Mimi answered slowly.

I gave Mary Anne the thumbs-up sign and left.

Mary Anne said that right from the start, Mimi was, well, difficult. Not mean or anything. But for instance, as soon as I was gone Mary Anne suggested to Mimi, "How about working on your flash cards?"

And Mimi replied, "Oh, Mary Anne, why do we not watch the . . . the . . . big box?"

Mimi *never* watches television. Well, hardly ever. So this was pretty unusual.

But Mary Anne didn't want to argue with Mimi. She decided that maybe listening to people talking would help Mimi's speech, so she found a talk show on TV. Unfortunately, it wasn't a very interesting show. It was about tax reform or something. Mary

Anne was bored immediately, and after about five minutes, she realized that Mimi wasn't even looking at the screen.

Mary Anne jumped up, flicked off the TV, and said, "Come on, Mimi. It's a beautiful day. Let's sit on the porch and I'll help you with your flash cards."

Mimi heaved a big sigh, but apparently couldn't think of anything to say. She let Mary Anne help her out to the porch.

When they were settled, Mary Anne held up the top card.

"Kitchen," said Mimi.

"No, *chicken*," Mary Anne told her.

Mimi remained silent.

"Say *chicken*," Mary Anne prompted her.

"Chicken," whispered Mimi.

I could just picture the two of them on the porch with the flash cards. Mary Anne was wearing a jeans skirt, a pink and white striped blouse, and shoes with no socks. I'm sure she was perched on the edge of her chair with her feet crossed. One hand was probably holding up the cards, and the other was probably playing with her hair.

Mimi would have been sitting just as primly in her chair, only settled well back in it, since her balance wasn't very good. She had put on a blue trousers suit that morning, and I had helped her choose a little gold peacock to pin on her blouse. Lately, she had taken to sitting stiffly and sort of cradling her useless right arm in her good left one.

Mary Anne held up the next card.

Mimi looked thoughtful. Then her face grew pink. "*Hitsuji*?" she suggested after a moment. "No . . . no . . ."

"It's a sheep, Mimi," said Mary Anne.

"Ah. Mmm . . ." Mimi's speech was disappearing, along with her nerve.

"Say it," said Mary Anne.

This may have been the real beginning of the problem. I'm not sure. The thing about Mary Anne is that although she's shy, she can sound sort of schoolteacherish sometimes. In fact, she said recently that she wants to be a teacher one day. Maybe Mimi thought Mary Anne was being pushy, or treating her like a child. ("Say da-da, Lucy. Say da-da. Oh, what a good girl!")

"Say it," Mary Anne said again.

"Sheet."

"No, sheep. *Puh, puh*." Mary Anne emphasized the p-sound at the end of the word, which I'm sure Mimi had heard just fine and had meant to say. It just hadn't come out right.

"*Sheep*. PUH PUH," Mimi repeated loudly.

Mary Anne hesitated then. She wondered if she should forget about the cards, but she remembered my saying that if Mimi wanted to get better, she would have to drill, drill, drill every day. Even Saturday and Sunday.

So Mary Anne held up the next card. It showed a baseball bat—for some reason, one of the toughest words for Mimi to remember.

"Mmm," said Mimi. "Mmm . . ."

"No," said Mary Anne. "Buh, buh."

"Buh . . . buh . . . be *quiet*!" said Mimi as loudly as she could. She got unsteadily to her feet. "Be *quiet*!" she shouted again. She started to teeter off the porch into the house.

Mary Anne stood up nervously.

"And leave alone! I can do myself!" said Mimi.

"All right. All right. I'm just coming along behind you. I won't help you," said Mary Anne. She followed Mimi. What, she wondered, should she do if Mimi locked herself in her bedroom?

But Mimi made her way into the kitchen, holding onto her right arm the whole way, even though Mum and I had told her many times to use the cane she'd been given by her physiotherapist.

In the kitchen, Mimi sat down huffily for a few moment. Then she stood up again and began slamming the cupboard doors.

"Mimi?" asked Mary Anne. "What—"

"Special tea," Mimi managed to say. "We need it."

"Oh," said Mary Anne, relieved. "You're right. We do. How about, um, how about . . ." (Poor Mary Anne was so nervous about upsetting Mimi that she hardly knew what to say.) "I could get out the special cups and the pot, if you'll find the tea."

"Yes, yes." Mimi began to calm down.

Twenty minutes later, the tea was before them. Mary Anne had made it (following Mimi's garbled instructions), but Mimi was able to pour lefhanded.

She and Mary Anne each took a sip.

"Ah," said Mimi. "Good."

"Wonderful," agreed Mary Anne. "We haven't had special tea in a long time."

"Mary," said Mimi, "I am sorry. I did not mean to . . . talk at you."

"That's okay," said Mary Anne. "I think I deserved it."

"No one deserves rude." Mimi put down her cup and held out her left hand. Mary Anne took it. Mimi smiled at her. "All forgive?"

"Yes," said Mary Anne. "And I have a suggestion. Let's play hooky."

"Hooky? Oh . . . yes!" Mimi laughed.

Mary Anne laughed too.

They spent the rest of the morning watching game shows on TV. Mimi got pretty good at *Wheel of Fortune*. I decided that she should watch it every morning.

13th CHAPTER

On the day before Lucy Newton's christening, I worked with Mimi in the morning, as usual. She and I had never discussed her blowup at Mary Anne, and Mimi had been quite cooperative with me, my parents, and her therapists since then. We could see improvement every day. Her speech was getting better and her limp was going away. She still didn't have much use of her right arm, though, and the occupational therapist worked hard with her to increase the use of her left hand. That was difficult for Mimi, since she used her hands a lot—cooking, embroidering, knitting, sewing. And no matter how well she learned to use her left hand, there were some things she'd never be able to do one-handed. I found her bag of knitting needles stashed in the hall cupboard one day.

Mimi was sad and disappointed, but she

wouldn't complain.

After Dad came to take Mimi to the hospital that day, I went to the Newtons' house. Mrs Newton was in a panic. Jamie had a cold and Lucy was cutting a tooth. Both of them were crying.

The dining room was a shambles. Mrs Newton had set out every plate, dish, and piece of silverware she planned to use at the party the next afternoon. And by each dish and bowl was the food that was going to go on it or in it. There were packets of decorations, stacks of plates for the guests, and boxes of cocktail napkins and matches that said Lucille Jane Newton and the date of the christening on them in silver letters. And there were little notes on yellow paper stuck everywhere. They said things like: *Remember carrot sticks in fridge, Don't forget to salt*, and one I didn't understand at all that was stuck to an empty jar and read, *Auntie Nora's swizzle sticks.*

Mrs Newton looked as much a wreck as the dining room. She was wringing her hands and surveying the room warily, as if it were going to crumble away at any moment.

"Oh, Lord, what if it *rains*?" she exclaimed. "We'll have to hold this thing in*side*."

"Well, the Babysitters Club will be there to help you," I reminded her. My friends and I had been invited to the christening and the party as "paid guests". We were going to keep an eye on Jamie and Lucy, and help Mr and Mrs Newton pass food, fill trays, make ice cubes, and do other party stuff.

"Claudia, how would you like to decorate the garden tomorrow?" Mrs Newton asked me. "That is, if it doesn't rain. You're so good at things like that."

"I'd love to," I told her. "When should I come?"

"Let's see. The service will be at two. Why don't you come over around noon? You could help get the children dressed afterwards." Mrs Newton glanced at the sniffling, tear-stained Jamie and Lucy. "Oh, I hope they're better by then," she added.

"By head hurts," wailed Jamie.

"Wahhh . . ." added Lucy pitifully.

Mrs Newton looked pained, but she turned the children over to me and got to work. While she bustled around with her party things, I rubbed teething medicine on Lucy's gums, handed tissues to Jamie, and tried to keep both of them happy and quiet by reading them picture books. Jamie's current favourite story was *The Saggy Baggy Elephant*, and we read that one six times.

When it was time for me to leave, Jamie smiled and said he felt a lot better. Only he didn't sound any better. What he had said was, "Thacks, Claudy. By head does't hurt iddy-bore. I feel buch better."

"Keep your fingers crossed," Mrs Newton said as I started down the front steps.

"Oh, I will," I told her. "All of them. My toes, too."

Of course, I didn't really keep all my fingers and toes crossed. But as I was getting dressed for the christening the next morning, I crossed two of my fingers briefly, and hoped for good weather and healthy kids.

I chose a new outfit, one I liked a lot. It was a big, loose white shirt with black splotches all over it, and white pants that came to just below my knees. My shoes (and I might point out that I'd had a fight with Mum over permission to buy them) were dainty gold sandals that laced partway up my legs. Then I put on my pink flamingo earrings and a pink bracelet that said CLAUDIA in heart-shaped beads. Finally, I plaited my hair into four long plaits, tied a ribbon around the top of each, and fastened the ends with butterfly clips.

I was all ready. I wasn't wearing a very churchy outfit, but after all, it was Saturday and we weren't going to an actual church service—just to a ceremony in a church.

A little while later I found myself in the Newtons' garden, surrounded by balloons, lanterns and miles of crepe paper.

I hung everything as artfully as I could. Then I asked Mr Newton if there happened to be a couple of strings of Christmas lights handy. Surprisingly, there were. I arranged the strings on some bushes by the back porch and plugged them in. The twinkling gold lights made the yard look festive.

I called the Newtons outside.

"It's lovely!" exclaimed Mrs Newton.

"You did a fine job, Claudia," added Mr Newton.

"Is this all for Lucy?" asked Jamie, who had miraculously recovered from his head cold.

"Well, it's all for Lucy's party," his father told him.

"I thought so," said Jamie. He disappeared indoors.

"Oh, dear," said Mrs Newton, "I think we've got a problem. The children are well, but Jamie's suffering from jealousy."

"I'll start getting him dressed," I said. "It's almost one o'clock. Kristy and the others will be here in half an hour."

I found Jamie in his room, sitting sulkily on his bed.

"Time to get dressed," I said cheerfully.

"For the party?" asked Jamie.

"Yup."

"Nope."

"What do you mean, nope?"

"I'm not getting dressed."

"Yes, you are. Look." I held out the new

clothes Mrs Newton had bought him—a very smart little outfit: khaki slacks, a white shirt, a navy-blazer, and brogues. "See how grown-up you'll be? Just like Daddy."

Jamie hesitated. "All right," he said grumpily after a few moments.

He let me help him with the buttons and laces. When we were finished, I gasped. Jamie didn't look like the little Jamie Newton I knew. He looked like a real boy. Shocked, I led him to the kitchen where Mr and Mrs Newton were. They must have been more used to him than I was, because all they said was how nice he looked and how well his blazer fitted.

"Shall I dress Lucy now?" I asked.

"I'll do it, thanks," replied Mrs Newton, "but come and give me a hand. I can't wait for you to see her dress."

When Lucy was dressed she didn't look any older or younger than usual, but she did look like an angel. Her christening outfit was a white gown with lots of lace and ribbons, tiny pearl buttons, and a matching cap. We finished dressing her just as Kristy, Mary Anne, Stacey and Dawn showed up.

There was plenty of oohing and aahing, and I think every one of them said at least once, "Isn't she *cute*?"

Lucy smiled at us from under her cap, and Jamie glared at us darkly.

Trouble was brewing.

The christening ceremony at the church went by quickly. The guests and we baby-sitters sat in the first few rows of pews, while the Newtons stood at the front of the church with the minister and the man and woman who were going to be Lucy's godparents.

Lucy let out a little cry when the minister touched her forehead with the water, and Jamie kept leaning over to examine his new shoes, but otherwise things went well. Unless you count the very end of the ceremony, when the Newtons were walking down the aisle towards the back of the church, and Jamie turned around and called over his shoulder to the minister, "Hey, God bless you!"

Everyone laughed, but it didn't matter, because the christening was over and it was time to go to the Newton's for the party. The members of the Babysitters Club got ready to switch from being guests to being helpers.

Mr Newton drove us from the church to the party. Mrs Newton put us to work right away. Kristy and Stacey were to pass out hors d'oeuvres, Mary Anne and Dawn were to help set up the food table, and I was to watch Jamie.

Lucy apparently wasn't going to need much watching. She was the centre of attention, passed adoringly from one pair of arms to the next.

Jamie was torn between watching all that, and not watching it. When he wasn't watching, he tried to perform daredevil tricks on his climbing frame.

"Hey, Gram! Look at me!"

But usually Gram (Or Gramps or Auntie Nora or whoever he was calling) was too enthralled with Lucy to pay much attention to him.

"Roarrr!" shouted Jamie, standing at the top of his slide and beating his chest. "I'm King Corn!"

The only attention that stunt attracted was from his mother. "Honey, not so loud, please."

"Anyway," I whispered to him as I helped him off the slide, "it's King *Kong*, not King Corn."

"Oh."

When the food had been eaten and the guests were happily stuffed, Kristy and the others helped clear the table. Then they began to pile it up with gifts the guests had brought.

"Presents!" yelped Jamie eagerly. "Maybe they're for me!"

"I . . . I don't think so," I told him.

"Why not, Claudy? Who're they for?"

"Well, I think they're for Lucy. For her christening."

"All of them?"

"Probably."

"Are you sure?"

Jamie just couldn't believe that the entire stack of presents before him was for Lucy. And, in fact, he was right; not all of them were for Lucy. There were a few small things for him: some Match Box cars and a tiny teddy. But the majority of the heap was dresses and stuffed animals and toys for Lucy.

Jamie made his unhappiness plain. "Leave me alone," he told me crossly.

I knew how he felt, so I did leave him alone. The party was sort of coming to an end, anyway. I joined my friends, who were looking at the Polaroid pictures Mr Newton was taking. It was fun to watch each print change from a brownish blank to a clear colour photo.

I'm not sure what made me look up to see who was holding Lucy at the moment, but I did—and I couldn't see anyone holding her. So I scanned the garden and saw that she'd been placed in her bouncy walker chair. She was sitting by one end of the food table, next to a half-empty jug of fruit punch that had been left out. As I watched, Jamie spotted both Lucy and the punch. He darted toward her, lifted the jug, and—

I ran across the garden as fast as I could, knowing I'd never reach them in time. I could just picture Lucy's beautiful gown all stained with red punch.

"Jamie!" I shouted. "No!"

But before the words had actually left my mouth, Jamie was putting the pitcher back on the table. And by the time I got to him, he was tickling Lucy's bare feet.

"Jamie," I gasped, "I thought you were going to pour that punch on your sister."

Jamie looked at me guiltily. "I was," he said, "but I changed my mind."

"How come?" I asked.

Jamie shrugged, then frowned. "'Cause I love her," he said at last. "She *is* my sister."

Hmm, I thought, remembering when I'd raised my hand to hit Janine, but had stopped just in time.

The party ended a little while later. Jamie's words didn't come back to me until I was on my way home. Then I began to think about Janine. Janine was my sister and I was hers. I supposed we loved each other, although we'd never actually said so. I hadn't thought much about it. Mostly what I thought about was how much attention Janine got from everybody. Janine was such a brilliant student. Janine was going to be a physicist. Don't interrupt Janine, she has to study. Janine this, Janine that.

It was kind of the way Jamie probably felt about Lucy. Lucy was so pretty. Lucy did such adorable things. Be quiet, Lucy's asleep. Lucy this, Lucy that.

And yet—I knew that Lucy wasn't more special to anyone than Jamie was. Did that mean that I was as special as Janine? And underneath, did I really love Janine the way Jamie said he loved Lucy? *And*, if *I* loved Janine, did *she* love the rest of us back—but just didn't know how to show it?

I wasn't sure at all.

14th CHAPTER

I struggled through our front door after the party that afternoon. My arms were loaded with things. Mrs Newton had sent my friends and me home with leftover party stuff. I had a stack of Lucy napkins, a container of pastries, some biscuits, some peanuts, and half a bag of M&M's.

"Hello!" I called.

"My Claudia?" came a tentative voice from the back porch.

"Hi, Mimi!" I ran to her, and showed her the things from the party. "They had special napkins and matchbooks made," I told her. "Here. Do you want to try a pastry? They're really good."

Mimi took one and began eating it neatly, using her left hand.

"Hey," I said suddenly, "where is everyone?" Mimi wasn't supposed to be left alone.

"Your parents had to . . . to leave," Mimi replied carefully. "Janine is here."

"Where?" I asked.

"Room."

"She's in her room? Is she working?"

"Think so."

"Are you all right down here for a while?"

"Yes. Surely."

I ran upstairs, pounded on Janine's door, then let myself in without waiting for her to answer.

"Claudia!" she said, frowning. "Is something the matter?" She was in front of her computer, as usual. I was surprised her face hadn't turned green from the glow yet.

"Mimi is downstairs all by herself. She's not supposed to be alone."

"I've been right here," said Janine uncomfortably.

"You're supposed to be *with* her," I pointed out. "Can't you do *any*thing for this family? Is it too much to ask that you spend an hour with our grandmother?'

Janine dropped her hands into her lap. "I just couldn't," she mumbled. "Mimi asked me to sit with her, but I didn't know what to *do*. You're the one who's been spending so much time with her."

"You were great with her in the hospital," I said. "You could talk to her even when she couldn't talk back."

Janine shrugged. "Well, anyway, no one

wants me as part of this family."

"What?"

"You're always pushing me into my world and out of yours."

As usual, I didn't understand what she was talking about.

Janine gave another exasperated shrug and turned back to her computer. "Go away," she said, not bothering to look at me. "Mimi prefers you to me, anyway."

"Janine, wait," I said. "I want to talk to you. Can't you turn that thing off for a minute? Whenever it's on, you look at it, not at me. Besides, I think your face is turning green."

Janine gave me a hint of a smile. "All right," she said. "Just let me save this." She pressed a few keys, waited a moment, then reached around to the side of the computer and touched something or other that made the screen go blank.

I sat down on Janine's bed, and she swivelled around in her chair to face me. "What do you mean," I asked, "about pushing you into your world?"

"I mean," replied Janine, "that all I ever hear is, 'Janine, go study,' or, 'Janine, don't neglect your schoolwork.' Nobody ever asks me to accompany them somewhere or to help them—and then, more often than not, you accuse me of foisting extra work onto your shoulders."

"But you do!" I exclaimed. "You sit

around in your room with your books while I have to cook, go to the hospital, work with Mimi . . ."

"Recall, if you will," said Janine, "what happened when Mum and Dad made the decision to rearrange our schedules—"

"Our lives," I interrupted.

"—in order to work with Mimi."

"I got stuck with the mornings and had to drop out of the play group, while you got off scot-free," I said.

"No," Janine went on. "Let me refresh your memory. I started to speak and you rushed into the conversation, *volunteering* your mornings. Mum then thought that was such a wonderful arrangement that I had to pretend I wouldn't have been able to help Mimi in the first place. And what about the day Mary Anne was asked to attend to Mimi? No one told me that was to happen. If someone had mentioned it, I could have arranged to miss a class. But no one thought to inform me. It's as if I don't exist."

"Well—"

"How about those times you blamed me for not helping you with dinner? Did I realize that task had fallen to you? No."

"But—"

"I am many things, Claudia, but I am not psychic. I do not have ESP."

"But Janine," I said, "You're everyone's favourite. You're so clever—"

"*I'm* everyone's favourite!" she cried.

"No, *you* are. You're popular and pretty—"

She stopped. We smiled at each other.

"Look," I said, "maybe we haven't been good about including you in things, but this business is not all our fault. It's—it's a two-way street," I said, quoting my father. "Maybe we wouldn't have been so quick to put your studies first if you hadn't always made us feel that your work was so important to you."

"It *is* important to me," said Janine. "But not more important than my family."

"You know what?" I said slowly. "I think you ought to talk to Mum and Dad. I think you should tell them this. Mimi, too. I bet they don't have any idea how you feel."

Janine turned her head away. "I don't know . . ."

"And if you can't talk to them," I said, "then show them."

"How?"

"Start spending some time outside your room. Do you really have to study non-stop?"

"No."

"Then spend some time with us. The next time Mimi wants company drill her on her flash cards. Or help her learn to use the special equipment the therapist gave her to teach her to do things one-handed. Or just talk to her.

"Or some evening when it's about six o'clock," I went on, "go down to the kitchen and see if someone needs help with dinner. It's like . . . I don't know. Maybe if you change, Mum and Dad and Mimi and I will change, too."

Janine nodded her head. "I see," she said. "Yes. That's very sensible . . ."

"But don't change *too* much," I added. "Mum and Dad'll die if they don't get a physicist out of this family."

Janine laughed.

I stood up.

"I'll tell you something," said Janine. "For a little sister, you're pretty smart."

"*Moi*?" I said, grinning.

"*Toi*," Janine replied with a smile. It was the closest she'd come to making a real joke in a long time.

Janine stood up, too. "I wonder . . ." she started to say.

"What?" I asked.

"I wonder if it's too late in the day for special tea with Mimi. Let's see. Mum and Dad will be out for a while . . . No, I don't believe it's too late."

"Not if you start right now," I said encouragingly.

Janine straightened up her desk. Then I followed her out of her room, but I let her go downstairs alone while I went to my own room. A half hour later I crept down to the kitchen. There were Mimi and Janine, sitting across the table from each other. They were drinking tea from Mimi's cups, and were involved in a conversation about being left-handed versus being right-handed. Truthfully, the conversation sounded a little dull. But Mimi's eyes were sparkling, so I knew she was very, very happy.

15th CHAPTER

July was over. The play group was over. Summer holiday was half over. A new family had moved into Kristy's house. And Mimi was still improving. It was a different sort of summer—a summer of change.

I remarked on that to Mimi one hot, damp afternoon as we sat on the porch, trying to keep cool. Mimi was fanning herself with a delicate Japanese fan that she could open and close expertly with her left hand. I was aiming a tiny battery-operated fan directly at my face and neck, which were hotter than the rest of me, since my hair clung stickily to them. I couldn't find a good place to rest the fan, so I just held it and moved it slowly around.

"Time is change," Mimi told me importantly.

I frowned. "I don't understand."

"As long as there is time, there is change."

"You mean things are always changing?"

Mimi nodded.

"Sometimes they seem to change faster than other times," I said. "I mean, look at everything that happened just this month. We had a play group. Kristy moved out. That new family moved in—the Perkinses. You got sick, and then you got better . . ."

"Have you met these Perkinses?" asked Mimi.

But suddenly I found that I couldn't answer her. Over and over I heard myself say, "You got sick, you got sick." A huge lump was building up in my throat. I turned my fan off and set it down.

"Mimi, I'm sorry," I whispered, unable to look at her.

"Sorry? For what?" Mimi became very concerned. She snapped her fan closed and leaned toward me. "What is it, my Claudia? What is wrong?"

"I gave you the stroke, didn't I? I was rude to you that night, and then you went to your room and the next thing I knew, you had fallen on the floor."

"Oh, my Claudia," murmured Mimi. "Is that what you think?"

I nodded miserably. "It's the truth, isn't it?"

"No. It is not the truth. I had not been feeling well for a long time. Very tired. Did you not notice?"

I thought hard. "I suppose so."

"Look at me, my Claudia. This is an old baby, I mean, body. It is winding down. All parts have been working hard for many, many years. So, one of them wore out. That is all."

I tried to smile.

"Do you believe me?" asked Mimi.

"I want to."

"I can't make you belive me, but I will tell you again. What I said is the true . . . the truth."

"Honest?"

"Yes. Honest."

I turned my fan back on, feeling lighter. I was just about to ask Mimi if we could use her tea things to make special iced tea, when we heard a car door slam in front of our house. A few moments later, Janine appeared.

"Hi," she greeted me. She crossed the porch and gave Mimi a kiss on the cheek. "Hello, Mimi. How are you?"

"Fine, thank you," replied Mimi, even though I knew she was as uncomfortably hot as I was.

"I'm starved," said Janine. "I didn't get to eat lunch today. As soon as I have a snack, would you like to take a walk, Mimi?"

"A walk?" Mimi and I repeated at the same time. Mimi had rarely left the house since she'd come home from the hospital, except of course to go back to the hospital for therapy.

"We'll walk down the shady side of the street," said Janine.

"Well . . ." began Mimi.

I thought about it. With her cane, Mimi was pretty steady on her feet. Her physiotherapist had told her that light exercise would help. I didn't see why she couldn't go outside, as long as someone was with her. And it was *very* nice of Janine to make the offer.

"I think it's a great idea," I told Mimi. "Wouldn't you like to take a walk? Janine will be with you."

"All right," said Mimi slowly. Then she began to smile. "A nice idea."

I stood at the front door a while later, watching Janine and Mimi cross the front lawn, arm in arm. "Time is change," Mimi had said. The more I thought about it, the truer it seemed. It was an intelligent thought from an intelligent woman. I remembered how, not long ago, I had compared Mimi to Lucy Newton. How could I have done that? Mimi wasn't like a baby. At least not any more. She was my grandmother, and I was glad to have her back.

"Club notebook?"

"Check."

"Club record book?"

"Check."

"Treasury?"

"Check."

"M&M's?"

"Check."

We giggled. The members of the Babysitters Club were gathered in my room, preparing for a meeting. Kristy, taking charge, was seeing that we were prepared.

I passed around the M&M's, proudly wearing my newest pair of earrings. They were green, shaped like bottles, and said COCA-COLA on them.

Everyone crowded around for a look.

"Okay," said Kristy after a moment. "Down to business."

But before she could say another word, the phone rang.

"I'll get it," I said, reaching for the receiver. "Hello. Babysitters Club . . .Yes? . . . Yes? . . . Oh, sure. I just need a little information first."

When I hung up a few minutes later, everyone was looking at me eagerly. They knew we had new clients. "Well?" asked Kristy.

"It's the people across the street in your old house," I said.

"Mr Perkins?"

"Well, it was his wife calling. She read the flier we left in the mailbox, and she needs a sitter on Saturday afternoon. There are two little girls. Myriah is five-and-a-half, and Gabbie is two-and-a-half. I've got all the details."

Mary Anne checked the calendar in our record book. Kristy ended up with the job for the new clients.

"Lucky!" I said. "We'll be dying to hear. Mrs Perkins sounds really nice."

Ring, ring.

"I'll get it this time," said Dawn, diving across me. "Hello. Babysitters Club . . . Hi, Mrs Pike . . . *Really*? You're kidding! . . . For two *weeks*? . . . When? . . .Oh." (Dawn's "oh" sounded very disappointed.) "Well, I'm sure someone—What? *Two* someones? Okay. We'll have to do some checking. Permission and stuff. We might not be able to get back to you until tonight . . . You would? Yeah, that'd probably make a big difference. Okay. And *thanks*. 'Bye."

"What, what, *what*?" cried Kristy, even before Dawn had put the receiver back on its cradle.

"You will *never* guess," said Dawn.

"So *tell*." Kristy's eyes were bulging right out of their sockets.

"The Pikes are going on holiday this month. Two weeks in—"

"Sea City. We know," said Kristy. "The beach in New Jersey. They go every summer."

"Well, *this* summer," said Dawn, "Mr and Mrs Pike want some time to themselves, so they're looking for two mother's helpers to come along on the vacation. Two of *us*."

"Aughh!" Everyone began squealing and jumping around.

"*Which* two of us?" asked Kristy, suddenly sober.

"Any two. Mrs Pike said she'll be happy to talk to our parents. But I can't go," said Dawn. "I'm spending the first two weeks of August in California with my dad. Remember?"

"And we're going on holiday," I reminded my friends. "The doctor said Mimi is well enough."

"Well, I'm positive Mum won't let me go," said Kristy. "She wants all us kids around for the rest of the summer. We had a family meeting about it just last night. She says we have a big job ahead of us: learning to get along as a family. She even wants Karen and Andrew to spend extra time at Watson's—I mean, at our house—so we can really see what our new family is like."

"Well," said Stacey, "that leaves you and me, Mary Anne. I haven't got any plans. How about you?"

"Me, neither," replied Mary Anne.

"It won't be easy to convince my parents to let me go," said Stacey.

"Or to convince my father," added Mary Anne.

"But I have this funny feeling," Stacey went on, "that pretty soon you and I are going to be getting ready for surf, sun and fun!"

"Yeah!" said Mary Anne enthusiastically. "Sea City, here we come!"

The Babysitters Club

BOY-CRAZY STACEY

1st CHAPTER

"Mum?" I said. "How do you think you're supposed to behave in a mansion?"

My mother looked up from the letter she was writing at the desk in our study. "What, Stace?" she asked.

"This is the evening we're all going over to Watson's. I mean, to Kristy's. And I want to make sure I do everything right."

"You've been to Mr Brewer's house before, honey," replied Mum.

"I know, but not just for a normal visit. Kristy says all her neighbours are really fancy. Remember how we had to fix up Louie the day before the Thomases moved, just so he would look as nice as all the other dogs in the new neighbourhood?"

My mother smiled. "Sometimes Kristy gets carried away. You know that. I think you should just go over there and behave the same way you would have in Kristy's old house."

"Really?"

"Really. When are you supposed to be there, honey?"

"In about an hour. Mr Kishi's driving Claudia and Mary Anne and me over as soon as he gets home from work."

"And will you be—"

"Yes, Mum. I'll be careful about what I eat."

"Stacey, there's no need to be rude."

"But you know I'm always careful. And Kristy is really nice about making sure there's plain popcorn or fruit or something for me. Besides, this is just a *little* party. Just supper. And then I'll be home."

The members of the Babysitters Club were all going over to the new home of Kristy Thomas, our club chairman. She and her mother and brothers had moved there not long ago when her mother got remarried to Watson Brewer, this really nice guy who also happens to be a really rich guy. He lives in a neighbourhood where the gardens are big enough for swimming pools or tennis courts, and all the houses are set way back from the road. Some of them are hidden by walls or bushes.

Until she moved, though, Kristy had lived in an ordinary old house on ordinary old Bradford Court, next door to her best friend, Mary Anne Spier, who's our club secretary, and across the street from Claudia Kishi, our vice-chairman and *my* best friend. It was Kristy's idea to start a business doing baby-sitting for the families in our neighbourhood, and it worked out really well. The four of us, plus Dawn Schafer, who lives not far away, meet for about a half an hour three afternoons a week in Claudia's bedroom. Our clients phone us looking for baby-sitters and they almost always get one, since they reach five sitters (I should say, five *qualified* sitters) at once.

We have a record book with all sorts of information including our schedules, and Mary Anne keeps track of our jobs and who's available to sit when, and things like that. Kristy insists that we also keep the Babysitters Club Notebook, in which each of us has to write up every single sitting job we do. Then the book gets passed around so the others can read about what happened. It's pretty useful.

This summer, our club branched out a little. Last month, July, we did our regular baby-sitting *and* held a play group. We held it right here in my garden. The neighbourhood kids came over three mornings a week for games and stories and art projects. It worked out really well.

But July was over. It was the beginning of August. And for the first time since the club began almost a year ago, at the beginning of seventh grade, we baby-sitters were going to be scattered, split up. Before that happened, Kristy wanted to have a get-together. And she wanted to have it at her new house. That was fine with the rest of us. We love Watson's house, even though it makes us a little nervous sometimes.

I went to my bedroom and began looking through my wardrobe. Why hadn't I done this earlier? I realized I would have to choose my outfit very carefully. I wanted to be casual enough to have fun, but sophisticated enough to look impressive in case any rich neighbours dropped by. I also wanted to be cool since it felt like it was about 150 degrees outside. I changed my mind six times before I decided on this new pink shirt I got the last time we went back to New York City to visit friends. Big, bright green and yellow birds were splashed all over it. It was gigantic, so it would be cool. I put it on with a pair of baggy shorts, looped a wide green belt around my middle, and hunted up some jewellery—silver bangle bracelets and a pair of silver earrings shaped liked bells that actually ring when they dangle back and forth.

I'm working on making Mum and Dad let me get my ears pierced a second time so I can wear two pairs of earrings at once, but so far, no luck. I pretty much grew up in New York—we just moved here to Stoneybrook, Connecticut, a year ago—and I have sort of wild tastes. My parents have let me get away with a lot of things fashionwise, but they draw the line at two earrings in each ear. They said I would look like a pirate, although I, personally, have never seen a pirate with more than exactly one earring. I pointed out that if I *did* get my ears pierced again, probably no one would mistake me for a pirate, but Mum and Dad failed to see the humour in that.

Beep! Beep!

I heard honking and looked out my window. The Kishis' car was in my driveway. Mr Kishi was at the wheel; Mimi, Claudia's grandmother, was next to him; and Claudia was in the back seat with Mary Anne Spier.

"I'll be right there!" I shouted.

I thundered down the stairs. "'Bye, Mum!"

"Wait, Stacey," she said, coming into the front hall.

"Mum, I have to go!"

My mother thrust a small, foil-wrapped package into my hand. "Here. Take this with you."

"What is it?"

"Apple slices."

'Mum, I promise you there will be stuff I can eat at Watson's. He's got the biggest kitchen I've ever seen. I'm sure, somewhere, there's an apple." I handed the package back to her. "Put them in the fridge, okay? I'll eat them tomorrow."

My parents worry about me constantly because I've got diabetes. That means I have to be very careful to eat a certain amount of sugar every day—not too much and not too little. If I'm not careful, my blood sugar level goes all haywire and I can get really sick. My parents are always afraid I'll sneak off and eat junk food. I've been tempted, but I've never done it. Why would I want to get sick?

I dashed out of the front door. "See you!" I called to Mum.

My father was gardening in one of the flower beds. It's his favourite early evening activity in the summer.

"'Bye, Dad!" I called.

"'Bye, honey. Be careful."

Be careful. I should have known. But I reminded myself that they're a lot better than they used to be. Just a little over a year earlier, my parents practically wouldn't let me go to school.

I scrambled into the back seat of the Kishis' car. "Hi, everybody! Hi, Mimi!"

Mimi eased herself around and smiled. "Hello, Stacey," she answered slowly. (Mimi had a stroke this summer and she's still recovering. She moves awkwardly and has some trouble speaking.)

I could tell that Claudia and Mary Anne were as excited as I was about going to Kristy's. The three of us were wriggling around like puppies. But we quietened down when we reached Kristy's new neighbourhood. And by the time Mr Kishi had pulled into the circular drive and Watson's house had loomed into view, we were positively silent.

I think it was the sight of Kristy that brought us back to reality. She was sprawled outside the elegant front door of Watson's house, eating an ice-lolly, reading a magazine, and wearing cut-off jeans and a holey white T-shirt that said I ♡ MY followed by a silhouette of a collie. Her feet were bare.

The sight was refreshing. I knew then that my mother was right. No matter what Kristy's house looked like, Kristy was still Kristy. I wouldn't have to behave any differently.

Dawn arrived just as the back bumper of Mr Kishi's car was disappearing at the other end of the drive.

"Hi!" she cried, leaping out. "See you later, Mum!"

The five of us faced each other eagerly.

"Well, come on!" said Kristy.

We entered the front hall of her house and greeted her mother and Watson in the living room. Then we raced upstairs and down a hallway to the room Kristy had chosen for her bedroom. Watson's house is so big that Kristy and her three brothers each got a room of their own when they moved in. And even so, Watson's two little children from his first marriage, Karen and Andrew, who don't even live with him full-time, have their own rooms for when they visit, plus a playroom, and there are still a few guest rooms left over. It makes me sort of breathless. I mean, when I lived in New York, we had what was considered a pretty big apartment, and it only had four bedrooms, one of which was hardly big enough for a bed.

In Kristy's room, we all plopped down on the new duvet on her new bed, arranging ourselves around Louie, her collie, who was sprawled on his back.

"Where are your brothers?" I asked.

"David Michael's around somewhere," replied Kristy. (David Michael is seven.) "And Sam and Charlie are over at a neighbour's house using the pool." (Sam and Charlie are older, in high school.)

"Are sandwiches okay for dinner?" Kristy asked us. "Mum and I made a whole stack of them this afternoon. There are a couple of plain tuna fish for you, Stace."

"Great," I said. "Thanks."

I glanced at Mary Anne Spier. As I mentioned earlier, Mary Anne is Kristy's best friend, and Claudia is mine, but it's funny the way things work out. Mary Anne and *I* were going to be spending the next two weeks together. I was a little nervous about it. We are *so* different. Mary Anne is really shy; I'm pretty straightforward. Mary

Anne is kind of young; I'm sophisticated. Mary Anne has no interest in boys; I had a couple of boyfriends in seventh grade.

As if reading my mind, Claudia said to me, "Are you all ready for the Pikes, Stace?"

"I hope so," I replied. "I've never spent two weeks with eight kids before. At least I'll have Mary Anne to help me."

"You guys are so lucky," said Kristy wistfully. "Two weeks at the beach."

"Two weeks of chasing after Claire, Margo, Nicky, Vanessa, Byron, Jordan, Adam and Mallory," I pointed out.

"Well, I'd go to the beach in a second, even if I had to be a mother's helper," said Kristy.

As uncertain as I was about going off with Mary Anne, I had to admit I was excited. The members of our club baby-sit for the Pikes often, and not long ago, Mrs Pike had called to say she wanted two of us to go along with them as mother's helpers when they take their summer holiday down in Sea City, New Jersey. Mary Anne and I were the only ones available.

It was all part of why the Babysitters Club was going to scatter. In just a couple of days, Mary Anne and I would be off to Sea City, Claudia and her family were going on a quiet holiday to a mountain resort in New Hampshire, and Dawn and her younger brother were flying to California to visit their father. They hadn't been in California in seven months, since their parents got divorced and Mrs Schafer decided to move back to Connecticut, where she grew up.

"I can't believe I'm stuck here in Stoneybrook while you guys get to go to all these great places," wailed Kristy.

"It *is* sort of ironic," spoke Dawn. "I mean, here you are in this mansion with a rich stepfather . . ."

"I know," said Kristy, looking a little pouty. "But Mum is determined to make our 'new' family work out. She wants us all together for a while."

Kristy's mum appeared at the door just then, carrying a big tray loaded with drinks and the sandwiches. As soon as she left, we dived into the food as if we hadn't eaten since July. When we were finished, we fooled around with new hair styles, and I tried on some of Kristy's clip-on earrings to see how I'd look if my parents were to go crazy or something and let me pierce my ears again after all.

"Uh-oh," said Dawn suddenly, looking at her watch. "It's almost nine. My mum said she'd pick me up between nine and nine-thirty."

"My dad's coming soon, too," said Claudia.

"I won't see you guys for over *two weeks*!" cried Kristy.

"Hey," said Mary Anne, "I've got an idea. Let's exchange our holiday addresses.

Then we can all write postcards to each other."

Kristy found some index cards in her desk drawer and we wrote down our addresses for each other.

"I've got an even better idea," Kristy said. "Stacey and Mary Anne, why don't you write me a postcard every day describing your job with the Pikes? Later, we'll enter them in the notebook. That way, we'll keep it up-to-date and official."

"I might baby-sit for my old clients when I go back to California," said Dawn. "If I do, I'll send you notebook entries, too."

We talked and made plans busily. We could hardly believe it when David Michael called, "Mr Kishi and Mrs Schafer are here!"

We baby-sitters looked at each other. Kristy began to cry. Then Dawn. Then Mary Anne. Then Claudia and me.

"I'm going to miss you!" wailed Dawn.

"I'm going to miss you and be bored!" added Kristy.

"I've never been away from home alone before!" cried Mary Anne.

We all began hugging each other. Kristy handed out tissues. As soon as we'd calmed down, Dawn moaned. "Two whole *weeks*," and the hugging and crying started again.

A few minutes later, Claudia, Mary Anne, and I climbed into the back seat of the Kishis' car. We sniffled all the way to Bradford Court.

I was miserable . . . until I got to my room and looked at my new bikini and began thinking of sunshine and the ocean and cute boys in bathing trunks and the boardwalk the Pike kids were always talking about. A little flutter of excitement crept into my stomach and pushed away the stone of misery. By the time I went to bed I was so excited about Sea City, New Jersey, that I couldn't sleep.

2nd CHAPTER

There is nothing like ringing the doorbell at the Pikes' house. If the kids are at home, there is an actual stampede to get to the door.

Mary Anne and I stood on their front stoop the next afternoon. "Brace yourself," I said.

I rang the bell.

Pitter-patter, pitter-patter. Feet were running toward us.

Thump, thump, thump, thump. Thud, thud, thud, thud.

Crash.

The inner door was flung open. There stood Claire, Margo, Nicky, Vanessa, and Jordan. They looked flushed and breathless.

"Hi!" squealed Claire. Claire is the youngest Pike. She just turned five. Margo just turned seven, Nicky is eight, and Vanessa is nine. Jordan is ten, but he's not an ordinary ten-year-old—he's a triplet. Byron and Adam are his identical brothers. The oldest Pike is Mallory, who's eleven. She's a really good kid and usually gives us baby-sitters a hand. She even helped out at our play group last month.

I opened the screen door, and Claire grabbed my hand. "Come inside," she said urgently, tugging at me.

Not to be outdone, Margo grabbed Mary Anne's hand. "Yeah, come on in."

Vanessa, who is usually quiet, began jumping up and down. "Tomorrow, tomorrow, we go to Sea City!" she cried. "We'll see the beach and the shells so pretty."

Nicky rolled his eyes. "Do you have to rhyme *every*thing?" he asked.

"Yes," replied Vanessa. "Because I'm going to be a poet."

"You didn't rhyme *that*," Nicky pointed out maddeningly, and Vanessa stuck out her tongue at him.

"Mu-um!" yelled Nicky. "Vanessa stuck her tongue out at me!"

We were standing in the narrow front hallway. Mary Anne and I were pinned against a cupboard door.

"Okay, kids," called Mrs Pike, as she ran in from the kitchen. "Give Mary Anne and Stacey some breathing room."

The Pikes backed off.

Mrs Pike had invited us over that

afternoon to discuss the trip and to explain our responsibilities. She ushered us into the living room and shooed the children outdoors. Then she began talking.

"Mostly," she said after a while, "you'll just be giving Mr Pike and me a hand since, of course, we'll be there, too. But we would like some time to ourselves. So there will be afternoons or evenings when we'll go off to do things on our own. Then you'll be in charge."

Mary Anne and I nodded. I was beginning to think that "mother's helper" was a pretty funny term, since Mary Anne and I were going to be helping Mr Pike as much as Mrs Pike. Maybe we should be called parents' helpers.

"Have you ever been to the Jersey Shore?" asked Mrs Pike.

"Nope," said Mary Anne.

"Once," I replied.

"Well, Sea City is a medium-sized town. There's a lot to see and do and you'll be perfectly safe on your own. Just keep a careful eye on the children. There's traffic to watch for, but there's also the ocean."

Mary Anne and I nodded again.

"As you know, Mr Pike and I don't believe in making rules for the children or forcing them to do things they don't want to do. But we do make one beach rule which we expect everyone to stick to: Absolutely no going in the ocean—not even wading—

before nine A.M. or after five P.M. Between nine and five the lifeguards are on duty, unless it's raining. Then you can swim as much as you want as long as you stay in front of the lifeguard station. Is that clear?"

"Yes," we said.

"I don't mean to sound harsh. It's just that the ocean can be so dangerous. But believe me, there are plenty of other things to do in Sea City. There's Trampoline Land and miniature golf. There's the pier with an amusement park. There's a cinema and shops and so many places to eat you can smell Sea City before you see it!"

I giggled.

"It's a great place for kids," Mrs Pike added. "We've been going there for nine years. I know you'll have a good time."

Mrs Pike went on to tell us about the house they always rented, food shopping, dividing up chores, and stuff like that. Then I told her about my diet and about the injections of insulin I have to give myself every day. Although the Pike kids don't know I have diabetes, Mr and Mrs Pike do, and they wanted to be sure I'd feel comfortable on the trip, and that they had the right kind of foods on hand for me. It was very nice of them.

Mrs Pike had had to do a lot of fast talking to convince my parents to let me go to Sea City. It would be the first time I'd been away from Mum and Dad longer than overnight since I'd got diabetes almost two years ago. They didn't even think about letting me go until they'd looked up a couple of doctors in Sea City and spoken to them over the phone.

Mary Anne and I left the Pikes' that afternoon practically crackling with excitement. We were to leave at eight o'clock the next morning. It was time to go home and pack.

"I already packed," Mary Anne confided. "I couldn't wait. I'm scared, but I'm really looking forward to this. It's my first time away from my father, my first trip to the beach—and my first bikini! Dad said I could get one as long as the bottom part was decent."

Mary Anne's father used to be really strict with her. He's still a little strict, but he's much better. It's because Mrs Spier died a long time ago and he's raised Mary Anne by himself. He loosened up a lot, though, when Mary Anne finally began standing up to him.

When I got home, I went to my room, opened my suitcase on my bed, and began carefully laying my clothes in it—last year's bikini, the new bikini, two bright sundresses, sandals, shorts, tops, a nightshirt. Then I snuck over to my bottom bureau drawer, removed a bottle labelled SUN-LITE, and buried it under my clothes. I was determined to come home with lightened hair. My hair is already blonde, but I wanted it Sun-Lite blonde. However, if Mum saw the bottle, I'd be dead.

I hid it just in time, because the next thing I knew I heard my mother's footsteps on the stairs.

"Honey?" Mum called.

"In my room," I replied. "I'm packing."

Mum came and perched on the edge of my bed. She watched me toss things into the suitcase. "Do you have everything?" she asked.

"I think so. Mary Anne and I asked Mrs Pike about clothes and stuff this afternoon. She said no one dresses up in Sea City. A sundress would be fine if we went out to dinner."

"Do you have something to do down there?"

"Something to *do*?! I've got eight kids to watch."

"I know, but I'm sure you'll have a little time to yourself. Do you have a book or some embroidery?"

I held up both—an Agatha Christie mystery, and this swan I'd been embroidering for about five years.

Mum nodded. "What about stamps? Do you have stamps so you can write postcards?" She was looking more and more nervous.

"No. But I'm sure there's a post office in Sea City."

"I'll get you some stamps," Mum said suddenly. "Be right back." She dashed into her bedroom and I could hear her rummaging around in her desk. When she returned, she handed me a strip of postcard stamps.

"Thanks," I said. I tucked them into my purse.

Next Mum asked about toothpaste. But I knew what she really wanted to ask me. She wanted to know if I'd been responsible enough to get together everything I'd need for two weeks of insulin injections. Finally I gave in and showed her. I opened the special travel kit she'd bought for me.

"See?" I said. "Everything's there."

"What about—"

"The doctors' numbers are in my purse. Mrs Pike wrote them down, too. And she knows all about my diet. We talked about it today."

"Oh, Stacey," said Mum suddenly. "I'm so worried. I'm going to worry for the next two weeks."

"You really don't have to," I told her. I sat next to her on the bed. "The Pikes have a phone, remember? You can call if you want. And Mrs Pike would call you if anything *did* happen—not that it's going to," I added quickly. "And don't call a lot, okay? I don't want the Pike kids to think I'm a baby. Then they'd never listen to me."

Mum looked at me for the longest time. Finally she opened her arms. I leaned over and we hugged. Mum cried. I cried a little, too. It's awfully hard helping your parents grow up.

But it has to be done.

3rd CHAPTER

Saturday afternoon

Dear Kristy,

Hi! We made it. The drive down here was wild, but we arrived unharmed. Do you like this postcard? Mary Anne and I found a shop with these really wild cards. Here are some things to put in the Baby-sitters Club Notebook: Sometimes the Pike kids get carsick. Claire is still in her silly stage. She calls her mother "Moozie" and her father "Daggles". That's all for now. More tomorrow! 'Bye!

Luv,
Stacey

The next morning, I discovered the meaning of the word *madhouse*.

Mary Anne and I arrived at the Pikes' early. My dad drove us over. If you think Mum and I had been tearful the day before, you should have seen Mary Anne and her father. It was like Niagara Falls—for both of them. I've hardly ever seen a man cry.

But Mary Anne's tears were dry by the time we reached the Pikes'. My father pulled up in front of the house. He started to help Mary Anne and me with our suitcases.

"Just drop us off, Dad," I said. "Okay? You don't need to come with us or anything."

Dad was understanding. He simply gave me a hug, waved to Mr Pike, then turned around and drove off.

Mr Pike was struggling with the luggage rack. Actually, with two luggage racks. So many of us were going to Sea City that we had to drive down there in both of the Pike's large cars.

While Mr Pike tried to fit suitcases into the luggage racks, Mrs Pike and Mallory kept carrying boxes and things out of the house and depositing them by the cars.

"Hi, Stacey! Hi, Mary Anne!" cried Margo.

Claire ran out of the house and joined her sister. I'd never seen anybody so excited. She looked as if she'd just had about ten cups of coffee.

"Hi, hi, Stacey-silly-billy-goo-goo!" Claire screeched. "Hi, Mary Anne-silly-billy-goo-goo!" She was galloping around in circles.

I rolled my eyes at Mary Anne. Claire was going through this incredibly silly stage. It could drive you crazy.

Mr Pike finally finished hefting all the suitcases onto the luggage racks and securing them with rope. He turned around. Seven boxes were at his feet. "What's all this?" he demanded.

"Bedding," replied Mrs Pike.

"Toys," added Nicky.

Mr Pike groaned.

Forty-five minutes later, everything was loaded into or on top of the cars, including the people. I was sitting in the back seat of the car Mr Pike was driving. Next to me was Nicky. Between us was a box. At our feet was a large thermos. Sprawled out in the very back were Claire and Margo. Mallory was sitting up front with her father.

"You guys comfortable back there?" I asked the girls.

"Yup," replied Margo. "We have everything we need."

"So I see," I said. "Colouring books."

"Crayons," added Claire.

"Pillows," Nicky pointed out, turning around.

"Crackers," I said. "Sick Bucket . . . Sick Bucket? What on earth is that?" Between the girls was a red plastic bucket. It was carefully labelled PIKE SICK BUCKET in big letters.

"In case we get carsick," said Claire.

"Be sure to drink a lot of grape juice this morning," said Nicky, grinning wickedly. "That'd look neat coming up. Purple puke."

Claire and Margo laughed hysterically.

I closed my eyes. I absolutely can't stand it when someone gets sick. When I opened them, I caught sight of Mr Pike looking at me in the rearview mirror.

"Don't worry," he said. "We rarely have to use it. We've only had a few emergencies that I can remember."

I smiled with relief.

Everyone was settled in the two cars. Mr and Mrs Pike had rolled down their windows and were callng last-minute instructions to each other. Things like, "It's the Garden State Parkway, not the New Jersey Turnpike," and "Ice-cream stop at Howard Johnson's," and, "Try to follow me, but if we get separated, remember the real estate agent in Sea City is Ellen Cooke."

At last we backed out of the driveway.

"Good-bye, house!" called Nicky.

"Good-bye, house-silly-billy-goo-goo!" called Claire.

"Good-bye, Stoneybrook. Sea City, here we come!" added Mallory.

"Hey, Daggles-silly-billy-goo-goo,"

Claire said to her father. "Guess what."

"What, sweetie?" replied Mr Pike, trying to cross a junction with a four-way stop.

"That's what!"

Mr Pike made it through the junction and noticed a rope from the luggage rack flapping against the windscreen. He pulled to a stop and got out to fix it.

"Are we there already?" asked Claire.

"We're still on our own *street*, stupid," Nicky said in disgust.

"Don't call her stupid," said Mallory, without even turning around.

"Stacey-silly-billy-goo-goo?" asked Claire.

I hesitated, not wanting to fall into the trap Mr Pike had fallen into. "What?" I said at last.

"How much longer?"

"Several hours," I replied as Mr Pike got back in the car. "It's a long drive. Why don't you and Margo open your colouring books? You can each make a picture to give your mum when we get to the beach."

The girls opened their books and began sorting through their crayons. Nicky took a horrible-looking green monster out of his pocket and started to play with it. In the front seat, Mallory was reading *The Secret Garden*. We pulled onto the highway.

Everything was peaceful for about half an hour—until Mrs Pike edged forward and passed us in the next lane. For some reason, we all happened to look up as the car went by. So we all saw that Jordan was holding up a big piece of paper in the side window that read BARFMOBILE. Jordan was pointing his finger at us and grinning. Obviously, he meant *we* were the Barfmobile.

"Barfmobile!" yelped Nicky. He sounded highly insulted. "You guys have any paper back there?" he asked, turning to his little sisters.

"Sure," replied Margo. "Paper, scissors, crayons—"

"Give me a piece of paper, quick," said Nicky. "And a red crayon."

Margo handed them to him. Nicky rested the paper against the box and began scribbling.

"What are you writing, Nicky-silly-billy-goo-goo?" asked Claire about twelve times.

Nicky held up his masterpiece.

The paper read VOMIT COMET.

"That'll show them," remarked Mallory.

"Hey, Dad," said Nicky, hanging his arms over the front seat. "Speed up."

"Why?" asked Mr Pike.

"I want you to pass Mum."

"Sorry, Nick-o. The traffic is too thick. Maybe when it clears up a little."

"Okay." Nicky flopped back into his seat, pouting.

The little girls went back to their colouring. Mallory returned to *The Secret Garden*.

But Nicky kept peering out the window, trying to spot his mother's car. "Jingle bells," he sang softly. "Batman smells, Robin laid an egg." He turned to me. "Get it, Stacey? *Robin* laid an *egg*?"

"I get it."

"Jingle bells, Batman smells, Robin laid an egg . . ."

"Nicky, I really hate that song," said Mallory.

"Okay. Jingle bells, Santa smells, Rudolph broke his—Hey! Here we go!"

The traffic was very heavy. The cars in Mrs Pike's lane were edging along, but the ones in our lane were suddenly moving a bit faster. As we passed the other Pike car, three things happened at once. Nicky triumphantly held up his sign and was rewarded with dirty looks from the triplets. Claire called, "Hi, Moozie-silly-billy-goo-goo!" to her mother. And Margo grabbed for the Sick Bucket and whimpered, "I don't feel too good."

"Uh-oh," I said.

"Darn," said Nicky. "She hasn't had any grape juice yet."

Poor Margo looked so miserable, I couldn't turn away from her, even though if I saw her throw up, I'd probably have to use the bucket myself. She turned a wicked shade of green, but nothing happened.

"She might feel better if she sat up front," suggested Mallory.

"If you're going to trade places, do it carefully," said Mr Pike grimly.

"Oh, boy!" squealed Nicky. "The last time this happened, Margo puked while she was climbing over the seats."

"Great," I muttered.

The girls managed to switch places. Mallory accidentally kicked Mr Pike in the shoulder, but Margo's breakfast stayed down.

"Jingle bells, Santa sm—" began Nicky.

"Nicholas, if we hear that song one more time . . ." threatened Mr Pike. He was trying to pass a truck.

"Okay," said Nicky. "Jingle barf —"

"*Nicholas*!"

"It's not that song!" Nicky exclaimed. "It's a different one." But he kept quiet after that.

"How many more minutes?" asked Claire.

"About fifteen and we'll stop for ice-cream," said her father.

What a relief! The ice-cream break was just what we needed. Mary Anne and the Pike kids (including Margo, who claimed to be starving) slurped up their ice-cream cones. Mr and Mrs Pike had coffee. And I managed to find an ice-lolly that was made with fruit only—no sugar. It was great. It's nice not to be left out of *every* food treat.

We climbed back into the cars and began the rest of the trip to Sea City. After a while, the ground began to look sandier. The trees became scrubbier and shorter. And finally Mallory spotted a sign that said SEA CITY, EXIT 10 MILES.

"Oh, boy!" she whooped.

The rest of us cheered.

Soon we were driving off the exit ramp, Mrs Pike behind us, and turning onto a causeway that crossed some marshy land. The air smelled of salt.

"Hey, there's the cow sign!" cried Nicky pointing.

I looked to the right and saw a sign-post with a three-dimensional purple cow. It was an advertisement for cream.

"There's Crabs for Grabs!" said Mallory as we passed a restaurant.

"There's the suntan girl!" Margo dissolved into giggles as we passed another sign-post, this one showing a puppy pulling at the bottom of a little girl's bathing suit, showing off her splendid tan line.

"Why did Mr Stupid tiptoe past the medicine chest?" shrieked Claire. "Because he didn't want to wake up the sleeping pills!" she answered herself.

"Okay, settle down," I told her.

The Pikes fell into silence as we entered Sea City. They looked awed, and I could see why. Their senses were suddenly overloaded with great kid stuff: the smell of hotdogs and fried food and the sea air, the sounds of the waves and of kids shouting and laughing and calling to each other, but mostly the sights. We passed Trampoline Land and miniature golf and souvenir stands. We passed shops and restaurants and ice-cream parlours. And in the distance was a pier with arcades and a ferris wheel and a roller coaster and probably plenty of head-spinning rides. And beyond all *that* gleamed the ocean.

4th CHAPTER

Saturday night

Dear Claudia,

Hi! We've been in Sea City for half a day now. You should have seen the kids today after we got here. We went exploring as soon as we had unpacked, and they were *so* excited! There's so much to do here!

After we looked around the town we took a walk on the beach. I saw the most gorgeous boy! He's a lifeguard, and he's the guy of my dreams! See ya!

Luv,
Stace

Mr Pike cruised down a wide street in Sea City. (He called it the main drag.) There were palm trees in front of a lot of the stores, but they were all plastic! I suppose Sea City wasn't really palm tree country. Anyway, after a while he turned down a side street and stopped in front of a little pink house surrounded by white gravel. A sign in the yard read ELLEN COOKE, ESTATE AGENT. Mr Pike went inside. He returned a few minutes later with a ring of keys and a folder full of brochures and ads and even an uninflated souvenir beach ball. We drove off again.

"I claim the ball!" cried Nicky.

"No, me!" yelled Margo.

"No, me!" yelled Claire.

I grabbed the beach ball and sat on it. "Guess what," I said. "The beach ball is either everybody's or nobody's."

"Thank you, Stacey," said Mr Pike.

"But it can't be everybody's," said Nicky.

"Then I guess it's nobody's," I replied.

"If it's nobody's, then I claim it!" Nicky retorted gleefully.

Luckily, just then we turned into a drive.

"Here we are!" announced Mr Pike. "End of the line! Everybody out."

"Yeah! Hurray!" We tumbled out of the car. Mrs Pike parked next to us, and the triplets and Vanessa tumbled out of her car. The Pike kids were all jumping around and yelling. No wonder. The air smelled *wonderful*. It wasn't just the salt. It was something else that I couldn't describe, a freshness that was different from country air.

"We're back, we're here, we've come once more, to our gingerbread house by the white seashore!" sang Vanessa.

"Hey, that was good one," said Byron appreciatively.

I took a look at the Pikes' rented house. We were facing the back, but even from there I could see that it *was* sort of gingerbready—with carved railings and posts and eaves and edges. Very old-fashioned. It was large and rambling, painted yellow with white trim. I glanced at Mary Anne and could tell that she had already fallen in love with it. I knew she was mentally writing a postcard to Dawn, describing the house and its view of the ocean.

"Do you rent the same house every year?" I asked Mallory as we unloaded boxes from the car.

"Yup," she said. "And we're so lucky. I mean, right on the beach and everything. In the evening we sometimes sit on the front porch and just stare out at the ocean. And when it rains . . ."

"Yeah?"

"I go up to this room on the third floor and sit on this window seat and watch the lightning and the waves crashing and everything."

I shivered. It sounded very romantic.

"Plus," added Mallory, "the lifeguard stand is right in front of our house. We can walk out of the front door and straight into the ocean for a swim."

The driveway was behind the house, and we were carrying things in through the back door. Inside, Mrs Pike was directing traffic.

"Why don't you take the same rooms you had last year?" she suggested. "Boys in the big bedroom at the end of the hall. Claire and Margo, in the room next to Daddy and me. Vanessa and Mallory, the pink bedroom. Oh, and Mal, show Mary Anne and Stacey the yellow bedroom, okay?"

Mary Anne was looking around the house, wide-eyed. The rooms on the first floor were big and bright and airy. I saw a living room, a sunporch, and a kitchen before Mallory whisked us up the wide staircase to the second floor.

The second floor consisted of a hallway, bedroom, and bathrooms.It reminded me a little of Watson's house, only it wasn't nearly as big. Mallory opened a door towards the end of the hall.

"This is the yellow bedroom," she said. "If you don't like it, there are a couple of rooms on the third floor, or you could trade with somebody."

"Oh, no, it's perfect!" Mary Anne breathed. "Just perfect."

It was a pretty room, I suppose, although

not really to my taste. It was old-fashioned, with two high dark wood beds, a bare wood floor, and yellow flowered wallpaper. It did, however, have a view of the beach. Out our window was sand and sun and the lifeguard stand.

"This is great!" I said to Mary Anne as soon as Mallory had left. "What a view. Come on, let's unpack. Then we can help the kids unpack, and after lunch, we can go out and do something."

We did just that. We emptied our suitcases, putting things in the tall bureau between our beds, or hanging them in the wardrobe. Then we gave the Pike kids a hand. While Mr and Mrs Pike were still unpacking boxes and opening windows and making grocery lists, Mary Anne and I made sandwiches and served them up at the table in the kitchen.

As we were finishing lunch, I made the mistake of asking, "So what do you guys want to do this afternoon?"

"Go to the beach," said Mallory.

"Go to the arcade," said Jordan.

"Go swimming," said Adam.

"Go to Trampoline Land," said Nicky.

"Make sandcastles," said Claire.

"Go on the ferris wheel," said Margo.

"Go to Ice-Cream Palace," said Byron, who loves to eat.

"Look for shells, look for shells, washed

to shore by the ocean swells." (That was Vanessa, obviously.)

Mary Anne and I glanced at each other. Mary Anne raised her eyebrows. "Well," she said slowly, "maybe we can do everything . . . sort of."

"How?" asked the kids.

"Yeah, how?" I asked.

"We'll go exploring," replied Mary Anne. "Stacey and I haven't been here before. Why don't you take us on a tour? You can show us everything. We probably won't have time to go on rides or play games, but at least we can see the town."

The triplets were the first to okay the idea, and the others quickly followed. Fifteen minutes later, Mary Anne and I were herding the Pike kids out of the back door and down the street.

"Where do we start?" I asked.

"The main drag," replied Adam promptly.

"Yeah, that's good," said Mallory. "We'll walk right through town, and then go over to the pier and come back home that way."

Walking "right through town" took just under two hours. At least one Pike wanted to stop at nearly every place we passed. Nicky wanted to see how much it cost to jump on the trampolines this summer. Byron wanted to see if the price of ice-cream cones was the same, and whether Ice-

Cream Palace still had cherry vanilla. Mallory and Vanessa ducked into every souvenir shop along the way. They exclaimed over the little animals made of shells (which *were* pretty cute) and Sea City hats, towels, mugs, T-shirts, shorts, and postcards.

We almost had tears when we passed a penny sweet store called Candy Heaven and Byron discovered two quarters in his pocket and started buying up—but only for himself. The others wanted sweets, too. Luckily, Mary Anne and I had just enough change to buy each of them a gobstopper. And Mary Anne bought a tiny chocolate teddy for herself, but I had to go without, of course. When we left Candy Heaven, all you could hear was *slurp, slurp, slurp*, and exclamations of, "Mine's turning blue now!" or, "Hey, look! Mine's yellow!" or, "When mine gets smaller, I'm going to bite it in half and look at all the layers."

We proceeded along the main drag.

"There's Burger Garden!" said Byron, as we passed a tacky-looking restaurant. It was surrounded by a "garden" of plastic flowers. The outside tables were in the shape of mushrooms, and the waiters and waitresses were dressed like animals.

"Ask Claire what this place is called," whispered Jordan.

"What's this place called?" I asked her.

"Gurber Garden."

Jordan hooted. "She never says it right!"

We continued on our way. "There's Candy Kitchen," said Margo. "That's where we get fudge. It's yummy-yummy!"

"And there's miniature golf," pointed out Jordan.

"That looks like fun," I said. "They didn't have miniature golf in New York City. Have you ever played, Mary Anne?"

"A couple of times. There's a miniature golf course near Shelbyville in Connecticut."

I kept looking. I looked so long that Adam said hopefully, "Maybe we could play now."

"Sorry, kiddo," I told him. "I wish we could, too, but we don't have any money. I'm sure we'll come back, though. It would be fun to play sometime."

We stood around and watched a while longer. Then we continued with our exploring. It took us another hour to walk along the pier and finally we ended up on the beach in front of the Pikes' house.

"Can we go in the water?" asked Nicky.

I looked at my watch. "Nope. Sorry," I said. "It's five o'clock. The lifeguards are getting ready to leave. Besides, you guys aren't wearing your swimming costumes."

"Can't we even go wading?" Nicky pressed.

"Please, please, please? Just to our knees?" added Vanessa.

"No," I told them. "You know the rules."

"You could make a sandcastle or look for shells," suggested Mary Anne.

Nicky pouted. "That's girl stuff," he announced. "I know. We'll play paddle ball." He ran into the house to get rackets and balls.

Mary Anne and I settled ourselves in the sand. We watched the rest of the Pike kids run around, laughing, glad to be at the seashore finally. I looked at the other people on the beach. They were mostly families. Then I watched the lifeguards. They had jumped off of their wooden stand and were pulling on blue windbreakers that said SEA CITY COMMUNITY BEACHES. One had dark, curly hair; the other wavy, blond hair. They looked about seventeen years old.

As the blond one leaned over to fold his towel, the sun caught his hair, making it gleam. And at that moment, he glanced up. He saw me looking at him, and gave me a smile and a little wink.

He was gorgeous. Absolutely gorgeous.

He turned back to his towel and I let out my breath in a shaky gasp.

"Oh, wow," I whispered to Mary Anne. "I'm in love."

"Huh?" she said, frowning.

"I'm in love," I repeated, "with that gorgeous lifeguard."

Mary Anne just shook her head. I knew she thought I was crazy.

5th CHAPTER

Sunday

Dear Kristy,

Here's something for the notebook: Pikes get up early. See ya! Stacey

Sunday

Dear Claudia,

I'm in LUV with that blond, tan hunk of a lifeguard! Today I found out his name. It's Scott. And I think he likes me. Later! Luv,

Stace

P.S. I can't let Mary Anne see this card. She doesn't understand about Scott at all. She thinks I'm looney tunes.

"Stacey?" whispered a small voice.

I pulled the covers over my head, hoping the small voice was part of a dream. It was Sunday morning. Very early Sunday morning. Something had awoken me from a sound sleep.

"Stacey?" whispered the voice again, more urgently.

"Mmphh."

"STACEY-SILLY-BILLY-GOO-GOO?"

"WHAT?" I sat up in bed like I'd been shot out of a cannon. "What is it?"

Margo was standing in the doorway to our bedroom. Claire was next to her.

"We want to go to the beach," said Margo.

"What's going on?" asked Mary Anne sleepily from across the room.

"These two want to go to the beach and it's the middle of the night," I said.

"No, it isn't," replied Margo. "The sun's almost up."

"Mr Sun-silly-billy-goo-goo!" cried Claire.

"Shh, you guys. It's too early for the beach. It's even too early to get up. Come in bed with me."

The girls scrambled for my bed, but three of us were a tight squeeze, so Claire got in bed with Mary Anne instead. We all went back to sleep. We didn't wake up until we smelled breakfast cooking.

"Mmm," I mumbled. "Scrambled eggs. Bacon. Toast."

"Daggles-silly-billy-goo-goo is making breakfast," Claire announced.

Mary Anne and I got dressed and the four of us were downstairs in ten minutes. The other Pikes had gathered. Mallory and Adam were already in their swimming costumes. But Nicky, Vanessa, Byron, Jordan and the little girls were still in their pyjamas. I had a feeling it might take a while to get eight kids ready for the beach.

"Good morning!" Mr Pike greeted us. "I'm the chief cooker of breakfast around here. Are you hungry?"

"Starved!" Mary Anne and I replied.

"Good," he said. "Stacey, come and give me a hand at the stove."

"I'm not much of a cook," I told him.

"That's all right," he replied when I'd reached his side. He lowered his voice. "I want to make sure you can eat what I'm fixing. Pancakes are out, right?"

"Right," I said, looking longingly at a pan of pancakes warming up in the oven. Pancakes used to be my favourite breakfast.

"Toast?" he asked.

I read the ingredients on the bread wrapper. "That's okay," I told him.

"Bacon?"

"Fine."

"And the main course—cheese omelettes," he said proudly.

"Oh. Um, no. It's the processed cheese. I can't eat it."

"No problem. I'll scramble you up a couple of plain eggs, okay?"

"Great," I replied. "Thanks."

Mr Pike didn't look at all put out, but I felt terrible. A mother's helper wasn't supposed to create extra work for her clients. I began to feel apprehensive. What if Mallory or one of the younger Pike kids wanted to know why I was on a diet when I'm already pretty thin? But I put my fears aside, and felt better by the time breakfast was over and no one had mentioned my scrambled eggs or the fact that I had turned down "yummy-yummy" pancakes in favour of plain old toast.

No sooner had the last bite of breakfast been eaten, than Jordan yelled, "Beach!" and the Pikes turned into a human tornado. Six of the kids needed to change into swimming costumes. We had to find eight towels, two umbrellas, some chairs, four buckets and spades, four paddleball rackets and balls, books, a pack of cards, several tubes of sunscreen, T-shirts, and drinks. And that was just for the kids. Mary Anne and I had to get ourselves ready, too.

Mary Anne, ever-organized, had packed her beach bag the night before. Neatly arranged in it were a hairbrush, sunglasses, a headband, and a copy of *A Tree Grows in Brooklyn*. I threw together a similar bag, remembering to toss in the bottle of sun-lite. Then we prepared to peel off our shorts and shirts, revealing our bikinis.

"You first," I said to Mary Anne.

"No way. You first."

I'm not shy. I whipped off my clothes. Underneath was my new bikini. It was skimpy (and we're talking *very* skimpy) and yellow, with tiny bows at the side on the bottom part. And if I do say so myself, the top part was filled out pretty nicely.

Mary Anne's eyes nearly bugged right off her face.

"Oh, my—" she started to say. "Well, that does it. I'm not taking *my* clothes off. I'll sit on the beach in a shirt and jeans. I'll wear an evening gown if I have to."

"Come on, Mary Anne," I said. "It can't be that bad. Let me see."

"No."

"Mary Anne, the kids are waiting. They want to hit the beach. They sound desperate. Off with your clothes."

Slowly Mary Anne removed her shirt and shorts. Underneath was a perfectly nice pale blue bikini with white stripes running diagonally across it. It wasn't quite as skimpy as mine, and the top wasn't filled out at *all* (Mary Anne and Kristy are just about the shortest, smallest girls in our year), but she looked fine. I told her so.

Reluctantly, she helped get the kids organized. The ten of us struggled out the front door and across the sand. About halfway to the water, Mallory suddenly said, "This is a good place."

The kids dropped the junk they were holding and ran, leaving Mary Anne and me to set up our spot. It was nine-thirty and the lifeguards were on duty, so we knew the kids were pretty safe by the water. We spread out towels, opened the umbrellas, set out the beach chairs, and were ready.

I rubbed some sun-lite in my hair. "Sun, hit me with your rays," I said. I oiled myself up with sunscreen and sat back in a chair.

"Hey!" yelped Mary Anne. "We forgot to put lotion on the kids. They'll be as red as lobsters if we're not careful."

We had to round up all the kids and make sure they got lathered with sunscreen. Then we turned them loose again.

I put on my shades. I put on my visor. I sat back in my chair again. The sand was white and warm. The sky was a brilliant blue. In front of me, the ocean crashed and foamed. This was the life.

I gazed around. Not far away, a mother and three little kids were parked. In another spot were a mother, a father, a grandmother, and a little boy about Nicky's age. With some interest, I watched two boys, one about seven, one about four, tugging at the hands of an older boy (fourteen?) and pulling him impatiently along the beach. The older boy was trying to carry a bundle of towels, an umbrella, and a baby. They stopped near us. The boy reminded me of me. He spread out their towels, rubbed sunscreen on the children, and then let the boys run to the water while he stayed under the umbrella with the baby.

Was the boy their brother? I didn't think so. He was fair-skinned with light brown hair, while the children had olive complexions and masses of black curls.

I nudged Mary Anne. "See that boy over there?"

She nodded.

"I think he's a guy mother's helper."

"Really?"

For the next fifteen minutes or so, Mary Anne and I kept an eye on the Pike kids, watched the other mother's helper, and just enjoyed the beach. Of course, I had checked out the lifeguard stand. Two guys were on duty, and they were cute, but neither one was the hunk I'd seen the day before.

"Stacey?" said Mary Anne after a while. "Look at Byron."

I searched the shoreline. I saw Mallory, Jordan, Adam, and Nicky shrieking around in waist-high water. Claire, Margo, and Vanessa were crouched in the wet sand at the water's edge, making castles that were meant to be washed away with each wave. But Byron was hanging back, alone. He was sitting in dry sand, staring out to sea.

"What's wrong with him?" I wondered.

"He hasn't been near the water since we got here. He hasn't even stuck a toe in."

"He does know how to swim, doesn't he?"

"I know for a fact that he does. I remember when the triplets were taking lessons at the Y," replied Mary Anne.

My attention was drawn away from Byron by something very interesting. A jeep was driving up the beach. It stopped by the lifeguard stand. Two guys wearing windbreakers got out. One removed a pair of mirrored sunglasses. It was the hunk! White sun screen and lip cream were smeared on his face, but it didn't matter. He was as gorgeous as ever. He was totally cool!

And he was changing places with one of the guards on duty! The hunk was now sitting just ten yards away from me. Unfortunately, I was facing his back.

"There he is! There he is!" I hissed to Mary Anne.

"Who?" She was still watching Byron.

"Him! That incredible hunk from yesterday. The lifeguard of my dreams. Oh, I am in love with him for sure. I mean it."

"You're not the only one."

"Huh?"

"Look." Mary Anne pointed to a group of girls about our age who had gathered at the base of the lifeguard stand. They seemed to have materialized out of thin air. They were giggling and talking and asking the guards questions.

My heart sank.

All morning I watched the lifeguards and the girls. I watched them much more than I watched the Pike kids. Mary Anne seemed a bit miffed, but I couldn't help it. I was in love.

How did those girls get so lucky? Not only did the lifeguards seem to know them, but they gave them the supreme honour of letting them do favours for them. Those girls brought them drinks and picked up anything that fell off the stand, and one was even asked to fix them sandwiches for lunch.

"Will you quit looking over there?" Mary Anne finally said crossly. "You're boy-crazy. Those lifeguards are much too old for you."

"They are not."

"Are too."

At that moment, three girls who were definitely in high school, maybe even in college, sauntered down the beach. The lifguards stopped talking to the younger girls surrounding the stand, and watched the progress of the older ones with interest.

"See what I mean?" said Mary Anne smugly.

"Oh, cut it out," I snapped. "You don't understand."

And that was all we said to each other until we rounded up the Pikes for lunch and a little break from the hot sun. The kids ate hungrily but didn't want to stay inside for long. They were soon clambering to get back to the sea and sand. I made them all put on sweatshirts and things, since their skin wasn't used to the sun, and I put on some extra clothes myself.

(Only Mary Anne refused to do this. She said she wanted to get a tan right away.) Then we ran out to the beach again. Mr and Mrs Pike decided to go into town.

The kids made a beeline for the water, despite the fact that I'd just told them not even to go wading until their lunches had had a chance to digest for an hour.

"At least Byron paid attention to you," Mary Anne pointed out.

"Yeah . . . Uh-oh."

I jumped up. At the water's edge, Adam and Jordan were splashing Byron.

"Stop it!" he shouted. "Cut it out!"

"Sissy!" Adam yelled back.

"Jerk!"

"Baby!"

"Ratface!"

"Okay, okay, okay," I reached the boys in record time. "What's going on here?"

"He started it!" Byron cried.

"I don't care who started it. I want to know what you're fighting about."

Mary Anne had run up behind me. When Adam made a grab for Jordan, she dived between them, separating them and almost losing her bikini.

"Byron is a baby!" exclaimed Adam. "He won't go in the ocean."

"And you're mad at him for that?" I asked.

"I want him to come in with us. Triplets stick together. He's ruining everything."

"I suppose the only choice is for the three of you to do something *out* of the water," Mary Anne pointed out practically, adjusting her bathing suit.

I turned around at that moment and saw the hunk watching us. He flashed me a grin. My knees melted. I just *had* to talk to him.

While Mary Anne took over with the triplets, I sauntered up to the lifeguard stand.

"Hey, cutie," said the hunk.

My knees practically disappeared, but I turned on all the charm I could find. "Do you have the time?" I asked. "My watch isn't working."

The group of girls around the stand looked at me warily. They backed off a couple of steps.

"Sure," replied the hunk. "It's two twenty-five."

"Thanks," I said.

Just as I was turning away, I heard a cry and the sound of sobbing. "Stacey!" shouted Mallory's voice.

Mallory ran to me, carrying Claire, whose

foot was bleeding. "She cut it on a shell," said Mallory.

"WAHH! Stacey," wailed Claire, holding out her arms to me.

I reached for her—and realized that the hunk was at my side. He was holding a first-aid kit. In no time, he had cleaned Claire's cut and put a Band-Aid on it. Claire and I both gazed at him adoringly.

As Claire ran off a few moments later, the hunk said, "Maybe we'd better introduce ourselves. I'm Scott. Scott Foley. I've been noticing you."

(The girls at the stand retreated even further.)

"I—I'm Stacey McGill," I told him. "Thirteen years old. Formerly of New York City." (Oh, I could just *die*! What a stupid thing to say.)

But Scott simply smiled again. "I'd better get back on duty," he said.

That afternoon, I talked to Scott several more times. I asked him about the weather for the next day. I asked when high tide would be. I pretended I really, really needed to know. Then, around four-thirty, Scott asked me if I'd mind getting him a drink. (*Mind?!*)

The girls left altogether. I had Scott to myself for the rest of the afternoon. I found out that he lived in Princeton, New Jersey, had recently turned eighteen, and was going to college in September. He *was* a little old for me, but I didn't care.

Just before supper that night, I escaped Mary Anne's accusations about how little help I was being, and ran across the beach and down to the water's edge. I stared at the spot where the lifeguard stand had been, and then at the tracks it left as it had been dragged back to the dunes for the night. After a moment, I knelt down in the wet sand. I found a piece of shell and carefully printed:

STACEY + SCOTT = LUV

Then I ran back to the house before a wave came in. I didn't want to see the words wash away.

6th CHAPTER

Monday

Dear Kristy,

A problem with Nicky. The triplets think he's babyish, so they don't play with him. But there are no other boys in the family, and he doesn't like getting stuck with the girls, especially Vanessa. I feel kinda sorry for him.

Luv,
Stacey

Monday

Dear Dawn,

Hi! How is sunny California? Guess what? I am sunburned. I look like a tomato with hair.

Love,
Mary Anne

Mr and Mrs Pike spent almost all of Monday on the beach with the kids and Mary Anne and me.

Scott wasn't on duty.

I was depressed.

But I felt better that afternoon when Mrs Pike said that she and Mr Pike wanted to go out to dinner—just the two of them—to this fancy restaurant in Jamesport, the nearest town, and gave Mary Anne and me enough to take the Pike kids out for the evening.

"Probably the best you'll be able to do with that is go to Burger Garden, which is fairly inexpensive, and get a treat on the pier later," said Mrs Pike.

At this, the kids became hysterical with joy.

"Gurber Garden-silly-billy-goo-goo!" exclaimed Claire.

"Burger Garden! What a way to end this bright and sunny day!" said Vanessa, who was sounding more like a greeting card with each poem.

The others cheered.

At six o'clock that evening we waved goodbye to Mr and Mrs Pike as they backed out of the drive.

"Well, let's go!" said Jordan.

"I want a double Crazy Burger with the works," announced Byron.

The kids looked at Mary Anne and me expectantly.

"You're all ready to go?" I asked them.
"Yup."
"You're all wearing shoes?"
"Yup."
"You've all been to the bathroom?"
"Yup."
"Really?"
"Yup."
"Wait a sec," said Mary Anne. "Where's Vanessa?"
"In our room. She's still getting dressed, I think," said Mallory.
I ran upstairs to the pink bedroom. Vanessa was slowly getting herself ready. Sometimes I think that if Vanessa ever had to race the tortoise, she'd lose.
"Ready?" I asked her.
"Almost."
"Everyone's waiting."
"I know, I know," she said frantically. "I just can't go. My feet are moving much too slow."
I laughed. "Come on, slowcoach." I tied her shoelaces and hair ribbons and she was ready.
We set off for Burger Garden, Mary Anne and Mallory leading the way; the triplets, Claire, Margo, and Nicky in the middle; and Vanessa and me bringing up the rear.
Considering the appealing places we passed on the way—Candy Heaven, souvenir stands, the Ice-Cream Palace—we

reached Burger Garden in pretty good time. The Pikes' excitement had been building with every step we took. As we approached the entrance, an explosion of chatter burst from them.

"We sit at mushrooms to eat!"

"Crazy Burgers have orange sauce on them 'cause the ketchup and mustard's already mixed together!"

"I want to ride the merry-go-round!"

"It's delightful, let's all blab it. The burgers here are served by a rabbit!"

"Last year there was a colouring contest and I won two Crazy Burgers and a Fantasy Fountain juice!"

Mary Anne and I looked around. Burger Garden consisted of a very informal indoor restaurant where you could sit at either tables or a long counter with high stools, and an outdoor garden. Despite all the kids spinning happily on the stools, the garden was obviously the more fun place to eat.

The Pikes headed for it immediately.

"I wanna sit by the merry-go-round!" cried Claire.

"Shh," I said. "We'll sit wherever we're seated. And we'll probably need three tables."

"There are some empty mushrooms over by the Enchanted Tree," said a large mouse. The mouse was holding menus in her paws. "This way, please."

"Well, this is a first," whispered Mary

Anne. "In fact, it's been a week of firsts. My first bikini, my first trip away from home, my first time at the Jersey Shore. And now, my first meal ever served by an animal."

I giggled. "Or eaten on a mushroom."

"By the Enchanted Tree, whatever that is," she added.

The mushrooms were sort of small, so we did need three. Claire and Margo ran to one and Vanessa sat down by herself. Then the triplets bunched up at the third mushroom. Nicky ran over to them.

"Go sit with Vanessa," Adam told Nicky.

"No, I want to sit with you."

"Us triplets are sitting alone," said Jordan.

"No, you're not, because I'm sitting with you," I said.

"No way!" cried Adam.

"Where will I sit?" exclaimed Nicky, downcast. "I'm not sitting with girls."

"Sit with us Nicky-silly-billy-goo-goo," said Claire.

"You're *girls*," said Nicky disparagingly.

Vanessa was still at a table by herself. "Hey, what's the matter, what's the fuss, sit with me, I'll—"

"NO!" cried every single one of her brothers and sisters.

"We don't want to eat with Elizabeth Barrett Browning," said Mallory.

"Who's Elizabeth Barrett Browning?" asked Nicky.

"A poet."

"A very good one," Mary Anne pointed out.

"Well, anyway, we don't want to—" Nicky began.

"Look," I broke in suddenly, "a six-foot mouse has been waiting about five minutes for us to sit down. If you guys don't find places, we're never going to eat."

Everyone dived for the mushrooms. Against my better judgment, I let the triplets sit alone. Mary Anne sat down with Claire and Margo, and I joined Nicky, Vanessa, and Mallory. Before he allowed us to open our menus, Nicky made Vanessa promise not to rhyme a single word during the meal.

"Are you happy now?" I asked him.

"Yup."

We opened the menus and took a look. It's a good thing I like hamburgers because, except for hotdogs and chili, the only main dishes on the menu were burgers. Twenty different varieties.

After a few moments, a large rabbit stepped up to us. "Hi, I'm Bugs," he said. "Any questions about the menu?"

"What's the Surprise Burger today?" I asked.

"That would be the burger with tofu and avocado."

Vanessa nearly choked.

She and Nicky and Mallory and I ordered

Crazy Burgers—burgers with bacon, Swiss cheese, pickles, and the orange sauce.

When Bugs moved on to the triplets, Nicky turned to me and said conversationally, "So one day this matta-baby comes up to me—"

"What's a matta-baby?" I interrupted.

"Nothing," replied Nicky. "Whatsa matta with you?" He pounded the table with glee.

Mallory rolled her eyes.

"Can I go see what the Enchanted Tree is?" asked Vanessa.

"Sure," I told her.

"It's—it's—you won't believe it!" she cried a few minutes later. She was running back to our mushroom. "It's just like in *Charlie and the Chocolate Factory*! That tree is growing chocolate bars!"

"Really?" asked Nicky, amazed.

"No, stupid. They're just hanging all over it. And they cost twenty-five cents apiece and so you buy one and if it has a gold wrapper inside you win a prize just like Charlie Bucket did only it's for Burger Garden food not the chocolate factory and I didn't rhyme a single word, Nicholas. So there."

Bugs came back and served us our drinks. At the next mushroom, the triplets shot their straw papers at each other.

"Well," I said loudly, turning to Mary Anne, "I think I'll go sit with the triplets."

"No, no!" said Byron hastily. "We'll stop. Really."

And they did.

All the Pikes behaved themselves. When the food was served, they ate it up without messes or squabbles. Later, after Mary Anne and I had seen what the bill came to, we let each kid buy a candy bar from the Enchanted Tree. Nicky got a gold wrapper! It turned out to be worth four free Burger Garden dinners. Suddenly the triplets were his best friends.

Mary Anne and I counted the remaining money and debated how to spend the rest of the evening. We decided to go to the pier for a while and then back to the Ice-Cream Palace before heading home.

On the pier, we gave each kid a dollar to spend, all we thought we could afford, not knowing how expensive the Palace might be. The kids planned and planned, each wanting to get the best and the most for his or her money. The only thing we said they couldn't do was go on the fast rides. I was not about to watch anybody throw up a Crazy Burger.

An hour later, Byron had ridden the ferris wheel twice; Vanessa had bought a little pink deer from the glass blower; Clare, Nicky, and Margo had tried the bumper cars; Mallory had bought a frog made out of seashells; and Jordan and Adam had been through the haunted house, and were mad at Byron, who had refused to go with them.

We arrived at the Ice-Cream Palace feeling ready to sit down for a while.

"Okay," I said, "I'm not going to have any ice-cream, so that means there's about three dollars for each of you," I was eyeing the menu. The Palace looked expensive.

"More than three," spoke up Mary Anne. "I—I don't think I'll have any, either."

"What's wrong?" I asked warily. "You look kind of funny."

"I don't know. I feel sort of hot all over."

"Your face is awfully red," I said.

"My skin feels stiff."

"Your *skin* feels—Just a second. Hold out your arms."

Mary Anne obliged.

I pressed her skin with my finger. A white spot appeared where my finger had been. It slowly turned bright pink—like the rest of her skin. "You're sunburned!" I exclaimed. "Eat some ice-cream. It'll probably cool you off."

We had enough money for everyone to have what he or she wanted, with two dollars and thirty-one cents left over.

We got back to the beach house shortly after nine. Mr and Mrs Pike were still out.

"You are *so* sunburned!" Mallory exclaimed to Mary Anne.

"Oh, I know. Don't remind me."

Mary Anne flopped down on her bed. She lay on her back with her arms stretched out, while I looked on helplessly. "What did I do to deserve this?" she moaned.

She'd been lying there for about ten minutes while the kids were supposed to be getting ready for bed, when a voice said, "Mary Anne? I brought you something."

"We all did," said another voice.

Standing in the doorway were the Pike kids, each in pyjamas, each holding something out to Mary Anne.

"It's for your sunburn," said Margo. "I brought you skincream."

"I brought you suncream," said Byron.

"An ice pack," said Jordan.

"Cold compresses," said Adam.

"Mum's aloe creme," said Vanessa.

"A fan," said Nicky. "To cool off."

"Teabags for your eyelids," said Mallory. "They really work."

"Butter," said Claire, offering Mary Anne a tub of margarine.

"Butter is for *real* burns, not sunburns!" screeched Nicky. He grabbed for his little sister, but Claire twisted away and fled to Mary Anne. Nicky followed. So did everyone else. They ended up on Mary Anne's bed in a giggly heap—margarine, ice, and all. I joined them.

I don't think I've ever laughed so hard in my life.

7th CHAPTER

Tuesday

Dear Claudia,

I know I'm supposed to be baby-sitting, but Scott was on duty today, and he's all I can think of. He gave me the most fabulous present, but I'm not going to tell you what it is. I'll show you when we're back in Stoneybrook. Say "hi" to Mimi!

Luv, Stace

P.S. Mary Anne thinks the gift is dumb. She doesn't understand.

Tuesday

Dear Kristy,

I'd never have suspected it, but Byron has a lot of fears. He's afraid to go in the ocean (even though he can swim), and last night when we went to the amusement park on the pier, he wouldn't go through the haunted house. We'll have to talk about this.

Luv, Stacey

On Tuesday, the weather was lovely. The beach looked like a postcard. Mary Anne and I took the kids out early, even before Scott was on duty. The air was cool, the sky was crystal clear with one or two fluffy white clouds that looked sort of like sheep, and the sun was all sparkly, but not hazy and blazy the way it would get during the afternoon.

Mary Anne came to the beach that morning wearing a long-sleeved caftan and a Boston Red Sox cap that Adam had lent her. She looked pretty weird—even weirder after she gooped on sunscreen and lip cream, then put on her sunglasses. As an added precaution, she sat under the umbrella. I didn't say anything. I knew she felt hot and uncomfortable.

The second the lifeguards showed up, the kids (except for Byron, of course) dashed into the water. I sauntered after them, but really as an excuse to say hello to Scott. He greeted me with, "Hey there, princess."

I thought I might pass out.

"Hi," I said. "Was yesterday your day off?"

"Sure was. I used it well, too."

I added that bit of information—*Monday is Scott's day off*—to my mental list of things I knew about him. I wished the list were longer.

Then I leaned casually against the lifeguard stand, almost as if I were posing. I glanced across the beach to see if Mary Anne was watching. But she was busy. Claire, Margo, and Vanessa, already dripping wet, were crowded around her, asking her to help them with something. And to my surprise, the guy mother's helper was leaning over behind Mary Anne, giving her a hand.

I didn't have time to think about that, though. Right then, things started happening pretty quickly.

First, a couple of the other girls showed up. "Hi, Scott," they said.

"Do you kids know Stacey McGill?" he asked.

Kids! He had called them kids! He must have thought I acted older then they did!

That was all the girls needed to hear. Scowling, they edged around to the other side of the lifeguard stand. "Hi, Bruce," said one, giggling.

"Hey, beautiful," replied Bruce.

More giggling.

I had Scott to myself again.

I looked back at our towels. Mary Anne was alone.

I was just about to check around for Claire and Margo when it happened.

"SHARK!" yelled a terrified voice from out in the waves.

In one second, Scott and Bruce were on their feet, binoculars to their eyes. Then they put the binoculars down, glanced at

each other, nodded, and began whistling people in.

FWEEEET! "Everybody in! Everybody in!"

FWEEEET! "Outta the water!"

Then Scott blew three short *fweets* and signalled to the guards down the beach, while Bruce signalled to the ones up the beach.

I've never seen people move so fast. Those in the ocean staggered out. Those on the beach ran to the water's edge. Frantically, I tried to round up the Pikes. I gathered Byron, Jordan, Nicky, and Vanessa in a matter of seconds.

"Mary Anne!" I yelled, spotting her caftan and baseball cap. "Where are the rest of the kids? We have to make sure they haven't . . . I mean—" I didn't want to say, Haven't been eaten alive by some relative of Jaws.

"I've got Claire and Adam."

"Oh, no! We're missing Mallory and Margo!"

"No, you're not. Here we are," said Mallory, running up to me, pulling Margo along.

"Oh, thank goodness."

Mary Anne and I counted the Pikes about five times before we were satisfied that they were all safe and sound.

"I want to see the shark!" cried Nicky, jumping up and down.

So did I. "Okay," I said. "Let's walk down the beach, away from this crowd."

Mary Anne and the other kids followed us. When we had a little space, we held our hands to our eyes, blocking the glare of the sun, and stared out to sea.

"I think I see something!" exclaimed Byron.

"Where?" we all asked.

He pointed. "See? Sort of over to the left?"

I could make out a faraway shape, but it looked like a sea gull bobbing on the waves.

Later, Adam swore he could see five fins circling around, but nobody else saw them. At last we gave up. We walked back to the lifeguard stand.

The crowd was dispersing. Scott and Bruce were back on duty. I saw a good opportunity to ask Scott a question.

"Hi," I said to him, leaning against the base of the stand and squinting up.

"Hi, love."

Love! Scott had called me love! Of course, he meant *his* love.

When I recovered, I managed to say, "So were there really sharks?"

"It looked that way. Sometimes it's hard to tell, but it's better to be safe than sorry."

"I'll say."

Scott wiped his brow. "It's going to be a hot one."

"So you want a drink or something?" I

asked eagerly.

"You bet, love. That'd be great."

I was off in a flash. I didn't even remember to tell Mary Anne where I was going. I grabbed a drink out of the Pikes' fridge, ran back across the sand, and handed the ice-cold can to Scott.

He held it against his forehead. "Oh, wow. That feels great," he said. Then he popped open the can, tipped his head back, drank half the can without stopping, and handed it to Bruce. Bruce finished it off practically in one gulp.

"That sure hit the spot, honey," said Scott.

I was dying. I was *dying*!

After lunch that day, Mary Anne and I stood at the water's edge. I alternately tried to coax Byron into the water (he staunchly refused, saying he didn't want to be eaten by a shark) and found excuses to talk to Scott. Every time I did, I noticed Mary Anne giving me dirty looks.

Well, could I help it if Scott needed a sandwich and then another drink? I'm sorry if she thought she had her hands full, but it wasn't *my* fault Adam dumped a bucket of water over Byron, or that Nicky disappeared for ten minutes. It turned out he'd gone back to the house without telling anyone, but Mary Anne panicked. She was just going to have to learn to cope with things like that.

At five o'clock, Scott and Bruce climbed down from their stand. Mary Anne called the Pike kids out of the water. "I think we should take them inside," she said to me. "Mallory and Jordan look kind of burned. And I know Claire's tired."

"Okay, you start," I told her. "I want to talk to Scott for a minute."

"*Sta*cey," she said impatiently, "there are two umbrellas, ten towels, a set of Tonka toys, buckets, spades, card games, suntan lotion, and beach bags to pack up."

"Well, you've got eight kids to help you," I pointed out. "Besides, I'll be there in a minute."

"You're getting paid as much as I am," said Mary Anne in a huff, "and *I'm* doing all the work."

She was sunburned, I forgave her.

Anyway, the guy mother's helper turned up to give her a hand. I realized that he had helped her look for Nicky earlier, too. So what was she complaining about?

While Mary Anne rounded up the Pikes, I watched Scott get ready to leave. Then I followed him as he and Bruce dragged the stand back to the dunes.

"Well," I said after a moment, "I guess I'll see you tomorrow."

The lifeguard jeep was driving up the beach to pick them up.

"Just a sec, Stacey," said Scott. "Hey,

man, you go on to the jeep," he told Bruce, "I'll be right there."

Did Scott want to be alone with me?!

Scott flashed me his hunk grin. Then he lifted his whistle from around his neck and handed it to me by the chain. "You sure were a lifesaver today, princess," he said. "Thanks a lot. I want you to have my whistle."

I held it with shaking hands.

"Well," said Scott softly. "I better go. See you tomorrow?"

"Yeah. Tomorrow. Definitely. Hey, and thanks, Scott. This is really special."

I watched Scott run across the beach to the jeep and vault inside without opening the door.

I knew he had meant to say more to me, but was too shy. Boys get that way sometimes. Anyway, he didn't need words to tell me what he meant. I already knew.

Scott was in love with me!

8th CHAPTER

Thursday

Dear Kristy,

Today the weather was awful. Stacey and I must have been out of our minds: we took the kids to the miniature golf course. But guess what? We had a great time. Sometimes I think that eight kids aren't any harder to take care of than two or three. The Pikes argue and tease, but they also help each other out.

Love,

Mary Anne

P.S. Stacey is being a real pain. She really is.

P.P.S. (Don't *ever* show this card to her.)

I guess we should have expected at least one rainy day while we were in Sea City, but the weather had been so nice that somehow we didn't. So we were all kind of shocked when we woke up on Thursday, shivering in our beds, to find a misty, grey sky and cool, damp air. It wasn't actually raining, but it was certainly no beach day. In fact, by nine-thirty the beach was still deserted and we realized that the lifeguards weren't even going to go on duty. Why couldn't this have happened on Scott's day off? I wondered.

"I think," said Mr Pike at breakfast that morning, "that today would be a good day to go to Smithtown.

"Oh, Dad, please. No. Not Smithtown," said Jordan, amid groans from his brothers and sisters.

"What's Smithtown?" asked Mary Anne.

"It's a dumb old town that's supposed to look like the seventeen-hundreds or something," said Adam.

"I always wear a frown when I go to Smithtown," added Vanessa.

"You've only been there once, honey," her mother pointed out.

"Once was enough," Byron whispered to Adam.

"Smithtown," said Mr Pike, "is a very nice restored colonial village. There are shops and houses, a church, a blacksmith shop, craftspeople . . ."

"Really?" said Mary Anne. That was just the kind of thing that would interest her.

"But you kids don't have to go if you don't want to," said Mrs Pike.

"Oh, thanks, Mum," said Mallory. "Are you and Dad going to go anyway?"

Mr and Mrs Pike looked at each other. "Why not?" said Mr Pike. "Can you kids find something to do today?"

"Oh, sure," I replied. "No problem."

(Mary Anne looked disappointed.)

So a little while later, Mr Pike gave Mary Anne and me some money and he and Mrs Pike drove off.

An hour after that, we were all bored silly. I'd written to my parents and my friend Laine in New York, and was tired of writing. There was no TV in the house, and the kids had already read, coloured, and tried to invent a game of catch they could play indoors without breaking anything. Mallory had been up on the third floor, watching the angry ocean from the window-seat, but was tired of it. Every suggestion Mary Anne or I made was met with a bored "nah".

"Well," I said. "It's not actually raining. We could go into town or to the pier."

"Yeah!" cried the kids.

"*If*," said Mary Anne, "you promise to wear jackets or jumpers."

"We promise."

It wasn't easy, but the ten of us agreed on

one thing we all wanted to do: play miniature golf.

It was late morning when we reached Fred's Putt-Putt Course. Because of the weather, a lot of other people had had the same idea we'd had, and Fred's was kind of crowded. There was a short line of people waiting at almost every hole.

The kids were undaunted.

"Come on. Let's get our putt-putt clubs," cried Byron.

"I want a five-iron," said Nicky.

"Silly," said Mallory, smiling. "You get putt-putt clubs according to your height. There are no five-irons or anything."

"Silly-billy-goo-goo," added Claire.

I rolled my eyes.

When we were all equipped with our golf clubs, we lined up at the first hole. The par was four. That means the average person needs four strokes to hit the ball through the moving arms of a windmill, around a corner, and into a little sunken cup.

Claire insisted on going first. Twenty-seven strokes later, her ball was in the cup. There were nine more of us to play. The people behind us, a man and a woman, began to look impatient.

"Mind if we play through?" asked the man. "There are just the two of us. It'll only take a few minutes."

"No," cried Margo. "It's my turn! I want

to go next!"

"Margo—" I said.

"That's all right," the man said to her. "You go on."

After Margo had tried eleven times to get her ball through the windmill, I thought the man would turn purple. Jordan told her she could pick it up and carry it to the other side.

"You go on through—sir," I said when Margo was finished.

"Thanks," he said with relief. He and the woman sped through expertly.

The older kids were somewhat better players. Mallory actually got her ball in the cup in the suggested four strokes. Even Mary Anne and I couldn't do that.

"Hey, you're good!" I said to Mallory.

"It was beginner's luck," muttered Byron, who'd taken twelve strokes.

The second hole looked a little easier. At the top of a short green ramp sat a clown's face with a blinking red nose. You were supposed to hit your ball into the clown's mouth, and it would come out of one of three holes on the other side. If it came out of the middle hole, you could get a hole in one—which is just what Nicky got.

"A hole in one! A hole in one!" he shrieked. "I did it! I never got a hole in one before."

Several people nearby smiled at him.

Adam had just scored an embarrassing

ten on the clown hole. Nevertheless, he punched Nicky affectionately on the shoulder. "Good going, little bro," he said.

Nicky beamed.

The people behind us—a family, now—were beginning to get that look that the man and woman had had earlier. I called Mary Anne and Mallory over to me. "I think," I said, glancing nervously at the impatient family, "that we'd better split into three groups and play separately. Otherwise, we're likely to get killed." After much discussion, Mallory agreed to play with the triplets, Mary Anne took Nicky and Vanessa, and I took Claire and Margo.

We lined up at the third hole, which had a royal theme and was called "Old King Cole Hole". Mallory and the triplets played through first, and went on to the fourth hole. A half hour later, they were waiting in line for the eighth hole, Mary Anne's group was playing the sixth hole, and Claire was taking her thirty-seventh stroke at "Old King Cole".

"Claire . . . dear," I said as sweetly as I knew how.

"What, Stacey-silly-billy-goo-goo?"

But before I could finish (and I hadn't even been sure what I was going to say), Margo interrupted.

"You know what I think?" she said. "I think we should make a limit. You can't hit the ball more than twenty times. Twenty is it. If you get to twenty, your turn is over."

I raised my eyebrows. Great suggestion!

But Claire was frowning. "What if my ball isn't in the cup yet?" she asked.

"Twenty would be a better score," I told her. "Remember, you don't want a lot of points. The person with the *fewest* points is the winner."

"Well, okay," said Clare.

The twenty-stroke limit made a big difference. Even so, by the time Mallory and the triplets were finished, we were only on the tenth hole, and Mary Anne was on the thirteenth. We let the older kids leave to look in shops, if they promised to stay nearby and not cross the busy main road. When Mary Anne and Nicky and Vanessa finished, they joined the others.

Then it was just me, Margo, Claire, and the putt-putt course. We were on the fourteenth hole. There were four more to go—five if you counted the "nineteenth" hole, which was really just a fancy way to return your ball to the rental shop.

On the fifteenth hole, Claire dropped her putt-putt club on the green. "I'm *tired* of this, Stacey. I don't *wanna* play any more." (She had just found out that her score was over two hundred.)

On the sixteenth hole, Margo did the same thing.

I didn't care. I was very tired of miniature golf, myself. "Okay," I said. "We just have to return our balls."

I led the girls to the nineteenth hole. Mallory had explained how it worked. You hit your ball up a ramp, it disappeared over the top, and ran down a chute back to Fred.

Thwack! My golf ball disappeared.

Thwack! Margo's ball disappeared.

Thwack! Claire's ball disappeard.

Then, *ding, ding, ding! Whoop, whoop, whoop*! The second Claire's ball sailed into the chute, lights flashed, bells rang, sirens wailed. Fred came rushing out of his shop.

"Congratulations!" he exclaimed. "Somebody has just won two free games here!"

"Me! Me! Oh, it was *me*!" Claire cried, jumping up and down.

"You're the lucky five-hundredth person to return your golf ball this week." Fred handed Claire two tickets for free putt-putt.

"Oh, please, Stacey, can Margo and I play again right now?" asked Claire.

I looked at the lines of people and "Old King Cole" and the swinging putt-putt clubs.

I was beginning to get a headache.

"Claire," I said, "you can use your tickets on the next rainy day."

"Okay," she said. "But you know what, Stacey? You're a silly-billy-goo-goo."

"You know what, Claire? You are, too."

Claire slipped her hand in mine, and she and Margo and I went off to find the others.

9th CHAPTER

Sunday

Dear Mary Anne and Stacey,

You will not believe what happened while I was taking care of David Michael, Andrew, and Karen this morning. It was a baby-sitter's nightmare. It all began when Watson told us he wanted his car washed. This is a warning, you guys. Never, never, ever, ever, EVER let little kids wash a car by themselves. This should be a Babysitters Club rule....

Kristy Thomas had been getting an awful lot of mail from Claudia and Dawn and Mary Anne and me—at least three postcards every day. And finally Mary Anne and I got a letter from her.

Believe it or not, we were all baby-sitting. Back in her old neighbourhood in California, Dawn was sitting for some of the families she used to sit for. Claudia and her family had travelled to an isolated mountain resort. Although it was quiet—the perfect place for Mimi to recover from her stroke—a lot of other families were staying there, too. Claudia had sat for a couple of them.

Of course Kristy was in baby-sitters' heaven. She was the only club member left in Stoneybrook, so she had all our clients to herself. But her most memorable baby-sitting job during the two weeks we were apart was not for another family, but for her very own stepsister and stepbrother, six-year-old Karen and four-year-old Andrew, and her little brother, David Michael.

Kristy's long letter told us about the entire incident. It began on Sunday morning when Watson Brewer announced that he and Elizabeth (Kristy's mum) were going to spend the day at an estate auction. Kristy didn't know what that was, and didn't ask.

Then her older brothers, Sam and Charlie, announced that they were going back to the old neighbourhood to visit friends for the day.

"I guess you're in charge then, Kristy," said her mother. "Can you baby-sit?"

"Sure," Kristy replied. She turned to David Michael, Karen, and Andrew. "What do you guys want to do today?"

"I'm busy," said David Michael. "Linny Papadakis is having a dog show. I'm entering Louie. Hey, do you want to come with me?"

"Yes," said Karen.

"No," said Andrew. (Andrew likes Louie all right, but he's afraid of most other dogs.)

"Karen, you can go to the dog show with David Michael," Kristy told her. "You could play with Hannie." (Hannie, Linny's younger sister, is a friend of Karen's.)

"That's okay. I'll stay with Andrew."

David Michael looked a little hurt, but didn't say anything.

Watson spoke up then. "I've got a job to be done," he said. "I need someone to wash the Ford."

"Oh, we'll do it! We'll do it!" shouted Karen.

"Can we use the hose and those big sponges? We'll do a great job, Daddy! Andrew and Kristy and I. We'll get your car cleaner than anything!"

The Ford is no big deal as cars go. In fact, it's sort of an emergency car. It's this old black thing that Watson used to drive years and years ago. He keeps it parked in a shed at the back of the property. (In his garage are a red sportscar and a fancy new car and the Thomases' green station wagon.) But Watson won't give the Ford away. He says you never know when you might need it. Kristy pointed out, though, that in all the time she's known Watson, he's washed the Ford twice, and driven it once.

But she didn't care. Car washing would be a good project for Andrew and Karen. So before everyone left that day, Watson drove the Ford out of the shed and parked it in the drive. Then he and Kristy's mother drove off in the sportscar, Sam and Charlie drove off in the station wagon, and David Michael led Louie, his fur brushed, his special plaid collar in place, over to the Papadakises'.

"Well?" said Kristy to Karen and Andrew. "Should we start?"

"Yeah! Yeah!" Karen jumped up and down.

"Okay," said Kristy. "First, we put on our swimming costumes. Then we get everything we're going to need."

Twenty minutes later, the three of them were standing on the drive amid buckets, sponges, cloths, and soap.

"All right, Andrew. Let 'er rip!" called Kristy.

Andrew twisted the nozzle of the hose. A fine spray shot out. But they had only just got the bonnet of the car wet when David Michael came slowly up the driveway with

Louie. Louie was limping and David Michael was crying.

Kristy dropped her sponge and ran over to them. "David Michael, what happened?" she exclaimed.

David Michael could barely speak. "I (sob)—at the dog show (hiccup)—a big dog came (sniff)—and (hic)—he growled at Louie (sob)—and Louie growled back (sniffle)—and the dog showed his teeth (hic)—and Louie showed *his* teeth (sob)—and the big dog ran at Louie (hiccup)—and Louie ran away (sniff)—and cut his foot on something (hic, sob, sniffle)."

Kristy examined Louie's foot. Sure enough the pad was bleeding. The cut looked pretty big. "Well," said Kristy, "we'd better bring Louie inside and figure out what to do. Come on, you guys," she said to Andrew and Karen.

"No, we want to wash the car," cried Karen. "We can do it ourselves. Really."

Kristy looked doubtfully at the kids. Then she thought, What could go wrong? It's a black car. If they don't get it very clean, no one will notice.

"Will you remember to keep the windows *closed*?" she asked.

"Yes."

"And don't spray anything but the car."

"Okay."

"And don't rinse out the sponges in the garden. The soap'll kill the plants."

"We won't."

After a few more instructions, Kristy took Louie and David Michael inside. She spread out a towel for Louie and gave David Michael some lemonade. Then she tried to clean Louie's paw.

"I think we'd better call the vet," she said after a few minutes. "Maybe Dr Smith will make a house call."

Dr Smith, of course, did not make house calls.

So Kristy began phoning around the old neighbourhood, trying to track down Charlie, since he could drive. While she was on the telephone, she noticed that Karen and Andrew ran in and out of the house a couple of times, but she didn't pay much attention.

Kristy finally reached Charlie at his friends the Ackermans', and he said he'd come right home. So Kristy made one more call—to the vet to say that Louie would be on his way out there soon. Then she decided she'd better check on Karen and Andrew. She went out the back door and approached the car from behind. It was just after noon and the sun was shining brightly. The Ford was gleaming.

"We've finished, Kristy!" cried Andrew.

"Yup, we sure are," said Karen. "I bet the car has never looked so shiny."

Kristy had to agree. The car looked shiny all right. In fact, it looked kind of . . . silvery.

Kristy's heart sank, but she managed to ask, "What, um, did you two wash this car with?"

"Oh," said Karen proudly, "we didn't use the sponges. They were no good. We used something better. These. Daddy always uses them to get pots shiny." Karen held out two pieces of steel wool.

"Oh, *no*," murmured Kristy. At last she dared to inspect the car closely. It was covered with big silvery-grey patches where the paint had been scubbed away. "You guys!" Kristy shouted. "You took the paint off! You can't wash a car with steel wool. Your dad wanted the Ford clean, not naked. Oh, no! What are we going to do?"

Kristy was a nervous wreck. As the afternoon wore on, Charlie came home and drove Louie and David Michael to the vet. Kristy cleaned up the mess in the driveway. She got herself, Karen, and Andrew dressed again. Louie returned with three stitches in his paw.

And then . . . Watson and Kristy's mum came home. They'd bought two crystal champagne glasses at the estate sale, which they brought inside and showed off proudly.

"Watson?" Kristy began, just as Watson said, "How did the car washing go? We haven't looked at the Ford yet."

Kristy, Karen, and Andrew glanced at

one another guiltily. "I think you'd better look now," said Kristy.

They all trooped outside. Kristy explained what had happened.

"Oh, no!" gasped Kristy's mother.

Watson turned slightly pale.

"I'm really sorry," said Kristy. "I should have been watching the kids more closely."

"I'm afraid I have to agree with you," replied Watson. "I know you had an emergency, but you *were* in charge, and you *should* have been keeping a closer eye on them. In a way it's all right, though. See, I'd been thinking of having the car painted. I've always wanted a purple car. But there was no real excuse to paint the Ford since we hardly ever drive it. Now I have an excuse."

"Paint the car?" repeated Karen with a gleam in her eye. "Can Andrew and I paint it? That would be fun."

Watson, Kristy, and Kristy's mother fixed their eyes on her.

"No," said Kristy's mother.

"Absolutely not," said Watson.

"When chickens have lips," said Kristy.

And that was the end of the car wash.

10th CHAPTER

K—

Sun.

Noth. new to rept. Kids fine. B. still afrd. of H_2O.

—S.

Sunday

Dear Claudia,

The most awful, humiliating thing in the world has happened. I can't believe it. I feel like such a jerk. Mary Anne tried to warn me about Scott but I wouldn't listen. She told me he was older. She told me this, she told me that. And I wouldn't listen. Oh, I am such a jerk. (I guess I've run out of room. I'll tell you the rest in the next postcard.)

Luv, Stace

I had to write *three* more postcards in order to tell Claudia the whole story. See, what had happened was completely unexpected—at least, it was unexpected to me.

We'd been in Sea City just over a week. I was having the time of my life. My hair was about two shades lighter, thanks to the sun, the salt, and of course my bottle of sun-lite. My skin was turning nice and brown. I had actual tan lines at the edges of my bikini. I also had another new bikini. I'd bought it on the main street one afternoon. It was pink, with palm trees and parrots all over it.

(Mary Anne had got rid of her sunburn, but she didn't have much of a tan. The only thing that happened when she sat in the sun was that her skin turned sort of blotchy and pink. So she covered up on the beach and stayed under the umbrella as much as possible.)

I wasn't having a bit of trouble with my diabetes, either. I'd been able to stay on my diet, and my mother had only called twice to see how I was doing. The Pike kids hadn't paid any more attention to that than they had to the fact that I never joined them in ice-cream or sweets or breakfast doughnuts. The best thing, though, was Scott. The bad weather had cleared up, and I saw him on both Friday and Saturday.

On Saturday Mr and Mrs Pike decided to go to Atlantic City for the day, so Mary Anne and I were on our own with the kids.

But by the end of the day, she practically wasn't speaking to me. She accused me of spending too much time with Scott.

Personally, I think she was jealous. And if I were Mary Anne, I'd have been jealous, too. That nerdy mother's helper had been hanging around her endlessly, and the two of them were always doing stuff with the kids, like building sand castles, or collecting shells to make a moat around the towels and umbrellas.

Mary Anne says I'm not spending enough time with the children, but I *am* doing something important when I'm on the beach. I post myself by the lifeguard stand and watch the kids when they're in the water—and Adam and Jordan are in the water non stop. I can't help it if Scott talks to me every now and then, or asks for a drink, or something.

"Sweetheart," he said to me on Saturday afternoon, "did anyone ever tell you you're beautiful?"

Immediately, my heart began to beat faster.

"No," I replied, which wasn't quite true. My parents are always telling me I'm beautiful, but they don't count. A blond-haired, blue-eyed, tanned, muscled eighteen-year-old hunk certainly counts, though.

Scott smiled down at me. He started to say something then, but suddenly he jumped up, blowing his whistle.

FWEET! FWEET! "You're too far out!" *FWEET!* "Too far out!"

"What were you going to say?" I asked him when the excitement was over.

"Oh," replied Scott, "you're—you're the greatest."

See? I thought. He wants to say more, but he's just too shy.

I wished Mary Anne had been saying a little more. Later that afternoon when I asked her if she wanted a drink, she just shrugged.

"I'll go back to the house and get you a really cold one," I offered.

"No, thanks."

"Well, I'm going to get one for me."

"'Kay."

I paused. Then, "See you," I said.

Those were the last words we spoke to each other for the rest of the afternoon.

Mr and Mrs Pike returned from Atlantic City in a great mood.

"How would you like the evening off?" Mrs Pike asked Mary Anne and me.

"We'd love it," I said. I tried to sound excited, but it was hard with Mary Anne so mad at me.

"Why don't you change out of your swimming costumes right now?" Mrs Pike went on. "We'll let you off the hook until ten o'clock tonight. You can join us for dinner—"

"We're going back to Burger Garden so I can get my free meals!" interrupted Nicky.

"—or you can go somewhere on your own," Mrs Pike finished.

"We'll think about it while we change," I said. "Come on, Mary Anne!"

We flew upstairs to our room. "Mary Anne, please don't be mad," I said. "It's only five o'clock. We have five whole hours to ourselves. We could go to the pier, eat supper, hang around, shop."

Mary Anne began to look a teeny bit interested. And by the time our bikinis were off, we had showered, and our clothes were on, she was actually speaking to me.

We selected our outfits carefully. Who knew who we might see on the pier at night. Cute guys . . . Scott . . . I put on a white cotton top over a pink cotton dress and tied a big white bow in my hair so that if flopped over the side of my head. Mary Anne couldn't find anything of her own that she really liked, so I loaned her my yellow pedalpushers, a yellow and white striped tank top, and an oversized white jacket. We looked at ourselves in the mirror. Pretty nice! We were ready for a night on the town!

Mary Anne and I went straight to the

pier. We ate hamburgers for dinner, which Mary Anne topped off with a couple of pieces of fudge that we had watched being made.

Then we wandered around.

We went to a souvenir stand. Mary Anne bought Sea City visors to bring back to Kristy and Dawn. I bought Claudia a bright yellow T-shirt. It didn't have any words on it, just a hunk surfer. The surfer looked kind of like Scott.

We went to the arcade and played ring toss and penny pitch. We didn't win a thing. I swear those games are rigged.

"Want to ride the ferris wheel?" Mary Anne asked as we left the arcade.

"Sure," I said.

We sauntered over to a ticket booth. The guy in the booth winked at us.

"Two for the ferris wheel, please," I said.

"Okay, cutie."

Cutie! In Sea City, there were adorable guys *every*where!

The view from the ferris wheel was great. When you reached the top, you were pretty high up. Below, lights twinkled in the houses along the beach, the moon cut a path of light across the ocean, and the pier looked like a fairyland.

I don't know quite what made me think of it, but while we were sitting so high up, gazing down at the lights, I suddenly said, "I should buy Scott a present."

"Hmph," was all Mary Anne replied.

Nevertheless, when the ferris wheel ride was over, I dragged her in and out of shop after shop. She waited patiently while I chose, then unchose, a book about shells and a blue hat (for when Scott was sitting in the sun); and while I decided for, then against, having a T-shirt printed up that said *Stacey + Scott = LUV*.

We were passing one of the many sweet shops on the pier, when suddenly I saw the perfect gift. I ran in and bought it. It cost almost ten dollars, but I didn't care.

Outside the shop I showed Mary Anne the present—a giant red satin heart-shaped box of chocolates.

"This'll really show him how I feel, don't you think, Mary Anne? . . . Mary *Anne*?"

Mary Anne wasn't answering, but she didn't look angry, just preoccupied.

I turned in the direction she was gazing.

"Wait, Stacey," said Mary Anne. "No."

But it was too late. I'd seen.

Snuggled up on a bench behind me were a girl and a guy. The girl was curvy and gorgeous and at least eighteen.

The guy was Scott.

They were kissing.

I turned back to Mary Anne. "Guess I won't be needing this," I said. I thrust the satin box at her. "You take it. You *deserve* it.

You were right all along. Enjoy your prize."
I burst into tears.

Mary Anne left the unopened box on a bench. Then she put her arm around me and walked me back to the Pikes'.

11th CHAPTER

Sunday night

Dear Dawn,

Stacey is still being a pain, but I feel bad for her because she saw Scott kissing another girl—a much older one—and she started to cry. How is California? I miss you. I'm thinking of getting another bikini at this store here called If the Suit Fits. Stacey got another one. Love,

Mary Anne

P.S. Stacey's been dyeing her hair!

P.P.S. Destroy this card in California!!

As bad as Saturday night was, Sunday morning was just awful. How could I go to the beach and face Scott? I decided there was no way.

After breakfast, I pulled Mrs Pike and Mary Anne aside. "I have a headache," I said. "Would it be all right if I didn't go to the beach this morning? I'd just like to take it easy. The beach gets so noisy."

"Of course," said Mrs Pike sympathetically.

"Sure," replied Mary Anne. But up in our room later, she said, "Thanks for sticking me with all the kids again. You know, last night you dragged me around to about a billion shops looking for a present for Scott. Then when you saw him with that girl, you practically blamed *me*. You are so rude. The least you could do is apologize."

"I'm sorry. I really am," I said.

But Mary Anne wasn't finished.

"If you actually had a headache, well, that would be one thing, but it's Scott, isn't it?"

I nodded.

"Boy." Mary Anne shook her head.

"Well, what are you complaining about?" I shot back. What was her problem? I'd already apologized. "That guy mother's helper will be hanging around."

"His name is Alex."

"He looks like such a nerd."

"Well, he's not! He's funny and nice.

And he's good with kids."

"Who are those kids, anyway?"

"They're Kenny, Jimmy, and Ellie. Ellie's the baby. And he *is* a mother's helper, but so what? . . . And don't change the subject!"

"What subject?"

"How you've made me do all the work so far."

"I have not."

"Have so."

I sighed. "I'm really sorry, Mary Anne," I said as I followed her downstairs. "I don't know what else to say."

Mary Anne ignored me. She opened the front door. "Come on, kids," she said to the Pikes. "Your mum and dad beat us to the beach this morning."

The Pikes ran outside.

But Byron immediately came back.

"Stacey?" he asked. "Can I stay with you this morning?"

"I suppose so," I replied, "but I'm not feeling very well. I just want to rest."

"I'll rest, too," he said quietly. He looked awfully serious.

"Okay. Go tell Mary Anne, so she knows where you are."

Byron disappeared. I was kind of glad he wanted to spend the morning with me.

As soon as he came back, he said. "Do you feel like taking a walk? Or are you too sick?"

"No, a walk would be nice," I replied. Then, remembering my "headache", I added, "As long as we go somewhere quiet."

"I know somewhere really quiet," said Byron earnestly. "Come on."

I left a note for Mary Anne and the Pikes. Then Byron led me out the back door, down the road across the main street, to the end of the road on the other side of the town.

"This is the bay side of Sea City," Byron informed me.

"Is Sea City on an island?" I asked incredulously.

"Nope, just a little piece of land that curls into the ocean like a dog's tail."

I smiled. "That's a very nice way to describe it," I told Byron.

The bay certainly was quiet. The houses there were even closer to the water than they were on the ocean side, but no one was outdoors. And the water was calm, like a big lake.

Byron waded out to his knees, shaded his eyes, and said, "See? You can see land across the water. That's the rest of New Jersey."

"Byron!" I exclaimed. "You're in the water!"

Byron looked down. "Oh, yeah," he said. "Hey, here's a little crab or something . . . Oops, there it goes." The something scuttled away.

"Go after it," I suggested.

Byron shook his head.

"Byron?" I asked. "Are you afraid of the water?"

"Not exactly."

"What do you mean?"

"I don't like the waves. They're too . . . rough. And I don't like it when I can't see the bottom."

So that was why he wouldn't go after the crab. He just didn't want to wade out any farther.

I reached for his hand. "It's really okay, you know," I told him.

Holding my hand, we waded out a few more steps. The water was over our knees.

"Stop!" cried Byron suddenly. "I can't see the bottom. How do you know we're not on the edge of a cliff or something?"

"I don't," I said. "But there's not a good chance of that. Anyway, if we were, and we stepped down, well, we could just turn around and swim to the shore, couldn't we?"

"Yeah . . ."

"I'll tell you something, Byron. It's smart to be a little afraid of things."

"It is?"

"Yes. Because if you aren't afraid, you might take dangerous chances. But if you're *too* afraid, then you'll probably miss out on a lot of fun."

Byron thought that over. He waded

around for a long time, looking for shellfish or for stones to toss. At one point, he said, "Boy, it's hot," and actually ducked under the water briefly.

We walked back to the house shortly after noon. Byron had made me feel as calm as the bay water. I decided I could face the beach. After all, Scott didn't know I'd seen him with the other girl, so it would just be a matter of avoiding him.

While Byron had been thinking and playing, I'd been thinking, too, and I'd worked out what had happened with Scott — or at least I thought I had. I decided that Scott really did like me, but just as a friend. Or maybe even just as a cute kid. He was, as Mary Anne had pointed out, too old for me. The girl I'd seen him with the night before had been much more his age. She was probably his girl friend. I began to feel silly. How could I have thought Scott loved me? He never kissed me, never held my hand, never asked me out. He just sent me off to do favours for him. Still, I couldn't hate him. He'd been nice to me. We'd had fun. He'd given me his whistle.

I was too embarrassed to hang around him any more, though. Scott might wonder why I was avoiding him. Then again, he might not even notice. Whatever I did probably wouldn't matter, anyway. I thought bitterly. Those other girls would step right back in and take over.

Byron and I returned to the Pikes' in time for lunch. When lunch was over, I whispered to him, "Ready for the beach?"

He nodded, looking scared but determined. Exactly the way I felt.

As it turned out, I didn't need to be scared. Just as we were heading across the sand, the lifeguard jeep pulled up, Scott jumped off the stand, traded places with another guard who'd been in the jeep, and rode away. The next day, I knew, was his day off. I wouldn't have to worry about him until Tuesday. But I couldn't decide whether to feel glad or let down.

Meanwhile, Byron had a terrific afternoon. He waded into the ocean almost up to his knees. While he couldn't be coaxed out any farther, this was good enough for Adam and Jordan. They could do plenty of splashing and shouting in knee-deep water.

I realized how much I'd missed the kids. I'd spent so much time thinking about Scott that I hadn't really been with the Pike kids. Even when I'd been *around* them, I hadn't been *with* them, if you know what I mean. Byron had shown me that.

Mary Anne seemed to be acting a little more friendly. I wasn't sure why, but it might have been the guy mother's helper—Alex, or whatever his name was. The two of them were playing with all eleven of the kids. Whenever I looked at Mary Anne, she was beaming. Her happiness must have cancelled out some of her bad feelings about me. I took advantage of her mood to be especially nice to her—and to apologize again.

So, by the end of the day, the triplets were together again, and Mary Anne and I were together again.

But Scott and I had come apart.

12th CHAPTER

Tuesday

Dear Kristy,

Byron went in the water! (Sort of.) I know what he's afaid of. We'll talk about it at the next meeting of the Babysitters Club. I heard a really funny joke today. I'll tell that at the next meeting, too.

Luv,
Stacey

Tuesday

Dear Claudia,

I'm IN LUV AGAIN! I met a cute guy named Toby. I mean, really cute. This one is my age, too. He has brown hair, brown eyes, and a few freckles. His clothes are extremely cool.

Luv ya,
Stace

Monday and Tuesday were gorgeous days. I'd been nervous about my decision to avoid Scott, but I didn't need to have been. The very thing that I thought would happen, did happen. All those other girls began hanging around him again, and he called them *cutie* and *beautiful*, just like he'd called me. I have to admit that hurt. I hadn't meant anything to him, after all.

But I stayed with the Pike kids, working hard, and Tuesday passed. Then Wednesday dawned — another clear, sunny morning.

"You know what?" Mary Anne said to me first thing that morning.

"What?" I replied.

"I think some of the kids are getting bored going to the beach every day. Maybe we should split them up. One of us can take the bored ones into town or something, and the other can stay on the beach with the rest of the kids.

"You know, that's a good idea. It's got so that Nicky looks a little green every time we mention the beach."

Of course, I was hoping to be the one to go into town, so I could avoid the beach for one more day, but Mary Anne ended up with that job because of her sunburn problem. She took Nicky, Mallory, Byron, and Margo to Trampoline World and the miniature golf course (Claire had decided she didn't care to use her free passes), and I took Claire, Vanessa, Adam, and Jordan to the beach. (Mr and Mrs Pike went to the pier!)

That morning, I had no sooner got the kids lathered up with sunscreen, and the chairs and towels set up, than I heard Claire's singsong voice proclaiming that someone was a stupid-silly-billy-goo-goo. I looked round. Not far away were Claire and one of the kids that Mary Anne's friend Alex took care of.

"Stupey-stupey-silly-billy-goo-goo!" Claire sang again. Hands on hips, she faced the little boy.

"Claire Pike!" I shouted, just as the boy burst into tears. I ran over to them. "Claire, what are you doing?"

"Nobody would play with me," she wailed, as if that explained everything. "They're all in the water and they won't play with me."

"So why are you calling this boy a stupey-silly-billy-goo-goo?"

Claire shrugged.

"Well, say you're sorry, and then go and lie down on your towel for ten minutes. I'll tell you when the time is up."

"Sorry," mumbled Claire, not sounding as if she meant it a bit. Then she marched off to our towels.

I looked over at Alex. He and another boy were playing with the baby (Allie? Ellen?) and another little kid on a blanket under an umbrella.

Heaving a deep sigh, I led the crying boy to them.

"Uh-oh," said Alex. "What happened?"

"Claire was teasing him," I explained, pointing to Claire, who was pouting on her towel. "I'm not sure why, but I'm really sorry."

"No problem," replied Alex cheerfully. "Kids are always teasing each other. Listen, you're Stacey, right?" He grinned, and I noticed that he had a very nice smile.

"Right," I said, "And you're Alex."

"Yup. And this is Ellie"—the baby—"Jimmy, Kenny"—who was drying his tears—"and Toby. Toby's my cousin. His family is staying in Sea City for a few days."

That was when I got my first really good look at Toby. He was about fourteen years old. (Perfect!) His brown hair was sort of waved back from his face. It was held out of his eyes with a blue headband. I was glad I could see his eyes, because they were a beautiful deep brown, almost velvety looking. A handful of freckles was sprinkled across his nose and cheeks. He was wearing plain white swimming trunks, but his shirt was amazing—tan with silly pictures of cowboy boots and cactuses all over it. And his sunglasses—black bands with narrow slits from side to side to see through. Totally cool. I wished Claudia had been there.

"Hi," I said, hoping I didn't sound too eager.

"Hi," he replied, sounding as eager as I had tried not to sound.

There was an awkward pause.

"Well," I said, "I'd better get back to Claire."

"Okay."

Disappointed, I wandered back to our stuff. But when Claire's ten minutes were up and the two of us began to amble toward the ocean, Toby ran after us. "Hey," he said to Claire, "do you know how to make witches' castles?"

Claire looked intrigued. "No," she replied. "How?"

Toby led us to a patch of wet sand just beyond where the waves were coming in. (I noticed, thankfully, that we were yards down the beach from the lifeguard stand.) He showed Claire how to drip the wet sand through her fingers to make weird, blobby fairy-taleish shapes.

Soon Claire was making a whole row of castles. She left Toby and me behind.

"Well," I said after a while, "where do you live?"

"Lawrenceville, New Jersey," replied Toby. "How about you?"

"Stoneybrook, Connecticut. But I grew up in New York."

"New York *City*?"

"Yeah."

"Wow."

Toby was fourteen. He was going to be a freshman in high school. He played soccer and football. His hobby was computers. He had two older sisters. His favourite group was Smash. His favourite food was peanut butter. He hated history and geography. He liked maths. He loved telling jokes. He didn't look at a single girl except me while we were talking.

By the end of the morning, he and I knew everything about each other. And the two of us and Claire, joined by Alex, his kids, and Adam, Jordan, and Vanessa, had built an entire village of castles. People walking along the beach would pause to watch us.

We hated stopping for lunch, but we had to. We were all dying of starvation. Afterwards, though, we came right back. The waves had destroyed part of our village, but we started building again, anyway.

"So," said Toby, as he topped off a large castle, "did you hear about the dying man named Al who wanted a city named after him?"

"No," I replied, smiling.

"Well, this guy Al knows he hasn't got much time left, so he says to his friend, 'Promise me they'll name a city after me.' And his friend says, 'I promise, Al.' And Al says, 'Will it be big?' and the friend says, 'Sure will, Al,' and Al says, 'Will it be pretty?' and the friend says, 'Count on it, Al.'"

"They named a city Al?" I interrupted.

Toby grinned and went right on. "And Al says, 'And you *promise* it'll be named after me?' and the friend says, 'You betcha, Mr Buquerque,' Get it?" said Toby. "The guy's name was Al Buquerque? *Al*buquerque? As in New Mexico?"

"I get it," I said. I fell over in the sand, laughing hysterically.

Claire pounced on me. "Stacey-silly-billy-goo-goo!"

And Vanessa commented, "Joking, playing in the sun. Now this is what's called lots of fun!"

I looked up at Toby. He looked down at me.

We began to laugh.

I was in love again.

13th CHAPTER

Friday

Dear Kristy,

The kids are moody. It's their last day here. They want to do everything "one last time." But they're also excited about coming home. I'll probably see you before you get this card!

Luv,
Stacey

Friday

Dear Claudia,

I'm going out with Toby tonight. For real! We have an evening on the pier planned. I'll tell you all about it when I see you.

Luv ya!
Stace

Friday was our last day in Sea City. The next morning, we would pack up the car and leave. I couldn't believe the two weeks were almost over.

Guess how Mrs Pike began our last day. She said to Mary Anne and me, "You girls deserve another night off. At five o'clock this afternoon you're on your own. Just be home by ten."

We were ecstatic! But we tried not to show just how ecstatic we were. We didn't want the kids to think we didn't enjoy taking care of them.

Friday's weather was not the greatest. It was in and out, cloudy and sunny. And rain was predicted for the next day. I thought that was a good thing, because going home would be easier if we weren't leaving brilliant sunshine behind.

However, despite the clouds, the kids wanted to go to the beach. "I wanna make one last witch castle," said Claire.

"We wanna play one last game of shark," said Jordan.

Each kid had a last "wanna". While they were taking care of the wannas, I said to Mary Anne, "I just had a great idea! What if Alex could get tonight off, too? Maybe you and I and Alex and Toby could go to the pier together or something."

"Together?" repeated Mary Anne warily.

"You know," I said. "A sort of, um, double date."

Mary Anne turned pale.

"Mary Anne, I said *double* date, not *blind* date. It's not as if you've never seen Alex before. You know him. You like him."

"But girls aren't supposed to ask guys out."

"Oh, Mary Anne, that is so old-fashioned. Besides, this is our last chance. If we don't say something, and we don't go out with Toby and Alex tonight, we'll probably never see them again."

"That's true . . ."

"Good. Now go ask Alex if he can get the night off."

"*Me?!* This was your idea."

"Yeah, but Alex is your friend," I told her.

Well, Mary Anne surprised me. She got up and walked over to Alex's spot on the beach. I watched her in her caftan and baseball cap. I wished I could hear what she was saying, but the wind was blowing in the wrong direction. All I know is that she came back with a grin on her face, looking a little smug, actually, and said, "We're on. We're supposed to meet them at Hercules' Hot Dogs at six o'clock."

Mary Anne and I spent almost an hour—from five until quarter to six—getting ready to see Toby and Alex. We didn't have much choice about what to wear, so we ended up in the same clothes we'd worn on our last night off, but we kept thinking of other things to do.

"I'd better file my nails," said Mary Anne. "They're all ragged."

"I better put on nail polish," I replied. "I've got pink sparkles and yellow sparkles. Want to borrow the yellow?"

"Sure! Oh, and I should put on hand lotion."

"My perfume!" I cried. "Where is it?"

"I don't know. Do you have any lip gloss?"

"Sure. Here . . . Ew! Look at my hair."

"Yours! Ew! Look at mine!"

Somehow, though, we were on our way to the pier at 5.45, and standing in front of Hercules' at 5.55. The boys showed up promptly at six.

Mary Anne elbowed me when she saw them heading toward us. "Doesn't Alex look great?" she whispered excitedly.

He did look great, but I thought Toby looked greater. (I didn't say so, of course.) Toby was wearing these baggy white cotton trousers and an oversized blue and white striped sweater. Totally cool.

"Hey," he said, taking me by the elbow.

"Hi," I replied. "I'm glad you could come tonight."

"Me, too."

"Are you guys hungry?" I asked.

"Starved," said Alex. "Let's eat."

Hercules' main feature was hot dogs that really were an entire foot long. We sat at the counter and gave our orders to a waitress. (I got a hamburger.) Mary Anne and I ate about two thirds of our food. The boys finished their hot dogs. Then they finished our food. Then they each ordered another dog. Mary Anne began to look a little green just watching them eat. They kept slathering the dogs up with mustard, and dumping spoonfuls of sauerkraut on them, while Toby told the longest joke in the history of comedy.

In order to get Mary Anne's eyes off the hot dogs, I nudged her and murmured, "Mary Anne?"

"Yeah?" she whispered.

"Would it be okay with you if Toby and I went off by ourselves for a while? I mean, would you feel okay about being alone with Alex?"

Mary Anne looked thoughtful. Then a slow smile spread across her face. "Yeah," she said. "I *would* feel okay!"

I grinned. If we hadn't been sitting in the middle of Hercules' Hot Dogs, I would have hugged her.

At last, the ends of the boys' hot dogs disappeared into their mouths. We left Hercules'.

"What do you want to do now?" asked Alex.

"Look around the shops," Mary Anne replied.

"Go to the arcade," I replied.

So we split up.

Toby and I played a dart-throwing game. I won a hat for him, he won a teddy bear for me. (Later I named the bear Toby-Bear.) It must have been beginner's luck (or maybe it was beginner's *love*) because after that we played three other games and didn't win anything.

It was starting to grow dark. "Let's walk around," I said. I liked just looking at the lights and listening to the pier sounds and smelling the pier smells.

We came to a shell shop and peered in. "Come on," said Toby.

Inside were shelves and bins full of nothing but seashells. I was poring through a box of tiny conch shells when Toby handed me a little paper bag.

"What's this?" I asked as we walked outside.

"Open it."

I did. Inside was a shiny pale pink shell.

"It's to remember me by," said Toby.

For some reason, I couldn't smile at him. I felt like crying, instead. "Thanks," I whispered.

Toby took my hand. "Hey, there's the Tunnel of Luv! Let's buy tickets for it!"

The Tunnel of Luv was like no ride I'd ever been on. It wasn't noisy, it didn't jerk you around corners, and nothing jumped out at you. Toby and I sat side by side in this boat shaped like a swan and floated lazily through a dark tunnel in which soft music was playing.

Just before we left the tunnel, Toby leaned over and kissed me gently.

My first kiss! I didn't believe it!

I knew I would never forget Sea City or the pier or the Tunnel of Luv.

Or Toby.

I would never, *ever* forget Toby.

14th CHAPTER

I didn't want Saturday morning to come. I wanted Friday night in Sea City to last forever. Toby and me in the Tunnel of Luv.

But there was no stopping Saturday. I woke up early that morning and lay in bed, just thinking and remembering. I looked over at Mary Anne, who was curled up in a ball. Her hair was falling across her face and she was breathing deeply.

Outside the window, the waves crashed, pounding the shore. The sky was a threatening grey. A lone sea gull wheeled low over the sand. The salt air came in our open window on a breeze that felt chilly. I pulled my covers more tightly around me. It seemed like the end of summer as well as the end of our vacation.

I was amazed at all the things that had happened in the last two weeks. I'd been away from home. I'd stayed on my diet and taken my insulin and hadn't got sick. I'd met two boys I liked, and one of them had kissed me.

I smiled.

Toby was going to come by that morning to say good-bye. I was excited and sad at the same time.

"Stacey-silly-billy-goo-goo?" whispered a voice.

I tiptoed to the door and opened it. There stood Claire. She was stark naked.

"Claire! What are you doing?"

"Looking for my swimming costume," she replied. "Will you come to the beach with me?"

"Sure," I said. An early morning walk might be nice. "But it's too cold for a costume. Why don't you get dressed very quietly? I'll meet you downstairs in a few minutes."

When Claire and I were dressed, we put on jackets and tiptoed out the front door of the Pikes' house. The sky and the ocean were almost the same colour—flat grey—but no rain was falling.

Claire ran to the water's edge.

"Don't go in!" I called after her.

"I won't," she said. "I'm just looking."

Claire stood and looked forever. I'd never seen her stay in one place for so long. While she was looking, I stooped down and picked up a piece of driftwood. Then I found a flat patch of wet sand and wrote.

STACEY + TOBY = LUV

I watched and watched, but the waves didn't wash it away.

At breakfast that morning, Mr Pike finished his eggs, wiped his mouth, and said, "Hey, hey, everybody! Guess what it's time for?"

"What, Daggles-silly-billy-goo-goo?" asked Claire, bouncing around in her chair.

"The . . . chore-hat!"

"Oh, no. Oh, no," moaned Mallory.

The triplets groaned.

Mary Anne and I looked at each other and shrugged.

"I've put the names of eight chores in the hat," Mr Pike went on. "Pass it around, kids. We have work to do this morning. And we have to leave by one o'clock."

Reluctantly, the Pike kids passed the hat. Each ended up with a chore such as sweeping the porch or collecting the sand pails. I realized we had a lot to do before we left for Stoneybrook.

"Stacey and Mary Anne," said Mrs Pike, "can you supervise the children's packing?"

"Sure," we replied.

A couple of hours later, the kids had finished their chores, and were fairly well packed-up. Mr and Mrs Pike were working away, but they turned us loose on the beach. Although the day was still grey, the air was warmer and it hadn't rained yet. The life-guards were on duty, so the kids ran to the water for a final swim.

Mary Anne and I sat down on our towels. (We hadn't brought anything else to the beach.)

"It's almost over," said Mary Anne sadly.

"It seems like we just got here," I told her.

"Yeah."

We hugged our knees and looked out at the ocean. Scott was on the guard station, but I barely noticed him. I was thinking of Toby.

Mary Anne looked dreamy-eyed. She'd already told me what she and Alex had done the night before. They'd sat by the ocean and talked, and then they'd gone through the Tunnel of Luv, too.

"Hey," she said. "Look who's coming."

Toby and Alex were heading across the sand with Kenny, Jimmy, and Ellie.

We waved to them. "Come sit over here," I called.

The boys came over, but they didn't sit down. "We're just out for a walk," said Alex.

"We have to get back, but we wanted to say good-bye."

"Oh, no!" cried Mary Anne. "I hate good-byes."

They had to be said, though, because the boys really couldn't stay.

Toby walked me away from the others so we could have a little privacy.

"Promise you'll write?" I said. We had exchanged addresses the night before.

"I promise. Do you?"

I nodded. I'm not much of a letter-writer, but maybe I'd feel different about writing to Toby.

"Well . . ." said Toby.

"Well . . ." I said.

"I guess this is it."

"Yeah, I guess . . ."

"I want to kiss you," Toby whispered, "but there are too many people around."

"That's okay, "I said. (The sixteen eyes of the Pike kids were boring holes into us, all the way from the ocean.)

"Will you remember me?" asked Toby.

"Always. By the shell and by the bear."

"I'll remember you by the hat." Toby was wearing it. He patted it fondly.

"Well," said Toby again. "'Bye, Stacey."

"'Bye," I replied.

I stayed where I was and watched him walk back to Alex and the kids. A few moments later, they started up the beach, leaving Mary Anne by herself. Toby turned around once to wave to me. Then they disappeared behind a sand dune.

I ran to Mary Anne. She was crying.

"Mary Anne!" I whispered. "All the kids are watching."

"I know, I know." She wiped her eyes. "I'm really okay."

I gave her a quick hug. "We'll talk about this at home tonight, okay?"

Mary Anne nodded.

My eyes drifted across the beach to the lifeguard stand—and Scott. For some reason, he turned around then. He saw me and waved.

I waved back. "Mary Anne," I said, "there's something I have to do. It'll only take a minute."

I ran across the sand to Scott.

"Hey, babe," he greeted me. "Long time no see."

"I've been busy," I replied vaguely. "We're leaving today."

"You are? Hey, too bad, love. I'll miss you."

What he'll miss, I thought, is someone to run errands for him. But somehow I couldn't feel mad about that any more, because I knew Scott really did like me, even if he didn't love me.

"Thanks again for your whistle," I said. "I'll always keep it." I'd never wear it, but I'd keep it to remind me of the first boy I ever fell in love with. I'd put it in a drawer, though. Not on a shelf, where I planned to sit Toby-Bear, or on my dresser, where I planned to put the seashell.

"Hey, Stacey!" Byron yelled to me from the water's edge. "Mum's calling us!"

I turned around. Mrs Pike was at the front door of the house, signalling to us. The rest of the Pike kids were wading ashore. Mary Anne was gathering up towels.

"I have to go," I said. "I hope you like college, Scott."

"Thanks. You be good now, babe."

I joined the Pike kids and herded them across the sand to Mary Anne. Just as we were running into the house, rain began to fall.

Claire burst into tears. "I don't want to leave!" she cried.

I picked her up and gave her a hug. "I don't want to either, but it's time to leave. Hey, you'll be coming back next summer. Think of that."

"Yeah," said Claire, sniffling. "And we can eat at Gurber Garden."

"And play miniature golf."

"And jump on the trapperleens." Claire began to smile.

When everyone was dressed, we loaded up the cars. We seemed to have an awful lot more stuff than we'd left Stoneybrook with. But after pushing and shoving and groaning, we found places for everything and everyone.

We split into the same travelling groups as before.

As we were pulling out of the drive, Mr Pike called to Mrs Pike, "First stop, Ellen Cooke's to return the keys. Next stop, Howard Johnson's."

"Jingle bells, Santa smells," sang Nicky.

"I *hate* that song, Nicholas," said Mallory.

"Good-bye, Sea City-silly-billy-goo-goo!" cried Claire.

"Where's the Sick Bucket?" asked Margo.

I sighed. We were on our way home.

15th CHAPTER

"Hi, Mum! Hi, Dad! I'm home!"

I let myself into our house, feeling absolutely exhausted. Claire had asked, "How many more minutes till we get there?" twenty-nine times between Howard Johnson's and Stoneybrook.

"Stacey!" My parents ran out of the kitchen and folded me into a happy three-person hug.

"How are you?" asked Dad.

"Did you have fun?" asked Mum.

"What did you do?" asked Dad.

"Did you take your insulin every day?" asked Mum.

"Look at your tan!" exclaimed Dad.

"What happened to your hair?" asked Mum.

Although we had left rain behind in Sea City the sun was shining in Stoneybrook. Mum and Dad and I sat out on our back porch and talked and talked. I didn't exactly tell my parents everything (I left out Scott and Toby), but I told them a lot. I told them how easy it had been to stick to my diet, and that I never once forgot my insulin. That was the truth. And I told them that the sun had lightened my hair. That was half the truth.

"What's gone on around here?" I wanted to know.

"It's been pretty quiet," said Mum. "Oh, before I forget, Claudia phoned about an hour ago. The Kishis are back, and she wants you to call her."

"Okay," I said, but I was in no hurry to move, I was too tired. Dad made iced tea and we sat on the porch and drank it as the sun dropped behind the trees in the yard.

I waited until after dinner before I went to my room and picked up the phone. I wished I had my own private telephone number like Claudia did, but I knew I was lucky even to have an extension in my room. I closed my door. Then I lay down on my bed.

I dialled Mary Anne. I was dying to call Claudia, but I knew Mary Anne needed me, and I really wanted to talk to her.

"Hi," I said when she answered. "It's me, Stacey. I wanted to see how you're doing."

"Oh, I'm fine," said Mary Anne. "I'm sorry I cried before. I just didn't think saying good-bye to him—Alex, I mean—would be so sad. I didn't—Oh, I don't know. I'm so embarrassed."

"Mary Anne, he's a *boy*," I told her. "And it's okay to like a boy."

"But I never liked one before. I've always been sort of afraid of them."

"Then I'm glad you met Alex. I'm glad he helped change your mind about boys. They're not alien creatures, you know."

Mary Anne giggled. "I know. Hey, Stace? I want to tell you something. I understand now how you felt about Scott at first. I'm sorry I gave you such a hard time about not helping out and everything."

"That's okay. I guess I really wasn't being very fair. I did stick you with more than your share of the work. And that wasn't right. Besides, when a person is baby-sitting, the kids should come first, no matter what. Do you forgive me?"

"Sure," replied Mary Anne. "Do you forgive me?"

"Of course."

"Hey," said Mary Anne, starting to giggle.

"Remember when all the Pike kids tried to give me sunburn remedies?"

"Yeah. And when Claire won those free games from Fred?"

"And the look on Adam's face when Nicky got the hole in one?"

"And the look on *your* face when Alex said he and Toby would double-date with us?!"

We were laughing hysterically.

"I wonder if anyone ever found the box of chocolates you left on the bench on the pier?" I went on. Thinking about Scott and the girl made me sad, but I could remember the chocolates and laugh, or look at his whistle and smile.

"Oh, I hope so," said Mary Anne. "Listen to me. I'm laughing so hard I'm crying." I could hear her sniffling and snuffling.

"Did you and Alex exchange addresses?" I asked.

"Yup." There was a pause. "We exchanged something else, too," she said finally.

"What?!"

"On the pier, on Friday night. I didn't exactly tell you the whole story."

"Yeah?"

"We found this place where you can buy rings and have stuff engraved on them. They were only five dollars each. So he has a ring with my initials, and I have one with his."

"Ooh, Mary Anne, a ring!" I exclaimed. "That sounds serious."

"Well, it isn't," she replied. "I mean, not really."

"Are you going to wear it?"

"On a chain around my neck, not on my finger. I don't want Dad to see it. He'd probably lock me up until I'm twenty-one."

"Maybe not," I said.

"Maybe not," she agreed.

"Listen, I have to go," I told Mary Anne. "Claudia called this afternoon, and I haven't called her back yet."

"Okay. I guess I should call Dawn and Kristy."

"Mary Anne?"

"Yeah?"

"I'm really glad we got to know each other better."

"Oh, me, too!"

"Well, 'bye."

"'Bye."

I pressed the button, listened for the dialling tone, and called Claudia without even hanging up the phone.

She answered on the first ring. "Aughh! Hi! I can't believe I'm talking to you! How come it took so long for you to call? How are you? How was the trip? Oh, I got all your postcards! I'm really sorry about Scott."

I laughed. "How are *you*?"

"Great. Our vacation was fabulous! It was good for Mimi. She's getting better. And there were arts and crafts at the place we went to, and I threw a pot."

"You *what*?"

"I threw a pot."

"Why?"

"I mean, I *made* a pot—you know, on a potter's wheel. That's what it's called. Throwing a pot."

"Oh."

"The teacher said it was the best one she'd ever seen a beginner make. So Mum and Dad said maybe I could take a pottery class here when school begins."

"That's great . . . Did you meet anyone interesting?"

"You mean, any interesting guys?"

"Of course."

"Of course."

"You did?"

"Yeah. His name is Skip. He's three. I baby-sat for him."

"No, seriously!" I cried.

"Seriously," said Claudia, "there weren't any guys my age up there. Unfortunately. But I was busy enough just reading your postcards. So what finally happened with Scott and Toby? And what was the great present Scott gave you?"

"Oh, Scott gave me his lifeguard whistle. I'll show it to you sometime. And he and I are friends, although we'll probably never see each other again, or even write. And Toby and I are, well . . ."

"*What*?!"

"On our last night in Sea City, Mrs Pike gave Mary Anne and me the evening off, and we went on a double date with Toby and his cousin Alex."

I could almost hear Claudia's jaw drop. "Mary Anne went out on a double *date*?"

"Yup."

"With a *boy*?"

"What else?"

"I can't believe it. I can't believe it."

"And she really likes the guy," I added. "Anyway, after we ate supper, we split up, and Toby bought me a pink seashell to remember him by. He won a teddy bear for me, too. We're going to write to each other. I hope."

"He sounds really nice, Stace," said Claudia.

"Yeah . . ."

"How are the Pike kids?"

"Oh, they're fine. I think they had a great time. I feel like I know them so well now—I mean, *understand* them. You know why Nicky's a pest?"

"Why?"

"Because he wants to be 'one of the guys,' but sometimes the triplets don't let him play with them. Then he feels left out of the whole family. And Byron's different than we thought he was. He's quieter than Adam and Jordan, more serious. Kind of sensitive. And Vanessa can drive you crazy with this poetry kick she's on, but she's really a good little kid. Oh, and Mallory was a *big* help. We put her in charge of a few of the kids sometimes, and she did fine. Listen, when are we having our next Babysitters Club meeting? Monday?"

"I think so. We're all back."

"Great. I can't wait to talk to Dawn and see how California was. And Kristy must have had a trillion sitting jobs while we were all away."

"There's only one bad thing about all this," said Claudia.

"What?"

"The summer's almost over. School's going to begin again."

"Yeah," I replied, "but not for two weeks. And you don't know *what* could happen in two weeks. Almost anything. After all, in two weeks I found my first real love, lost him, found another, and got my first kiss."

"Your first *kiss*! You didn't say anything about that!"

"Oh . . . didn't I?" I replied casually.

"No! Tell me."

"Okay."

I knew we'd be on the phone for at least an hour, but who cared? After all, I was in love.

The Babysitters Club

THE GHOST AT DAWN'S HOUSE

1st CHAPTER

"Aughhh!"

‘Hi! Hello!"

‘Oh, wow! Look at your tan! That's disgusting!"

"Your hair, Dawn! It's even blonder than before!"

It was the first meeting of the Babysitters Club since Kristy, Claudia, Stacey, Mary Anne, and I (Dawn Schafer), had been separated. It had been our longest separation since the beginning of the club. Two whole weeks. And we'd been scattered from here, in Stoneybrook, Connecticut, all the way across the country to California.

Claudia Kishi and her family had taken a trip to a resort in New Hampshire. Mary Anne Spier and Stacey McGill had got jobs (through the Babysitters Club) as mother's helpers, and had gone to Sea City, a New Jersey beach, with the Pike family. Poor

Kristy Thomas hadn't gone anywhere. She'd stayed here.

I was the one who went to California. I went with my little brother, Jeff. Our parents got divorced last winter and Mum moved Jeff and me from nice, warm California to freezing cold, snowy Connecticut. (Well, it was cold and snowy when we moved here. Now it's August, and hot and humid.) Mum chose Stoneybrook because she grew up here, and her parents still live here. Anyway, it was sort of a messy divorce, and Jeff and I hadn't seen Dad in ages, so Mum arranged for us to spend the first two weeks in August with him.

We got to fly by ourselves and everything. Since we were travelling alone, we were given all sorts of special attention. One stewardess slipped us free headphones. We saw a film starring Chevy Chase. Jeff laughed so hard he was nearly sick, but he recovered in time for dinner and managed to collect extra desserts from all the people around us who didn't want theirs—five in all. (Ordinarily, we're really into health food, but Jeff goes sort of crazy over chocolate cake.) Next, Jeff collected all the packets of salt, pepper, creamer, instant coffee, and sugar he could find. He saved them in a sick bag. The sick bag is now sitting on his desk at home.

Anyway, you'd think the aeroplane was the highlight of our trip, but of course it wasn't. What came next was not just California, but two weeks of Disneyland Daddy – you know, two weeks with a man who hasn't seen his kids in months and feels *really* guilty. Guilty enough to take time off from work and give them a whirlwind holiday of beaches, amusement parks, shopping, dinners in restaurants, movies, treats, surprises . . . It was spectacular – except for the fact that a Disneyland Daddy doesn't feel like your father any more. But I suppose he's better than no father at all.

However, California was over now, and I was back. All the members of the Babysitters Club were back. And we still had two glorious weeks of summer holiday left before we began school.

As usual we gathered for our meeting in Claudia's bedroom. Claudia is the vice-chairman of the club and the only one of us who has not just her own phone, but her own personal phone number. She's even listed separately in the Stoneybrook telephone directory as *Kishi, C.*

"Well, let's get down to business," said Kristy, our chairman. Kristy was the one who'd had the original idea to form the club.

The Babysitters Club is really more of a business than a club. The five of us meet three times a week at Claudia's. People call us when they need a sitter. They're willing to wait until our meetings to call, because they reach five of us at once, so they know they're practically guaranteed a sitter. No more calling all over town to track down someone available.

We're very official and responsible about running our club. This is mostly due to Kristy, even though she does get bossy about things every now and then. We keep a record book full of information – the phone numbers and addresses of our clients, an appointment calendar, and a list of our earnings. (We each get to keep whatever money we make, but Kristy always likes to know how the club is doing overall.) We also have a notebook, a sort of diary, in which we're supposed to write up every job we go on. Then we pass the book around so we can all read what's happening with our clients. It's very helpful. But sometimes it's a pain writing about the jobs. Not all of them are that interesting. Of course, there *was* the time Kristy ended up dog-sitting instead of baby-sitting. And the time Mary Anne was baby-sitting for a little kid who got really sick, and found out just how helpful the emergency number can be in a real emergency.

Kristy opened the record book to the appointment pages in case a phone call should come in.

She leaned back in the director's chair and crossed her arms. "I move that we start this meeting by discussing the baby-sitting experiences we've had over the last two weeks."

(We'd all done some sitting, even Claudia and I, who'd technically been on holiday.)

Claudia grinned. "I move that before we start talking, we have a little snack," she said.

Claudia, the junk-food addict, pulled a book off her shelf, opened it, and removed a bag of chocolate buttons. It was a hollow book! Claudia has sweets and stuff hidden all over her room, but she'd never gone so far as to use a hollow book before!

"Where'd you get that?" I asked.

"I bought it at a flea market. Isn't it great? I got this, too." Claudia held out her hand and showed us a ring with a fierce, green dragon's head on it. Claudia, who is Japanese and exotic-looking, loves wild clothes and jewellery.

"Ahem," said Kristy impatiently.

Claudia hurriedly passed around the sweets which Stacey and I turned down. (Stacey's a diabetic - no sweets for her.) Then she replaced the chocolate buttons in the book and tossed a packet of crackers to Stacey and me.

"Let's start with Mary Anne and Stacey," I suggested. "I bet they had the most interesting experiences."

Mary Anne and Stacey, by the way, are our secretary and treasurer. (In case you're wondering, I'm the official alternate officer. I take over the duties of anyone who has to miss a meeting.)

Mary Anne and Stacey looked at each other. They exchanged a grin.

"You start," they said at the same time. Then they laughed.

I couldn't help feeling just a teensy bit jealous. Mary Anne is my best friend in Stoneybrook. She was the one who introduced me to Kristy and the others and got me into the club. Of course, Mary Anne already had a best friend (Kristy), but she's kind of shy, and she's always been envious of Stacey, who's sophisticated and grown-up. Now it looked as if Mary Anne and Stacey shared something – something the rest of us weren't a part of.

"I'll start," Stacey said after a moment of giggling. "First of all," she began, crossing her long legs, "we had a great time. I like the Pikes – all of them – a lot." (There are eight kids in the Pike family.) "We did the usual beach stuff – swimming, sun-bathing, miniature golf. Claire is *still* going through that silly stage. She calls everybody a silly-billy-goo-goo. Vanessa has decided she wants to be a poet, so she speaks in rhyme."

"Really?" I said. I couldn't help laughing.

"Yup. It's true. And Byron can swim, but he's afraid of the water. It turns out he has a lot of fears."

"The most important thing about the Pike kids," added Mary Anne, "is something that's going on between Nicky and the triplets." (Nicky is eight. The triplets –

Byron, Adam, and Jordan – are ten.) "Nicky wants to play with his brothers, but they don't like to have him around. They say he's babyish. But if they won't play with him, that only leaves the girls, and Nicky says he doesn't like girls. So . . ."

"Trouble," I said, nodding. This was important, since I sit for the Pikes a lot.

"Now tell us about you, Dawn," said Stacey. "I've never been to California."

So I told them about Jeff and the trip and my Disneyland Daddy. "I only did a little baby-sitting," I added. "Twice I sat for the kids who'd been my favourites when I lived in California. They were our next-door neighbours. I mean, they are. I mean, they're still Dad's next-door neighbours. There are two kids, five and eight. And you won't believe what their names are. Clover and Daffodil."

"What?" screeched the others.

"Yeah. My dad says their parents were hippies in the sixties. Flower children, he calls them. I'm not sure what that means."

"It must mean you have to name your children after flowers!" Kristy hooted.

We all began to laugh.

"Anyway," I went on, "they remembered me, and we were really glad to see each other. They cried when I left. They thought I'd come back to California for good."

"Oh, that's sad," said Mary Anne. Mary

Anne is probably the most sensitive one of all of us.

"Yeah," I said. "But I'm sure I'll see them again. The next time I visit my dad."

"What about you, Claud?" asked Stacey. "Who'd you sit for?"

"Mostly this little kid named Skip," replied Claudia. "He and his parents were at the resort the whole time we were. It was no big deal. I just took him paddling and stuff. A couple of other kids, too."

"Well," said Kristy, "*I* had some interesting jobs while you guys were away."

"Oh, that's right!" I exclaimed, suddenly remembering. "You baby-sat for the Perkinses, didn't you?"

The Perkinses were special for two reasons. Not only were they new clients, but they had moved into Kristy's old house. Kristy lives across town now, which was part of the reason she'd stayed home for the past two weeks while the rest of us were away.

You see, I'm not the only one with divorced parents. Kristy's parents are divorced, too, only they've been divorced a lot longer than mine have. Long enough for Kristy's mum to get married again. Kristy was even in the wedding! And all the members of the Babysitters Club were guests. It was great.

But then Watson Brewer (that's Kristy's step-father – he just happens to be a millionaire) moved Kristy, her mum, her big brothers Sam and Charlie, and her little brother David Michael, across town to live in his mansion with him. It seemed like a fairy tale to me, but it has caused some problems. For one thing, we miss having Kristy nearby. For another, we have to pay Charlie to drive Kristy to and from our club meetings. Plus, Kristy's mum wants Watson and *his* two kids and Kristy and her brothers to become a real family. So . . . no holiday for any of them. Just plenty of togetherness at the mansion.

However, it was fun to have a new family in the neighbourhood. And the Perkinses have little kids, which is even better. Kristy had been the first to baby-sit for them. A sitting job right in her old house!

"It was weird," Kristy said. "There was my bedroom and my living room – with this strange furniture. I mean, you know, *different* furniture. But the girls are great. And Mrs Perkins is nice, too. I didn't meet Mr Perkins. The older girl, Myriah, is really clever. And she takes all kinds of lessons – ballet, tap dancing, swimming. And she's only five and a half. Gabbie is the little one. She's two and a half. She says sweet things like 'Toshe me up'. That's something she invented. It means, 'Pick me up and give me a hug.' And she kept calling me by my whole name – 'Toshe me up, Kristy Thomas . . . Want to see my room, Kristy Thomas?' I think you guys will like the Perkinses."

The phone rang then, and once it started, it kept on ringing. Everyone knew we were home from our holidays and back in business. Even Mrs Perkins called. By the time our meeting was over, we all had jobs lined up.

I rode my bike back to my neighbourhood, feeling great. There were new clients to meet, baby-sitting to do, and two weeks of the summer left!

2nd CHAPTER

It's amazing how different two people in the very same family can be. Take Jeff and me. We're pretty much alike, except for the obvious differences, such as that I'm a girl and he's a boy, and I'm thirteen and he's only almost ten. But then take Mum and me. (Or Mum and Jeff, for that matter.) I love my mother and we get along fine, but she's sort of like Oscar Madison in *The Odd Couple* and I'm like Felix Unger. Mum's not a personal slob like Oscar is, but she's forgetful and absentminded, and our house is usually a mess – except for my room. My room is the calm eye in the centre of a hurricane.

This is why I was not surprised to walk into my house after the Babysitters Club meeting to find a pair of hedgeclippers in the living room, a trail of popcorn from the front hall to the kitchen (that was Jeff's –

he's not a slob, but he *is* a nine-year-old boy), and a lot of other things that were in places where they didn't belong.

The mess has only grown worse since my mum got a job. Believe me, Jeff and I are happy that Mum is working – because *she's* happy she's working, and when she's happy, we're happy. But it does have its disadvantages. For instance, Jeff and I are now in charge of making dinner on week nights. At first we tried taking turns, but that didn't work out, since Jeff's idea of making dinner is getting a loaf of bread out of the bread tin.

Plus, Mum is so busy with her job that she doesn't have time for anything else. And I don't mean housework. I mean dating. In particular, dating Mary Anne's father. See, Mary Anne's mum died a long time ago, and after we moved here, my mother started seeing Mr Spier. Mary Anne and I were so excited! We thought we were going to get to be stepsisters. But I don't think that will happen now.

"Hey, Jeff!" I yelled. "Help me with dinner! Mum'll be home soon."

No answer.

"Jeff!" I called upstairs.

Still no answer.

Maybe he was in the barn.

I went out the back door, ran across the yard, and shouted into the barn. "JEFF!"

Thunk. What was that?

I stood still and listened. I could hear little rustlings. Far away, thunder rumbled.

I shivered. I love our old house, and the barn, but sometimes they give me the creeps. They were built in 1795, and there's just something spooky about a place that's been around that long. So many people have lived here . . . Some of them have probably *died* here, too. Right in the house or the barn.

"Jeff?" I said again, but this time almost in a whisper.

"BOO!" A figure leapt into view.

"Aughhh !" I shrieked. "Jeff, you nearly scared me to death!"

"Well, you scared *me*. You come screaming in here like some kind of I don't know what. You made me fall off the rope swing."

"Oh, was that thud you?"

"Yeah. What'd you think it was – a ghost?"

"Course not," I replied, sorry he'd put the idea in my head. "Come on. We have to make dinner."

Jeff and I made a salad with cottage cheese, pineapple, peaches, and coconut topping, and heated up a vegetable casserole Mum had made over the weekend. Then we brewed some herbal tea. Kristy teases us, but Mum and Jeff and I really like health food. We ate health food in California, and I think that's something about us that won't change, no matter how long we live on the East Coast.

"Boy, it's hot," I said, pulling my long hair away from my sweaty neck.

"I know," replied Jeff. "Sticky. Let's eat outside, okay? I could set the picnic table."

"Good idea," I said. I handed him plates, napkins, forks, and glasses, and he went outside.

I stood in our old-fashioned kitchen and stirred the tea. Then I poured it into a jug and added ice.

Suddenly the house seemed awfully . . . big. I heard a creak and looked over my shoulder. Nothing.

Describing the house as "big" was kind of funny, since it isn't. Big, I mean. Oh, it has plenty of rooms, but they're all kind of small. Mum explained to me that over the years, people have got taller. Back in 1795, I suppose we were still on the short side. At any rate, not only are the rooms in our house little and dark, but the doorways are low, and the steps in the staircase are low (and uneven). It's like a large, creepy dollhouse.

Since the house *is* so old, I have this theory that somewhere in it is a hidden passage. All old houses have them, don't they? Claudia, who loves mysteries, lent me a Nancy Drew book called *The Hidden Staircase*. On the cover, Nancy is pushing open a section of wall at the back of a cupboard and discovering a hidden staircase. I know there's a secret something somewhere in our house, too. I just *know* it.

"Dawn?"

I jumped a mile.

"Oh, Mum!" I said with a gasp. "You scared me."

"Sorry. I didn't mean to." She kissed my forehead.

"How was work?" I asked.

"Fine. Busy, though. I'm exhausted."

"I hope you're hungry. Jeff and I have dinner all ready. Jeff's setting the picnic table. It's so hot we thought we'd eat outdoors."

"Oh, that's fine."

Mum was looking more absentminded than usual. Sure enough, she took off her glasses and placed them carefully in an empty butter dish. I wonder if she does things like that at the office.

I checked her quickly to make sure she hadn't been wearing non-matching earrings or something all day. Luckily, she looked fine.

Mum and Jeff and I ate our picnic supper in a breeze that kept blowing our napkins away. At least it was cool.

"You know," said Jeff, chewing with his mouth open as usual, "it's getting dark very early tonight."

"Well, it *is* almost September," Mum pointed out.

"But it's only a quarter to . . . Hey!" I exclaimed. A fat drop of water landed on the back of my hand. Another landed on my head. "Uh-oh, it's raining!"

"And it's going to pour!" cried Jeff.

The sky wasn't just dark, it was black with heavy clouds.

BLAM! Thunder crashed. I remembered the rumblings I'd heard earlier.

"Everybody inside," said Mum. "Let's see if we can get all this stuff into the kitchen in one trip."

It wasn't easy, but we managed it. Jeff was the last one in and he raced through the back door just as a sheet of water came cascading down. Lightning streaked across the sky.

"Made it!" he exclaimed.

Later that night I settled into my bed with a library book. I'd had my name on the waiting list for that book for most of the summer. That was how popular it was. And no wonder everyone wanted to read it. It was called *Ghosts and Spooks, Chills and Thrills: Stories NOT to Be Read After Dark*. Well, it was after dark, but I'd taken the precaution of turning on every light in my bedroom. However, the storm was still raging outside. The wind was howling, the rain was pelting against the windows, and the thunder came and went, sometimes crashing loudly, sometimes just sort of grumbling in the distance. The grumblings were scarier than the crashes. They sounded like warnings of worse things to come.

I was right in the middle of "The Hand of the Witch" when the lights flickered. They dimmed, went out for a second, then came back on.

My heart began to pound. Weren't there tricky spirits called poltergeists that could cause things like that?

My window began to rattle. I know the wind was blowing, but I'd never heard such a racket.

As soon as the rattling stopped, I heard a rat-a-tat-a-tat on the wall.

That did it.

"Eeee-iii!" I shrieked.

Mum was up the stairs and in my room in about two seconds. "Dawn! What's the matter?" she cried.

"Mum, the lights are flickering and something's rattling my window and tapping on the wall."

My mother took a look at the book lying open on my bed. "Dawn," she said, giving me a wry glance, "there is a terrific storm going on out there. I'm surprised the electricity hasn't gone off completely. And *all* the windows in this old house are rattling. Those must be twenty-five-mile-an-hour winds out there. Now which wall is the tapping coming from?"

I pointed to the wall between my room and Mum's.

"Old houses make noises as they settle," Mum told me decisively. She closed the ghost-story book and laid it on my bedside table. "Why don't you go to sleep now, honey? It's late." She gave me a kiss and turned out the lights as she left the room, closing the door behind her.

I got up and turned two of the lights back on and opened the door a crack. *Sleep?* Was she kidding?

It was hours before I fell asleep. That was because I kept thinking I heard someone moaning. When I woke up the next morning, I still felt creepy.

3rd CHAPTER

The storm ended temporarily, but the rain didn't. The next morning was dreary, humid, and very rainy. I baby-sat at the Barretts' and the three kids, Buddy, Suzi, and Marnie, started out sleepy and moody, and slowly became wild and noisy. I was glad they only needed a sitter for the morning. Here's an example of why.

As I was leaving, I skidded a little on the wet grass, and Buddy shouted after me, "Have a nice *trip*." He laughed loudly.

Suzi, who's four, shrieked, "'Bye, Dawny-Dawny! Snap, crackle, pop!!"

Marnie, the baby, blew me a raspberry.

I have to admit, I was happy to get home. Jeff and I ate lunch. Then I went to my room. Another storm was brewing, and I was planning to read some more of the ghost stories and scare myself silly. But the sight of *The Hidden Staircase* on my desk gave me an idea. It was the perfect day to search – *really* search – for a secret passage in the house. I'd looked a couple of times before, but never very carefully or for very long.

I picked up the phone in Mum's bedroom and called Mary Anne.

"Hi!" I said. "Want to come over? I have this great idea. I want to invite the whole club to my house and we'll search for a hidden passage."

"Ooh," said Mary Anne. "Scary. I'd love to."

"Do you think the others are free?"

"I know they are. I was looking at the appointment calendar during the meeting yesterday. We all had jobs this morning, and we're all free this afternoon. Stacey's mother can probably drive us over."

"Perfect!" I said. "Listen, can you call Kristy? I'll call Stacey and Claudia."

"No problem."

An hour later, the members of the Babysitters Club were sitting expectantly in my bedroom.

"Now, we have to be scientific about this," I told them.

"Scientific?" asked Kristy sceptically.

"Well, sort of. See, there are certain things to do." I read them the pages in *The Hidden Staircase* where Nancy is searching Riverview Manor. "You tap on walls –"

"Why?" asked Kristy.

"To listen for any hollow sounds. A hollow sound might mean an empty space on the other side of the wall."

"And," added Claudia, who'd read a lot more mysteries than I had, "you have to feel around for springs or catches. And shine a torch over the walls. It might show up a secret opening you wouldn't notice otherwise." Claudia's eyes were sparkling. "*How* old is this house again, Dawn?" she asked.

I told her.

"Wow. I'd say we have a pretty good chance of finding something."

The storm that had been brewing finally let loose then with a terrific crash of thunder that banged the shutters and rattled the windows.

Stacey let out a little gasp. Then she giggled. "We're frightening ourselves, you know. This is just a silly storm."

"I know," said Mary Anne, "but it's fun to be frightening ourselves. We should take advantage of this super-creepy weather."

"Right!" I said. I couldn't wait to start!

"How do we begin?" asked Stacey.

"Let's split up," I suggested.

"*Split up?*" cried Mary Anne, "I'm not going anywhere alone!"

I could see her point. The house was dark and quiet. Outside, the rain was falling hard and the wind was howling. I happened to look out of my window just in time to see a bolt of lightning flash across the grey sky in a jagged streak.

I shivered.

"Well, we don't have to go alone," I said. "We can split up into teams, one with two people and the other with three."

Everyone agreed that that seemed safe.

"Kristy, why don't you and Stacey and Claudia take the ground floor," I suggested, "and Mary Anne and I will look around up here."

"What about the cellar and the attic?" asked Claudia.

We froze. They were bad enough on a nice, sunny day, but today . . .

"Maybe the five of us should search them together. Um, later," said Stacey.

"Or – or maybe not at all," I added.

"Why not?" asked Claudia. "Those would be great places for a secret passage."

"I know," I replied. "But, well, in this story I read – it was called 'Things Unseen' – this man moves into a really old house –"

"As old as this one?" whispered Mary Anne. A gust of wind blew the curtains against her face and she shrieked.

"Just about," I said, closing the window. "And he hears all these spooky noises coming from the cellar, and it turns out that years ago, a crazy lady buried her –"

"Aughh! Stop!" cried Mary Anne. "I don't want to hear the end of this."

"I do," said Kristy. "Leave the room

for a minute, Mary Anne."

"I'm not leaving the room. Not by myself!"

Stacey shuddered. "I'll go with you."

They went out into the hall, while I finished the story. When our screaming died down, they returned.

"Listen," said Kristy, "why don't you two scaredy-cats be a team, and Claudia and Dawn and I will be the other team?"

Stacey took offence. "Scaredy-cats?"

"And you can search downstairs," Kristy continued. "Jeff is there and the TV is on. It won't seem so spooky."

"I think that's a good idea," said Mary Anne hastily. "Come on. Let's go before they change their minds."

They clattered down the stairs.

"Let's search room by room," I suggested. "I can tap walls. Claudia, you feel around for hidden springs and buttons and things. Kristy, you shine my torch everywhere to see if the outline of a door or something shows up."

Kristy raised her eyebrows. She was used to being in charge. But this was *my* house and *my* search, so I thought I was entitled to give a few instructions.

We set to work. We searched Jeff's room first.

"Boy," said Kristy. "My brothers would kill me if I ever searched *their* rooms."

"Well, Jeff might kill me, too, if he knew

what we were doing," I replied. "But it's not as if we're searching his *stuff*. We're just looking at his walls."

"Oh, hey!" cried Claudia. "We should be checking the floors for trapdoors, too."

"On the first floor?" asked Kristy.

"You never know," Claud said.

Tap, tap, tap. I tapped and rapped every inch of Jeff's walls, but they all sounded pretty much the same.

Claudia followed me around, poking and feeling along the walls.

And Kristy crawled everywhere with her torch. She found two comics under Jeff's bed, but no trapdoor. We worked without speaking for a long time, and the only sounds we heard were our rappings and tappings, the pounding rain, and an occasional ominous rumble of thunder.

We didn't really find anything. There was an area near Jeff's desk where the moulding looked different than on the other walls, but no matter how much we poked and prodded, we couldn't find anything suspicious.

"Let's look in my room next," I said.

We started over again. I rapped, Claudia poked, and Kristy shone the torch.

"Nothing here!" said Kristy.

"Wait, I'm not finished," I said. "I've only done three walls."

Rap, rap, rap, rap, thud.

We all looked at each other.

"Did you hear that?" I whispered.

It was a definite hollow sound.

I was standing by my bed, next to the wall that separates my room from Mum's room. There was all this fancy moulding on the wall – one of my favourite things about the room – and Claudia immediately began running her fingers over it.

The three of us were expecting something to spring open or fly out at any moment, but not a thing happened.

"False alarm," said Claudia at last.

I knew she and Kristy felt as disappointed as I did.

"Hey, you guys," said Kristy, forcing a smile. "Let's show those two cowards downstairs how brave we are. Let's explore the attic."

"The attic?" I squeaked.

KER-RASH. A clap of thunder shook the house.

"I think that was a sign," I said. "A sign saying we'd be stupid to go in the attic."

"Oh, come on," said Kristy. "It's all this ghost stuff that's stupid."

Maybe to her. I couldn't stop thinking about "Things Unseen". Or another story I read where a man picks up a woman he finds hitchhiking one night. He decides to take her home, but when he gets to her house, she's disappeared – and the couple in the house say the woman was their daughter and had died ten years earlier.

Kristy grabbed my arm. "Come on."

I must have been crazy. I opened the door to the attic. We were greeted by stale, musty air, and the sound of the rain on the roof. We started to tiptoe up the stairs. The light switch was at the top. Halfway up, the door slammed shut.

"Yikes!" I cried.

The three of us piled back down the steps.

"I hope the door didn't lock behind us!" I whispered. We were closed into total darkness.

I was reaching for the handle when the door began to open slowly. We heard a low moan.

"Oh, no," I whimpered.

Then we heard a growl.

"You haven't got a dog, have you," said Kristy. It was a statement, not a question.

I shook my head, and looked at Kristy and Claudia with wide, terrified eyes.

Then the three of us let out eardrum-shattering screams.

"Gotcha!" Stacey and Mary Anne jumped out from behind the door. "Who are the scaredy-cats now?" asked Stacey.

"You guys nearly gave us heart attacks!" gasped Kristy.

Mary Anne and Stacey laughed hysterically. The three of us had to sit down to recover. We didn't think it was funny at all.

"Did you find anything?" I asked them, when I was able to speak.

They shook their heads. "But we haven't looked in the study yet," said Mary Anne.

We split up again. As soon as Stacey and Mary Anne had gone, I turned to the others and said, "This is war. We've *got* to get back at them."

"How?" asked Claudia.

"There's a heating vent in Mum's room that goes down to the study. I have an idea."

The three of us sat on the floor and crowded around the vent.

"Ow-oooh," I moaned into it.

Kristy and Claudia caught on immediately.

"Heeeelp meeee," wailed Kristy.

"Wheeeere aaaaaaam IIIIII?" whispered Claudia.

Then we moaned some more. The howling wind helped us along.

"Shhh," I said. "Listen."

Downstairs we could hear Stacey and Mary Anne shrieking.

I looked at Kristy and Claudia. We began to giggle. Then we took up the moaning again.

"Woooo . . . Ow-ow-ooooh . . . Oooooo-eeeeee . . ."

And then I felt a hand on my shoulder. I dared to look around. The hand was *green*.

"Kristy," I whispered. "Claudia."

We all looked up.

We were gazing into the green face of a deformed, one-eyed monster.

"BOO! Scared you!"

It was Jeff in a Hallowe'en costume.

"Aughh! Aughh! Aughh!"

Kristy, Claudia and I were screaming upstairs. Mary Anne and Stacey were screaming downstairs.

Jeff fell over laughing.

That was the end of our search for a secret passage. We didn't find a thing.

4th CHAPTER

Wednesday

I know Kristy said the Perkinses are nice, but I have to say, I really didn't want to baby-sit for them. I'm still mad (only a little) that they live next door, instead of the Thomases. Looking out my bedroom window just isn't the same anymore. (I look into Myriah's room now, not Kristy's.) But what I didn't know before this morning was that "different" could be fun, too.

I did sit for the Perkinses today and guess what -- Kristy was right. Myriah and Gabbie are great. And boy is there exciting news at the Perkins house! It sort of slipped out by accident while the girls were colouring.

I think I understand how Mary Anne feels about the Thomases and the house next door. Replacements can be hard to adjust to. Even if they're better than the original thing, sometimes you don't like them (at first) just because they're different.

Whatever Mary Anne's feelings, though, she *had* agreed to baby-sit at the Perkins home, so she turned up at ten-thirty on the dot on Wednesday morning.

She felt funny ringing the doorbell and not going straight inside like she used to do. Instead, she had to stand and wait. She heard a dog barking and feet running – not as many feet as when the Thomases lived there, but several pairs.

When the door was opened, two blonde-haired, brown-eyed faces were peering up at her. Behind them was a woman who was struggling to hold back a huge black dog.

There were a couple of moments of confusion.

"Chewy! Behave!" said the woman.

"That's Chewbacca, our dog," said the older of the two girls. "He's eight months old."

"I'm wearing Myriah's baldet shoes," announced the younger one, holding up her foot to show Mary Anne a pink ballet slipper.

Chewy struggled out of Mrs Perkins' grip, lunged for the door, and jumped up, resting his front feet on the door and grinning a happy doggie grin. In the process, he knocked the littler girl to the floor. She giggled and stood up unsteadily.

"Baldet shoes are slippery," she said.

Mrs Perkins got Chewy under control and let him out in the back garden. Myriah let Mary Anne in.

"Well, you're Mary Anne, right?" said Mrs Perkins as she returned.

Mary Anne nodded.

"I'm Mrs Perkins," she went on. "And this is Myriah," (the older one), "and Gabbie." (The one wearing the "baldet" slippers.) "Girls, this is Mary Anne Spier."

Myriah smiled shyly at Mary Anne.

Gabbie smiled, too. "Hi, Mary Anne Spier," she said, and she remembered that Kristy had said Gabbie called her by her full name.

"I'm going to the doctor for a check-up," Mrs Perkins told Mary Anne. "I have to run some errands, too. I should be back in about two hours. There are no special instructions, really. The girls will show you their playroom. And you can go outside, if you want." (The rain had miraculously stopped.) "Oh, one thing – leave Chewy in the garden. If you take a walk, don't try to take him with you. He's a bit of a handful."

"*He'd* take *us* on a walk, instead!" said Myriah.

After Mrs Perkins left, Mary Anne and the girls looked at each other. Sometimes a first baby-sitting job can be a little awkward, especially if you're on the shy side, like Mary Anne is.

But Myriah got things going. "Want to see our rooms?" she asked.

"Sure," replied Mary Anne.

"I have a doll," said Gabbie, skipping ahead.

"It's not really her doll," Myriah whispered confidentially to Mary Anne as they climbed the stairs. "It's mine, but I let her use it."

Mary Anne smiled.

"This is my room," said Myriah a few moments later. And Mary Anne found herself looking sadly around Kristy's old room. In place of her sports posters were animal pictures and a poster of a ballerina. In place of her desk was a dollhouse. It wasn't the same at all.

"Hey, let's go downstairs again," said Mary Anne huskily. "I want to see your playroom."

Gabbie turned and raced downstairs.

Myriah and Mary Anne followed. When they reached the playroom, Gabbie was already there, rocking an old Cabbage Patch Doll in her arms. "This is Cindy Jane, Mary Anne Spier," she said.

"Her name is really Caroline Eunice," Myria whispered. "Oh! There's R. C.!" she exclaimed suddenly.

A brown tabby cat sauntered into the room.

"R. C. stands for Rat Catcher," Myriah announced, "but he doesn't catch *any*thing. He's too, too lazy. Aren't you, R. C.?"

"Aren't you, R. C. ?" echoed Gabbie absentmindedly, as R. C. flopped over on his side and fell asleep.

"Now don't say everything I say," Myriah admonished her sister. Once again she whispered to Mary Anne. "The Gabbers is going through a stage."

"The Gabbers?" said Mary Anne.

"Yeah. That's what Mum and Dad and I call her."

Gabbie tossed Cindy Jane/Caroline Eunice to the floor. "Let's colour!" she said.

"Yeah!" agreed Myriah. "Let's colour. You want to colour, too, Mary Anne?"

"Colour with us, Mary Anne Spier," said Gabbie.

Myriah and Gabbie settled themselves at a pink and white table with pictures of Barbie dolls all over it.

"We always colour at our Barbie table," said Myriah.

Mary Anne squeezed into a little pink chair. She had to sit sideways at the table, since her knees wouldn't fit underneath it.

Myriah tore three pieces of paper off a pad and passed them out. She set a box of crayons in the middle. "Now colour, you guys," she said.

The three of them (even Mary Anne) got right to work. Both of the little girls sang to themselves as they coloured. Myriah sang "Take Me Out to the Ball Game." Gabbie sang "Hush Little Baby." Mary Anne raised her eyebrows. How had they memorized all the verses to those songs? Even Mary Anne didn't know them.

After a few minutes, Gabbie handed her picture to Mary Anne. It was a huge, jumbled scribble. "Look, Mary Anne Spier," she said.

"That's lovely!" Mary Anne exclaimed. She was about to ask, "What is it?" when she remembered something we Babysitters Club members had thought up. Instead of saying "What is it?" when we can't tell what a picture or an art project is, we say, "Tell me about it." That way, the kid doesn't *know* we can't tell, so his feelings aren't hurt, and he tells us what the picture is so we don't say anything stupid about it, like "I've never seen such a big elephant," when it turns out to be a picture of the kid's grandmother or something.

"Tell me about it," Mary Anne said to Gabbie.

"Okay. This is my mummy," said Gabbie, pointing, "and this is the baby growing in her tummy."

Once again, Mary Anne raised her eyebrows. She almost raised them right off her forehead. "The baby in her tummy?" she repeated. She glanced at Myriah.

"Yeah, we're having a baby," said Myriah nonchalantly. "Not for a long time, though. I hope I get a brother. We have enough girls around here . . . R. C. is a girl," she added. "The only boys are Daddy and Chewy."

"Wow! That's exciting!" cried Mary Anne. Actually, she felt even more excited than she sounded, but she knows how sensitive little kids are about new babies. She didn't want Myriah and Gabbie to think that they weren't important, too.

Mary Anne wanted to ask a lot more questions, but she didn't dare. She also wanted to call the rest of us baby-sitters with the exciting news, but she didn't dare do that, either. She knew she'd have to wait.

"Do you two want to take a walk?" Mary Anne asked Myriah and Gabbie. "It's so nice out. And yesterday was such an awful, rainy day. *I'd* like to go out."

"Okay," agreed the girls.

"Hey," said Mary Anne suddenly. "Do you know any other kids around here yet?"

"We know Kristy Thomas," said Myriah.

"Kristy Thomas," echoed Gabbie.

"Well," said Mary Anne, "I meant kids your age. Have you met Jamie Newton?"

"No," said Myriah.

"Or Nina and Eleanor Marshall?"

"No."

"Well, maybe you'd like to meet them. It would be fun to have friends around here, wouldn't it?"

"*Sure,*" said Myriah.

"*Sure,*" said Gabbie.

"And guess what – Jamie Newton has a baby, just like you're going to have. Only she's not a newborn baby any more. Her name is Lucy. Do you want to see her?"

"Yup," said Myriah.

"Yup," said Gabbie.

So Mary Anne walked the girls around the neighbourhood. By the time Mrs Perkins came home, Myriah and Gabbie had met Nina and Eleanor, Charlotte Johanssen, Mr and Mrs Goldman, Claudia's grandmother Mimi, and Jamie and Lucy Newton.

"Jamie has a new baby, just like we're going to have!" Myriah told her mother.

Mrs Perkins glanced at Mary Anne.

"The news sort of slipped out," said Mary Anne, "I hope you don't mind." She showed Mrs Perkins Gabbie's picture.

"I don't mind at all," said Mrs Perkins with a smile. "I suppose I just hadn't got around to mentioning it. But it's no secret." She paid Mary Anne and walked her to the front door.

"Are you going to come back again, Mary Anne?" asked Myriah. "I hope so, because

I didn't show you all the stuff in my room. Or in my goofy sister's room."

Gabbie smiled charmingly at Mary Anne.

"Of course I'll come back," replied Mary Anne. "And I'll show you something special, too. Right now. If you go up to your bedroom and wait by the side window, you'll have a surprise in a few minutes."

Mary Anne said goodbye to the Perkinses and raced home. She flew up to her bedroom. Then she stood at her open window. There was Myriah in *her* window.

"Hi!" called Mary Anne. "We can see each other!"

"Hey!" said Myriah. "We can talk to each other, too!"

"This'll be our special secret, okay?"

"All right!" cried Myriah.

Mary Anne turned away. Having the Perkinses next door still wasn't the same as having Kristy there. But Mary Anne didn't feel sad about it any more.

5th CHAPTER

"'Bye, Jeff! I'm going over to the Pikes'!" I called. "I'll be back in a couple of hours. Call if you're going to go anywhere."

"I'm not moving!" he shouted back.

The weather was unbearably hot, even for Californians like us. It was almost a hundred degrees and humid. Our old house isn't really equipped for air-conditioning, but there is one unit in the study downstairs. Jeff had been closed in with it all morning. I think that if he could have, he would have sat *on* the air-conditioner.

I'm sort of in charge of Jeff while Mum's at work, but I can go off and do things. Jeff is almost ten, and he's fairly responsible. All either of us really has to do is phone so the other one always knows where he or she is. And Jeff isn't allowed to have friends over if I'm not at home.

I made my way sluggishly over to the Pikes'.

Mallory, the oldest Pike, met me at the front door. "Guess what?" she cried. "All of us kids are here and *I'm* going to be the second baby-sitter! It was my idea, and Mum said okay!"

"Hey, Mal, that's great!"

Mallory is eleven and has always been a big help with her younger brothers and sisters. Until now, though, when all eight kids needed looking after, Mrs Pike would hire two sitters. Apparently, she'd decided that Mallory was old enough to be one of those sitters. That was fine with me. All of us baby-sitters like Mallory, and we've sometimes thought that one day she could join our club. She's younger than the rest of us, but she'd be really good.

"Hi, Dawn," Mrs Pike greeted me. "Let's see. Mallory's going to sit with you today. I'm sure she's told you that."

"Yes," I said with a smile. I glanced at Mallory, who looked as if she wanted to dance around with excitement and pride, but was containing herself in the interest of appearing grown-up enough to baby-sit.

"The triplets are in their room, practically draped over the air-conditioner," Mrs Pike went on.

I laughed. "Jeff's doing the same thing at home."

"Vanessa, Margo, and Claire are out in

the back garden playing in the sprinkler. And Nicky is . . . well, I'm afraid he's not in a very good mood today. He's in the playroom, sulking."

"Uh-oh," I said "That's too bad." I thought about what Stacey and Mary Anne had told us at the meeting the other day – that Nicky wants to play with the triplets, but they won't let him.

"He's having a tough time," said Mrs Pike, lowering her voice, "but he has to learn to deal with this."

"Tell Dawn about the two-block rule," Mallory spoke up.

"Oh, yes," said Mrs Pike. "You know how we feel about rules around here, except where safety is concerned." (There are almost *no* rules at the Pikes'.) "Well, Nicky's been complaining that we treat him like a baby, so we told him that he's allowed to go off on his own during the day, as long as he stays within two blocks of the house. Two blocks *is* a rule for him."

"Okay," I said.

"So if he disappears, don't panic."

I knew Mrs Pike was thinking of the time I'd been baby-sitting at the Barretts' and Buddy Barrett really *had* disappeared. We'd had to call the police and everything. So I was kind of touchy about little kids going off on their own. I appreciated Mrs Pike's understanding that.

Mrs Pike left a few minutes later.

Mallory looked at me expectantly. "Well?" she said. "What do we do first?"

"At your house," I replied, "I usually check on everybody, just make sure they're all accounted for. So why don't you go keep an eye on the girls, and I'll look in on the boys. Then I'll come outside with you. Maybe I can talk Nicky into playing in the sprinkler."

"Don't count on it," said Mallory darkly.

"Well, we'll see."

I went to the triplets' room first. Their door was closed to keep the cold air in. I knocked on it.

"Yeah?" called one of the boys. I wasn't sure which one.

"It's Dawn. Can I come in?"

"Okay."

I opened the door. The shades were drawn and the room was as dark as a room could be at two o'clock in the afternoon. The air-conditioner was going full-blast.

"What are you guys doing in the dark?" I asked.

"Playing with our glow-in-the-dark space creatures," whispered Byron.

"They're about to be attacked by the Wandering Frog People," added Jordan.

"Oh," I said. "Well, I just wanted you to know I'm –"

"*Shoof-shoof-shoof-shoof-BLAM!*" Adam shouted suddenly. He thumped a

Frog Person down on one of the space creatures.

"– here," I finished. I closed the door and left. The boys barely noticed.

Time to check on Nicky. I ran downstairs to the playroom. There he was, sitting in a ratty old armchair. A book was in his hands, but he wasn't reading it.

"Hi, Nick-O," I said.

"Hi."

"What are you reading?"

"Nothing."

"You want me to read to you?"

"Nah."

"Why don't you go out in the back garden? The sprinkler's on. You'll be much cooler there than you are inside. It's stuffy in here."

"Are the girls out there?"

"Yes."

"I'm *not* playing with the girls. I'm a boy. I'm supposed to play with the boys."

"Not necessarily," I told him.

"I want to play with the triplets!"

"Well, then, come on. Let's go and ask them."

Nicky looked at me with a hesitant smile. "Really?"

"Sure."

We were about halfway up the stairs when the triplets came stampeding out of their room. They were each wearing bathing trunks and carrying a towel.

"Dawn! Dawn!" cried Adam. "We're going swimming over at Joey's! We just called him. His mum said it was okay."

"She said we could bring a friend, too," Byron added.

"She *did*?" Nicky marvelled. "Oh, boy! Thanks! I'll –"

But before he could finish, Jordan said, "We called your brother, Dawn. It's all right if Jeff comes, isn't it? We said we'd tell you where he's going to be."

"Yes," I said with a sigh. "It's okay. Thanks for asking him."

Nicky watched the triplets run out the front door. He looked absolutely crushed. A few tears leaked out, which he tried to hide. After a few moments he said gruffly, "I'm going outside to play. *By-my-self*." He yanked the front door open.

"Two-block rule," I called after him.

"I know, I know, I know."

Nicky had been gone for about five minutes when I began to feel really bad for him. I decided I should find him and talk to him. I went outside and shouted his name over and over, but he didn't (or wouldn't) answer.

At last, I called Mary Anne on the phone and explained the situation. "Could you come and help Mallory so I can look for Nicky?" I asked her. "I'd really appreciate it. It would be a big favour."

Mary Anne arrived in a flash. I left her

and Mallory playing barefoot in the wet back garden with the little Pike girls. Then I started my search for Nicky. A two-block limit, which works out to a four-block area, is bigger than you think. I walked all around, through the Prezziosos' back garden, around the Barretts' property, even around my own house, calling for Nicky, looking for possible hiding places – in bushes, up trees.

Nothing.

I kept telling myself there were an awful lot of places a boy could hide. And I remembered what Mrs Pike had said – not to panic. But I couldn't help feeling just a *little* panicky. Why couldn't I find him? Maybe he wasn't within two blocks after all. If he was, surely he'd hear me calling.

"Nicky! NICK-EEE!" I shouted.

"Yeah?"

He'd appeared out of nowhere, looking dirty and sweaty.

I jumped a mile. "Nicky!" I exclaimed, half angry, half relieved. "Where were you?"

"Somewhere cool," he replied smugly. "The triplets didn't want me to come swimming with them, but I cooled off anyway. I showed them *and* I followed the rule."

I shook my head. "Come on. Let's go back to your house. You can shower off under the sprinkler . . . And don't scare me like that again!"

"Sorry," said Nicky. He smiled at me. I smiled back, glad the crisis was over, but thoroughly mystified.

6th CHAPTER

When I got home that afternoon, Jeff was still off swimming. I didn't like to admit it, but I was nervous about Nicky's disappearance. Things like that scare me to death. I'd never got over the time I couldn't find Buddy Barrett. Children *do* get kidnapped. And I'm afraid it's going to happen sometime while I'm baby-sitting. It's not impossible. In fact, it happens every day. You read about it in the papers or see it on the news. I heard that there are thousands and thousands of missing kids.

So could I help it if I panicked a little when I couldn't find Nicky?

I needed to relax. I took my library book out to the barn. Now, the barn is not the coolest place I can think of on a hot summer day – but it is the most relaxing. It's almost silent. There's not much in the barn that can make a sound, and the sounds are muffled.

Usually I climb up to the hayloft to find a comfortable spot to read, but heat rises, so there was no way I was going to be anywhere above ground on that day. I looked around for a place with enough light to read by. But instead I settled for a spot with a little dry hay scattered around that actually seemed cool.

I sat down, all prepared to open to "The Haunting of Weatherstaff Moor", but I had no sooner got into a comfortable position than I heard a crash.

The crash was *me*! I was falling.

I dropped down, down, like Alice through the rabbit hole.

"Help!" I cried.

Thump. I landed hard.

"Ow!"

I looked up. Although I'd only fallen about two metres it felt like two thousand. I was in darkness, but above me I could see a square of light, and beyond that, the beams in the roof of the barn.

I stood up shakily.

I was in some kind of cellar or tunnel. No wonder that spot I'd been sitting on had seemed cool. All that cellar air was circulating underneath.

Wait a second. Barns don't have cellars. Do they?

Maybe I was in – Nah. Impossible. Besides, what was I? Crazy? I was standing in a pitch-black hole. I had to get out.

I felt around gingerly. I was positive my fingers were going to touch spiders – fat, hairy spiders (possibly fat, hairy, *biting* spiders) – or slimy things.

But they didn't. Instead they touched a narrow wooden beam, and above that another, and another, and another. It was a ladder!

I climbed back into the barn and examined the top of the hole. I'd fallen through a trapdoor. It can't have been latched properly.

Okay, so in our barn was a trapdoor with a ladder leading down into . . .

I shrieked. I *had* found a secret passage! I really had! What else could it be?

I flew into our house, grabbed a torch out of a drawer in the kitchen, and flew back to the barn. I was feeling pretty brave, especially considering what a chicken I'd been about exploring the attic the other day. But that day had been dark and gloomy. It was hard to feel frightened with the sun shining so brightly. Besides, I'd found what I'd been searching for so desperately. How could I not explore my own personal secret passage?

I shone the light down the hole. There was the ladder I'd climbed up. I backed down it carefully, holding the torch in my left hand. When I reached the bottom, I examined the floor. It was hard-packed dirt. I shone the light around and saw that the passage veered off to the left – towards our house.

I began to walk. The passage sloped down slightly. I was moving through a tunnel of earth with a few support beams here and there. The only light was from my torch.

I edged forward for a good distance. I was moving slowly, and everything seemed sort of unreal. At long last, the passage began to slope upward.

I shivered. This was so exciting. If I were just a little older, I could be Nancy Drew. Wait until Claudia heard about this!

"Hey!" I exclaimed aloud. Ahead, my torch was shining on a dirt wall. After all this, had I come to a dead end?

No, the passage made a sharp right turn.

I rounded the corner – and drew in my breath.

I found myself facing a crude wooden staircase. My heart began to pound faster. I climbed the staircase slowly. Where was I? Somewhere inside our house? I felt like the mice in *The Tailor of Gloucester*, darting from house to house in their secret passageways.

At the top of the staircase the passage, which was now very narrow, and all wooden (I was sure, somehow, that I was between the walls of our house) took another turn, and then, a few feet beyond, really did come to a dead end. I began feeling the walls around me, and suddenly something made a loud clicking noise and the whole wall to my right swung away from me.

I gasped.

I was looking into my own bedroom!

I stepped inside. The wall that had swung open was the one with the fancy moulding that had sounded hollow the other day. The end of the passage was between my room and Mum's.

I was startled but immediately decided I wanted to explore the passage again more carefully. So I left the secret door to my room open (just in case), and stepped back into the passage. This time I kept the torch trained on the floor.

I blew up little flurries of dust as I made my way back to the staircase, crept carefully down the steps (who knew how sturdy they were?), and was soon back in the dirt tunnel.

And that was where I found it – the metal button. It looked positively ancient. I'd never seen one like it. It was sort of squashed in the middle, but I could tell that a design like a shield had been stamped on it.

A few feet further along I found something else I'd missed. A large tarnished buckle. It was too big for a belt buckle, and not quite the right shape. A shoe buckle? People hadn't worn buckles that size on their shoes since . . . the eighteen hundreds?

I felt a chill begin at the nape of my neck and creep down my back.

A key was the last thing I found. It certainly looked old – very long and narrow with a large ring to hold it by. How many years had the key been in the passage?

How many years had all the things been in the passage? More importantly, *why* were they there? Maybe they were all that was left of someone who had died in the passage – or worse, someone who had been locked up there to die. Maybe the poor prisoner had been trying to escape using the key. But he hadn't made it and had died a lonely, bitter death.

I knew it. I just knew it: *Our house was haunted*. It was haunted by the ghost of the secret passage. No one was going to believe it, but it was true. I remembered the rapping noises I had heard on the night of the storm. Now I knew what had really made them.

7th CHAPTER

Saturday

Thank you very much, Dawn. Because of you, we've all got ghosts on the brain. Even I do. How else can you explain what happened when I was baby-sitting for Karen, Andrew, and David Michael last night?

Well, it was a kind of wild night -- we had another storm -- but usually Karen's stories about Morbidda Destiny and old Ben Brewer don't really frighten me. What with the weather, though, and the gigantic house, and especially your tales about "things unseen," I guess the last straw was one of Karen's stories. So thanks a lot -- for the most embarrassing moment of my life!

The nice weather didn't last very long. By Friday it was gloomy again, and that night the skies let loose with a storm that my grandfather would have described as a "ripsnorter". I didn't know it then, but while Jeff and I were having a ghostly adventure in our old house, Kristy was having an adventure of her own in her new house.

Earlier that evening, she'd been left in charge of David Michael, and Karen and Andrew, who were visiting for the weekend. Her two older brothers were at a party, and her mum and stepfather had gone to the theatre in Stamford.

When everyone had left, the sky had simply been dark and threatening. An hour later, rain was falling, the wind was howling, thunder was crashing, and lightning was flashing.

Inside, Kristy was trying to interest the kids in a game of Snakes and Ladders, but it wasn't easy. Every time a clap of thunder sounded, David Michael shrieked, Andrew leaped into Kristy's lap, Louie the collie jumped (and skidded on the game board), and Karen looked disgusted and called everybody nitwits.

After that had happened three times, Kristy suggested, "Let's read a book instead of playing Snakes and Ladders. What should we read?"

"*The Little Engine That Could,*" said Andrew.

"*Fantastic Mr Fox,*" said David Michael.

"*Ramona and Her Father,*" said Karen.

Kristy rolled her eyes. "How about – "

"How 'bout if I tell a story?" Karen interrupted.

Kristy paused. Karen's stories are notorious. She never means to frighten anyone or to cause any trouble, but she always manages to.

"Do you know any nice, happy stories?" asked Kristy hopefully.

Karen thought for a moment. "Nope," she said.

"I want to hear a scary story," said David Michael bravely.

"You do?" asked Kristy incredulously, as thunder crashed and her brother jumped a metre in the air.

"Um . . . yes," replied David Michael.

"Me, too," said Andrew, not to be outdone.

Kristy thought that all this was a bad idea.

"Oh, we can tell scary stories any old time," she said. "Let's tell jokes instead. Knock, knock."

David Michael, Karen and Andrew glanced at each other.

"I *said*, knock, knock," Kristy repeated.

David Michael heaved a great sigh. "Who's there?"

"Banana," said Kristy.

"Banana who?" asked David Michael.

"Knock, knock."

"Huh? Wait, you were supposed to tell the joke part then."

"Trust me," said Kristy. "This one's a little different."

"Oh, all right. Who's there?" asked David Michael.

"Banana."

"Banana who?"

"Knock, Knock."

"Who's there?"

"Banana."

"Banana who?"

"Knock, knock."

"*Who's there?*" demanded David Michael.

"Orange."

"Orange who?"

"Orange you glad I didn't say 'banana'?" Kristy burst into giggles.

The three kids looked mystified.

"So," said Karen, "this is the tale of what made old Ben Brewer so weird."

Andrew and David Michael sat up straighter.

Kristy made a face and began to put the Snakes and Ladders game away. When she finished, she left the kids in the playroom, went downstairs, and straightened up the kitchen. She found a packet of biscuits in one of the cabinets, placed it on a tray with four glasses and a carton of milk, and took the tray upstairs to the playroom.

There she found Karen in the middle of her story.

"Ben Brewer had been sitting in his rocking chair by the fireplace in his bedroom for six hours. Just sitting. Outside, there was a big storm going on."

"Like this storm?" asked Andrew, wide-eyed.

"Yup," replied Karen. "And now . . ." (she lowered her voice dramatically) ". . . it was almost midnight."

"Oh, no!" yelped David Michael.

Karen nodded solemnly. "And you know what that means," she whispered.

Kristy joined the children on the floor. David Michael was leaning against an armchair. Andrew was sitting in the lap of a huge stuffed panda bear. And Karen, in the centre of the room, was also the centre of attention. As storyteller, she'd put on a witch's hat and a sparkly black mask, and was waving a wand around.

"It means," Karen continued, "that –"

KA-BLAM!

An enormous clap of thunder sounded. Everybody jumped – even Kristy.

"It means," Karen tried again, "that the headless ghost was going to come to Ben Brewer . . . and turn him into a crazy man."

"Ew," said Kristy.

"Ben Brewer was doing everything he

could think of to keep the ghost away. He had locked the door and the windows, and he wasn't going to leave the room. Not for anything. Not if he had to go to the toilet. He'd even put garlic all around the room."

"I thought garlic was to keep vampires away," said Kristy.

"Ben wasn't taking any chances," David Michael informed her.

"So imagine this," said Karen. "It's almost midnight, and Ben is locked up in that room. It's all quiet –"

"Except for the storm," said Andrew.

"And the fire crackling," added David Michael.

"And just think," said Karen. "This was happening right here in *our* house . . . in that room on the third floor." (Ben Brewer is Andrew and Karen's great-grandfather.)

"The room we never go in," whispered Andrew.

At that moment, Boo-Boo, the Brewers' fat cat, waddled in.

Karen pointed to him. "Boo-Boo knows about that room, Kristy. He knows it's haunted."

"The whole third floor is," said David Michael. He shuddered. "Boo-Boo doesn't go up to the third floor – *ever*."

Boo-Boo plopped down next to Karen. He sat on the floor with his tail twitching.

"Relax, Boo-Boo," said Kristy.

"He can't," Karen said. "Do you know

where we're sitting? We're right under Ben Brewer's room."

"Aughh!" cried David Michael.

"Karen," said Kristy, "the last time you told ghost stories, you said Boo-Boo won't go on the third floor because it's under the attic and the *attic* is haunted."

Karen paused. "Oh," she said. "Well, that's true. But Ben's room is haunted, too. So, anyway," she went on. "It was almost midnight. Just eleven more seconds." She paused. "Eleven . . . ten . . . nine . . . eight . . . seven . . . six . . . five . . . four . . . three . . . two . . ."

(Kristy noticed that she and the boys were all leaning anxiously toward Karen.)

"*One*," said Karen.

"What happened then?" whimpered Andrew. He sounded close to tears. Kristy pulled him into her lap.

"Ben thought there was no way to get in the room. But he was wrong. The ghost came down the *chimney*."

Everyone turned slightly and eyed the fireplace in the playroom.

"The ghost began to speak," Karen went on. " 'Oooh,' it wailed. 'I've come for you, Ben Brewer.' "

At that, Boo-Boo leapt straight into the air, darted through the door, and slid out into the hall, claws flying. Louie awoke, startled, heard Boo-Boo in the hall, and took off after him.

"It's Ben Brewer!" screamed Karen. "It's his crazy ghost! He was haunted – and now he's haunting us."

"Karen, calm down," said Kristy, whose teeth were chattering. "There is no ghost here."

"Yes, there is! That's why Boo-Boo and Louie are scared! Animals can tell when ghosts are around!"

Andrew burst into tears. "I don't want a ghost here!" he sobbed.

"There's *no ghost*," said Kristy. She stood up. "Anyway, it's bedtime."

"I want to sleep with you tonight!" wailed Andrew.

"Me, too!" cried Karen.

"Me, too!" cried David Michael.

Kristy admitted (but only to herself and later to the rest of us baby-sitters) that she was glad they wanted to sleep with her. And since she has this mammoth new bed in her room at Watson's, she figured they'd all fit. She hadn't counted on Boo-Boo and Louie joining them, but they did.

Kristy woke up the next morning when she heard whispering and snickering at her door. She blinked her eyes and struggled to sit up. Outside, the sun was shining. Next to her, Karen was sprawled on her back, her mouth open, and one arm slung across Andrew, who was sucking his thumb. On her other side David Michael was snoring lightly. Louie and Boo-Boo were scrunched up at the end of the bed.

"Look at that!" whispered a voice.

Sam and Charlie were peering into Kristy's room, trying to control their laughter.

"Hey, Kristy, what were you guys *do*ing last night?" exclaimed Sam. "You weren't by any chance afraid of the storm, were you?"

"No," replied Kristy. "Not exactly." She crawled over her brother and slid off the bed.

"Yes, you were," said Sam. "What a bunch of chickens."

"We were not," Kristy repeated more fiercely. "We were just . . ."

"Just what?" asked Charlie.

"Trust me," said Kristy. "It's a *long* story."

8th CHAPTER

Okay, so Kristy had a bad night. Maybe it was because of my ghost stories, maybe not. But she wasn't the only one having trouble during the storm. Jeff and I had a little trouble of our own . . . an adventure. And we weren't any braver about it than Kristy was with her adventure.

I did a strange thing after I found the secret passage. I didn't tell anyone about it. I'd been so excited – thinking I was like Nancy Drew and all – and then I was so scared when I realized the passageway had a ghost, that by the time I had climbed back into the barn and closed the trapdoor, I was totally confused. So I didn't call any of my friends to tell them the news, and I didn't show the passage to Jeff or my mum. I kept the secret to myself.

But on the night of the second big

storm – the night Kristy was baby-sitting for Andrew, Karen and David Michael – I was sitting for Jeff, and the haunted passage was weighing on my mind.

My mother left at seven o'clock that evening to go out on a date with this man named Mr Gwynne, which put me in a bad mood. I don't mind if Mum dates, as long as she dates Mary Anne's father. Mary Anne and I want to be stepsisters. But Mum had been going out with several different men. One of them was the son of friends of my grandparents, two were from her office, and a couple more were men she'd met at some party. I didn't like any of them, and I didn't want any of them for a stepfather. (I only wanted Mr Spier, because of Mary Anne.) Jeff didn't like any of the new men, either.

Tonight, Mum was going out with the son of my grandparents' friends. They were going to have dinner in a restaurant, then go to Granny and Pop-Pop's for dessert. I didn't like the sound of that – much too serious.

So I wasn't in a very good mood as my mum was rushing out the door. Usually I check her over to make sure nothing is mismatched or out of place. But that evening, I sulked in the living room and didn't look at her. If I'd looked at her and seen something wrong, I'd have to have told her. I couldn't let her go out wearing one hoop earring and one pearl earring, or just one false eyelash or something. But I figured that what I didn't know wouldn't hurt me – or her (much).

"I'm leaving, kids!" Mum called from the front door.

"'Bye," I said. I was sitting in an armchair, facing away from her. I didn't turn around.

"If it rains, close the windows."

"'kay."

"Dawn? Everything all right, honey?"

"Yup."

Mum hesitated. I couldn't see her, but I could *feel* that she was hesitating.

Jeff came crashing down the stairs, taking about three steps at a time.

"'Bye, Mum," he said.

"'Bye, honey. I just told Dawn – close the windows if it rains. Oh, and there's a casserole in the fridge. Remember, Dawn's in charge."

"Goodbye, Mum," I said pointedly.

Mum took the hint and left, and then I felt really bad.

Jeff didn't notice. "Let's eat," he said.

"All right." Maybe it would take my mind off Mum and the ghost.

Jeff and I heated up the casserole and made a salad. We ate our supper in front of the TV, watching a repeat of *All in the Family*.

"I hate this show," I commented.

"Me, too," Jeff replied.

"Why are we watching it?"

"I don't know. Because it's –"

CRASH

Thunder. Then rain poured down without warning.

"Windows!" I cried. We abandoned our meal and ran around, closing windows.

Then we tried to eat again, but we had no sooner settled down in front of the TV than the electricity went off. Since it was almost dark outside, it was pitch black inside.

"Yipes!" cried Jeff.

"I wonder if it's off everywhere or just in our neighbourhood," I said. *Or maybe*, I thought, *it's just us.* I shivered.

We stood at the front door and looked up and down our street. No lights anywhere, so the power was off in the neighbourhood, at least.

Maybe my mother would have to come home. Maybe the rest of her date would be off, along with the electricity. The thought cheered me.

"We better turn off the TV set so it won't come blaring on when the power's restored," I said. "And let's try to rinse off our dishes. Otherwise, they'll be impossible to clean later."

Jeff groped around and found a torch. We cleaned up the kitchen as well as we could. Then we wandered through the house.

"Well, this is boring," said Jeff.

"Yeah," I agreed.

"What can you do in the dark?"

I thought for a moment. I hadn't returned *Ghosts and Spooks, Chills and Thrills* to the library yet. I had two more stories to go. And there were a few I wanted to reread. I thought of the ghost in our secret passage and began to feel scared – not the awful kind of scared I'd felt several times earlier in the week – but deliciously scared.

"Hey, Jeff. Want to hear some really great stories?" I asked.

Jeff looked sceptical. (At least by the light of the flashlight, he looked sceptical). "What kind of stories?" he asked.

"Ghost stories," I whispered.

"Aw . . ."

"I know you don't believe in ghosts, but try to get in the *spirit* of things," I told him. "Get it? Spirit? Look. It's a gloomy, rainy, spooky night. Besides, what else is there to do?"

"Nothing," replied Jeff.

"Okay. Come on up to my room."

Ghosts and Spooks was waiting for us on my bedside table. We sat on my bed and I took the torch from Jeff and opened the book. First I read him "Things Unseen". Then I read him the story about the phantom hitchhiker. Then I read him "The Haunting of Weatherstaff Moor".

Before I got to one of the new ones at the end of the book, Jeff turned to me and said, "Let's stop now, Dawn."

"Had enough?" I asked.

He nodded. I couldn't tell if he was bored, scared, or sleepy.

"*Now* what should we do?" he asked. From the way he sounded, I decided he was bored.

"Let's try to play a game by torch," I suggested.

We tried. It was next to impossible. There was never enough light, even after Jeff perched the torch in a sort of sling made from a tea towel that he suspended from the edge of a table.

"I give up," I said.

Jeff yawned hugely. "What a waste of Friday night," he said. "Do you know all the great TV shows we're missing?"

"Wellll," I said slowly. "There *is* something we could do, and all we need is a torch."

"What?" Jeff looked mildly interested.

"Back to my room," I ordered.

I led Jeff up the stairs again and straight to the wall with the fancy moulding.

"Watch this," I said. "Here, hold the light."

I pressed the corner of the moulding (it hadn't taken long to work out how the catch worked), and the wall swung inward.

Jeff gasped. "Hey! Hey, what . . .?"

"I discovered this a couple of days ago," I told him. "It's a real, honest-to-goodness secret passage."

"I don't believe it," said Jeff flatly.

"Come on. Want to see it?"

I'd taken the button and buckle and key out of the passage and hidden them in one of my desk drawers. Somehow, without the *evidence* of the ghost, the ghost himself seemed less scary.

"Come on," I said again. I grabbed Jeff's hand and pulled him into the passage. "I didn't say anything because I – I just wanted a secret, I guess. But anyway, isn't this great?"

Wide-eyed, Jeff followed me through the passage to the rickety old steps. He had to walk behind me. The passage wasn't wide enough for two.

We were just about to start down the stairs when Jeff said, "Stop, Dawn. Look at that!"

"What?" I cried.

"Let me have the torch for a sec."

I handed it to him and he shone it against the wall near the top step. I could see something gleaming there. An image of the things I squirrelled away in my desk came to mind.

Jeff brushed aside the dust with his foot. Then he stooped down and picked up the object.

"What is it?" I asked. I tried to sound calm, but if my heart was beating as loudly as I thought it was, my brother could probably hear it, too.

Jeff examined the object in the light.

"It's a nickel," he said, sounding puzzled. "At least, it says 'five cents' on it, but it doesn't look like any nickel I've ever seen. There's a picture of an Indian on one side and a buffalo on the other. Maybe it's foreign . . . No, it's from the U.S."

"Indian-head nickels are really old," I informed him. "They made those nickels before the ones they make now. Let's see the date on that."

Jeff and I turned the nickel over and over and around and around, but it was rubbed so smooth we couldn't find a date.

"It must have worn off," said Jeff.

"Gosh, if it's worn off, this nickel must be ancient. It takes forever for metal to wear down."

"Yeah," agreed Jeff. "I wonder how it got here."

"Good question," I muttered, but Jeff didn't hear me.

"Well, let's go," he said.

Jeff was in front now and he led the way down the stairs. We had rounded the corner and were heading through the long tunnel to the barn when something crunched under my foot. I let out a cry. I was sure it was bones . . . part of a skeleton.

"What was that?" cried Jeff.

"Oh, I don't want to know," I moaned.

Jeff played the torch beam around on the floor. A few centimetres from my left foot, it lit up a small brown mound. Jeff and I bent down.

"I think it's part of an ice-cream cone," I said, although Jeff and I have eaten maybe two cones in our health-food lives.

"Really?" Jeff replied. "I thought ice-cream cones were kind of yellow and, you know, airy looking. And they have flat bottoms. Don't they? Remember that time Dad took us to Dairy Queen? What's left of that thing," he went on, touching the mound with the toe of his sneaker, "is brown and hard and has a pointed bottom."

"You know, I think this is an old-fashioned ice-cream cone," I said. I felt scared, awed, and excited at the same time. I wondered how long the cone had been in the passage. More important, I wondered why I hadn't seen either the cone or the nickel the other day. Can ghosts make things materialize? I was *sure* they hadn't been there before.

"Um, Jeff," I managed to say. "I don't want to scare you, but this passage is haunted – by an angry ghost. The ghost of someone who was locked up here to die a long time ago."

"Oh, for cripe's sakes," said Jeff. He gave me a really disgusted look. "You have got to be kidding."

"No, I'm not," I replied in a hushed voice.

"Okay," said Jeff, "the passage is

haunted . . . Prove it."

"I don't think I can *prove* it," I told him, "but I have been hearing an awful lot of weird noises lately. Mum keeps saying things like 'the house is settling'."

"She's right," said Jeff.

"Houses *moan* when they settle?"

Jeff looked startled. "Moan?"

"Yeah. Like this." I tried to imitate the moaning I'd heard.

"It could have been the storm," Jeff said, but he didn't look convinced, especially when I added disdainfully, "I *do* know the difference between something howling outside and something moaning inside."

"Well . . ."

"And," I went on, "the cone and the nickel weren't here the day I discovered the passage. I went looking pretty carefully, and I found a buckle and a button and a key. But these things weren't here."

"What are you saying?" asked Jeff, looking nervous in the flickering light.

"I'm saying that until right now, I didn't tell *anyone* about the passage. So no one's been in it except me, right?"

"Right."

"So where did the cone and the nickel come from?"

Jeff didn't answer. His eyes were growing wide, and he couldn't seem to close his mouth.

"There's only one answer," I told him.

"A ghost. And I'll tell you something else. I don't think I should have taken those other things out of the passage. I think the ghost is mad and wants them back. And we'd better not take these, either. Go and put the nickel back where you found it."

"*Me?* I'm not putting it back. Not alone, anyway." Jeff now looked truly terrified. His voice had risen to a squeak.

"Well, I'm not coming with you. We're much closer to the other end of the passage. I want to get out of here."

Jeff scowled at me. "Look at it this way," he said. "I've got the torch. If I go, the light goes with me. You'll be left alone in the dark."

I paused. He had a point. "Okay," I said. "Anyway, I just realized that we might as well both turn around now. We have to take the passage back to my room after all. It's pouring outside."

"Where *is* the other end of the passage?" asked Jeff.

"In the barn."

And at that moment we heard a creak, followed by a moan.

"Aughhh!" we yelled. Without another word of discussion, we turned and ran headlong through the passage, up the stairs, and back to my room. Jeff dropped the nickel somewhere as we ran.

9th CHAPTER

Somehow Jeff and I had managed to forget about the power failure. We had burst out of the passage and into my room, and I had slammed the wall shut behind us before we realized we were still in total darkness. It wasn't very comforting.

We flopped down on my bed, breathing heavily.

"It was the ghost!" I cried. "And he's carrying a grudge that's probably a hundred years old."

Cre-e-e-ak. Cre-e-e-ak.

Jeff and I jumped a mile. "I think the ghost's in the passage right *now*!" Jeff cried.

I'm sure I turned pale. I felt my knees go weak. "I'm calling Mum!" I announced, wondering if I could stand up without collapsing.

"Oh, good," said Jeff. He grabbed me at the waist, and followed me out of my room and into Mum's. We looked like two little kids playing choo-choo train.

As I reached for the phone, Jeff said helpfully, "I hope the telephone is still working."

I drew my hand back. "What if it isn't?" I whispered.

For a moment, neither of us spoke. At last, I reached my hand out again. I picked up the receiver and brought it to my ear very slowly. Halfway there, I could hear the dialling tone. "Oh, thank you, thank you, *thank* you," I said to no one in particular.

I figured Mum and her date would be at Granny and Pop-Pop's by then, so I called their house. Pop-Pop answered the phone, and I got carried away and told him we were having an emergency.

When Mum got to the phone, she sounded breathless and nervous. "Honey? Are you and Jeff all right?" she asked.

"Mum!" I exclaimed. "The power's cut off here, it's all dark, and there's a secret passage from my room to the barn – I know I should have told you about it, but I didn't – and Jeff and I looked in it, and we have a ghost."

"We heard noises!" Jeff shouted into the receiver from behind me.

"Dawn. Slow down. What are you saying?" asked my mother.

"I found a secret passage in our house. A real one." I paused. "Mum, the power's off here. Jeff and I are in the dark, except for a torch."

"I understand that, honey. But we've had power failures before. Now what is this about a secret passage?"

"You know how I'm always looking for one?" I asked.

"Yes."

"Well, I found one the other day. I promise, it's not a figment of my imagination or anything. But I kept it a secret. I didn't even tell Mary Anne."

"And where is this passage?"

"It runs from under the barn – there's a trapdoor in the floor – to my room. You know the wall with all the moulding? It swings out into my room when you press a corner of the moulding."

"Are you positive, Dawn?"

"*Yes.* Cross my heart and hope to die. And tonight Jeff got bored, so I decided to show him the passage. We'd almost got to the other end when we heard these noises. It really did sound like – "

Mum interrupted me before I could finish. "Trip and I will be right there. Sit tight, stay calm, and *don't* go back in the passage." She hung up.

"So?" Jeff said as soon as I'd hung up the phone, too. We both felt a little more relaxed. "What'd she say?"

"Mr Gwynne's name is Trip," was all I could answer. "*Trip.* Can you believe it?"

Jeff laughed. "Oh, yeah. Man, that is *so cool*," he said sarcastically.

"I bet he wears pink socks and alligator shirts and his friends call him, like, the Trip-Man or something."

"I bet he plays golf," said Jeff, with a snort of laughter.

"I bet his idea of an amusing afternoon is balancing his chequebook. And," I added, "I bet he has really short hair, wears wire-rimmed glasses, and has grey eyes, but wears contacts to make them look blue."

Jeff laughed so hard that he collapsed on the floor. I joined him – but mid-collapse I let out a yelp.

"What is it?" cried Jeff.

"What are we laughing for? That ghost could be sneaking into my room this very second. We've got to go and block the wall off!"

"In the *dark*?"

"Do you want the ghost in here with us?"

"No." Jeff flew out of Mum's room and into mine before I'd even got up off the floor. "Shove something in front of the wall," he commanded as soon as I ran in.

We moved my dresser in front of the door to the passage. Then we put a chair on top of it, and, puffing hard, slid my bed against the front of the dresser.

We were unloading books from my shelves and piling them on the chair and bed when two things happened at once: the power was restored, and Mum and Mr Gwynne came home. When the lights flicked on, Mum found Jeff and me standing on my bed, stacking books on to a pile of furniture. And Jeff and I saw two people standing in a doorway that we thought was empty.

Everyone screamed.

"What are you doing?" cried Mum at the same time that I yelled. "When did you arrive?"

Then we answered each other at the same time, too. "Keeping the ghost out," I replied as Mum said, "Just now."

"Whoa! Everybody calm down," exclaimed Mum's date.

Jeff and I jumped to the floor.

"Kids," said my mother, who was trying to catch her breath. "This is Mr Gwynne. Theodore Gwynne."

(My mother had no idea why Jeff and I looked at each other and began to laugh then.)

"And," she went on, ignoring us, "this is Dawn, and this is Jeff."

"Hi," the three of us said uncomfortably.

I have to admit that the Trip-Man didn't look exactly as Jeff and I had imagined, but he was pretty close. He was wearing glasses, but not wire-rims. The frames were tortoise-shell and very round. His blonde hair was short, but behind the glasses, his eyes were brown. He was wearing a suit and tie, so there were no alligators anywhere, and his socks weren't pink but his shirt was.

"Dawn," said Mum, sounding exasperated, "what are you and Jeff *do*ing?"

"Blocking the entrance to the secret passage so no one can come in."

"You mean the ghost?" she asked with a smile.

"Yeah."

"I thought ghosts could float right through walls."

"Um . . ." I said. (Why hadn't *I* thought of that?) "Of course they can. But the passage is his home base." What a stupid excuse. And now I had something new to worry about.

"Well, let's just see what we have here," said the Trip-Man.

He and Jeff and I moved the books and furniture away from the wall. Then I pressed the moulding, and the wall opened up.

Mum gasped. I don't think she'd really believed I'd found a secret passage until then.

The Trip-Man held out his hand. "If you'll let me have the torch, I'll go and take a look-see," he said.

A look-see?

Jeff handed him the torch.

"Oh, Trip, do you think you should?" asked Mum.

(Jeff and I dissolved into giggles again.)

My mother peered through the opening into the dark tunnel. She watched the Trip-Man disappear. "*How* did you discover this, Dawn?"

I told her the whole story, explaining where the passage led.

"I just can't believe it," said Mum. "I know this is an old house, but . . ." Her voice trailed off.

When the Trip-Man returned, he looked dusty but was in one piece. "There's no one – and *nothing* – " he added, looking at me, "in the passage. If you heard noises, I'm sure they were just – "

"The storm," I supplied. "Or the house settling."

The Trip-Man cleared his throat. "Right," he said. "By the way, I found this." He opened one hand and extended the ghost's Indian-head nickel toward me.

I just barely managed not to scream as I took it.

"I suggest," the Trip-Man went on, talking to Mum, "that tomorrow morning you work out some way to lock both entrances to the passage, or at least the entrance in the barn. I'm sure no one knows about the passage, but since it *is* another way into your home, you should lock it as you would any door."

"Definitely," agreed Mum.

"Well, that'll keep *people* out," I said, "but what about the ghost?"

"Dawn," Mum began warningly.

"There *is* one," I said. "The ghost of the secret passage." I explained how I knew that the passage was haunted.

My mother and the Trip-Man began to look incredibly impatient. They didn't even let me tell them about the ice-cream cone and the meaning of the nickel. Mum waved me to a stop.

A few minutes later, the Trip-Man left. Mum walked him out to his car.

Jeff reluctantly went to bed.

I looked around my room. No way was I going to sleep in there. I gathered up a blanket, a pillow, and *Thrills and Chills*. Before I took everything down to the living room, though, I opened the moulded wall a crack and tossed the Indian-head nickel back to the ghost in the passageway.

Mum went upstairs to her bedroom. I thought she was crazy. After all, the secret passage ran between our rooms. Mum was as close to the ghost as I was.

I was just settling down on the couch when I saw Mum's purse on the floor of the dining room. She is *so* scatterbrained. *I really should take it upstairs to her*, I thought, heaving myself off the couch. But when I picked up the purse, I saw that it had been sitting on something, a tattered old book called *A History of Stoneybrooke*. It must have come from Granny. She never sends any of us home emptyhanded. Sometimes she gives us food, but mostly little treasures and keepsakes. Mum says it's Granny's way of making sure she gives the things she loves best to the people she loves best before she dies. (As if she's going to die any time soon. She's only about sixty or sixty-three or something.)

The book I was holding was so old it was falling apart. The title was written in gold, but the gold had mostly rubbed off. The binding was peeling away, and two of the corners of the cover had cracked off. Gingerly, I opened the book to the first page. *A History of Stoneybrooke*, it said again. By Enos Cotterling. Copyright MDCCCLXXII. I dredged up an old arithmetic lesson (where was Stacey's maths brain when I needed it?), and decided the book had been published in 1872. Over a hundred years ago! Stoneybrooke . . . was that our town – Stoneybrook? When had the "e" been dropped? A line of teeny-tiny print said that the book had been published by Tynedale Press, right here in town.

I forgot all about Mum's purse and wandered back to the couch, turning pages as I went. The list of contents looked pretty boring – taxation, imports and exports, trade, growth of town, property laws. But the very last chapter sounded interesting. It was called, simply, *Legends*.

I turned carefully to the back of the book. Two pages fell out, and I replaced them guiltily, even though I knew I hadn't done anything wrong.

"Like most New England towns," the chapter began, "Stoneybrooke is replete with Indian myths and legends. But one local legend, not to be discounted lightly, is the unsolved mystery of Mister Jared Mullray." That did it. I was hooked. I started reading in earnest.

It seemed that long before Enos Cotterling had written his history, around the year 1810, a family in Stoneybrooke, the Mullrays, had fallen into financial trouble. They were deeply in debt to a banker named Mathias Bradford and couldn't pay their bills. The only things they owned that were worth much at all were their home, "a clapboard structure out past the Smythe property", and their small farm, Wood Acres. In order to pay off their debts, the Mullrays were forced to sell both, including their furniture and many of their belongings.

Old Man Mullray wanted to move up to Peacham, a tiny, young town in Vermont, and he convinced his wife, his daughter, his son-in-law, and their three children to move with him. There, he said, they could start again. But he could not convince his younger son, thirty-year-old Jared, to go with them. Jared, the author wrote, had never been "quite right in the head". He loved Wood Acres – a little too much.

Early on a Monday morning, the Mullrays packed a few personal belongings on to a cart, saddled up one of their horses, and prepared to leave. Mathias Bradford, who was going to sell off the farm, arrived with some men from the bank just as the Mullrays were tossing their last bag on to the cart.

"Jared!" shouted Old Man Mullray.

"I ain't leaving!" was the reply everyone heard. But Mr Bradford was to say later that it didn't sound as if his voice was coming from the house *or* the barn – sort of somewhere in between, although no one could *see* him anywhere.

(A clap of thunder sounded, and I shivered, pulling my blanket more tightly around me.)

Old Man Mullray glanced at his wife, who shrugged sadly. Then he flicked the reins, and the horse plodded down the lane. The Mullrays left Wood Acres behind forever.

Now, Mathias Bradford and four other men (one of whom was the head of the town council) had watched the Mullrays drive off without Jared, and they had heard his disembodied voice say that he wasn't leaving. But although the house and barn were searched thoroughly as every last stick of furniture and every last harness were sold off, no one ever saw Jared again. He simply disappeared.

A few people said he had packed up and moved to Alaska, but Mr Bradford didn't believe that. He had heard Jared and was convinced he'd never leave. The only question was – where *was* he? Soon another rumour began to circulate about Jared, and the people of Stoneybrooke were more inclined to believe this one. They thought that Jared, who couldn't bear to leave Wood Acres, was still there . . . somewhere. They thought he must know about some secret hiding place, and that he stayed there by day and scavenged for food at night.

Decades passed. By the time Enos Cotterling was writing his history, he presumed that Jared was dead. In fact, the story about Jared had become a ghost story. Jared, people said, had died in his secret hiding place, but his spirit remained. Wood Acres (which had been swallowed up by another, larger, farm and was no longer called Wood Acres) was haunted by Jared, who was always on the prowl not only for food, but for trinkets and things that he could sell in order to try to pay back Mr Bradford.

I put the book down thoughtfully. Wood Acres, a ghost, a secret hiding pl . . . A secret hiding place! Suddenly my arms broke out in crawly gooseflesh. I shivered so hard my teeth chattered.

It fitted! Everything fitted! Enos Cotterling hadn't described where Wood Acres was, but it must be my house and my barn! The house was old enough, it had once been part of a farm, and there certainly was a good hiding place on the property . . . a place you could yell from and sound as if you were between the house and the barn, yet not be seen.

There really was a ghost in our secret passage, and that ghost was crazy Jared Mullray!

10th CHAPTER

Sunday

There are times when I think babysitting is the hardest thing in th world. Last nigt was one those times. I was baby siting for Jamie Newton. And Lucy. Lucy was an angle, but Jamie wasnt. Boy! I have never seen him like that. all I was tryng to do was put him to bed. Thats all. I didn't have to give him diner or anything. I just had to get him to sleep. And I really wanted to too. Because there was this good porgram on tv I wanted to see it but Jamie WOULD NOT GO TO SLEEP!

It was eight o'clock when Claudia reached the Newtons'. Her job that night really should have been one of the easiest in baby-sitting history. Lucy was already in her cot and sound asleep. Jamie had already eaten dinner. Mr and Mrs Newton were only going to be gone for two hours. All Claudia had to do was put Jamie to bed – and the evening was hers.

That's how the evening *should* have gone. There was just one problem: Jamie didn't want to go to bed. I mean, he *really* didn't want to go to bed.

When Claudia rang the Newtons' door-bell that night, Jamie answered it. Right away, Claudia could tell he was wound up.

"Hi-hi! Hi-hi! Hi-hi!" he greeted her.

"Hi-hi, Jamie," said Claud.

Jamie was jumping up and down, up and down, like a yo-yo in blue jeans. "I learned a new song!" he exclaimed. "Listen to this: I'm in love with a big blue frog. A big blue frog loves me. It's not as bad as it may seem. He wears glasses and he's six foot three. Oh –"

Jamie's song was interrupted by his father. Mr Newton rolled his eyes. "I'm sorry I taught him that," he said. "He's been singing it *all day*. And there are several more verses."

Claudia laughed. "I think it's funny," she said.

"Only the first seventy-five times,"

replied Mr Newton, but he was smiling.

Mrs Newton came down the stairs as Claudia stepped inside. "Hi, honey," she said. "Well, the baby's asleep, and Jamie has eaten. I don't think he needs a bath tonight – "

"Yea!" interrupted Jamie.

"So just put his pyjamas on him. He's had a long day and should go to bed –" (she glanced at Jamie, who was listening intently) "– s-o-o-n," she spelled out.

"No fair spelling, Mummy!" Jamie protested.

"Okay," Claudia said to Mrs Newton. Then she added, "Don't worry, Jamie. We'll have fun tonight before you go to bed."

"Goody."

The Newtons left then, and Jamie began hopping up and down again.

"Okay, Jamie. Time to put your pyjamas on," said Claudia.

"Already?" he whined.

"Yup. It's almost bedtime. Come on upstairs."

"Just let me show you this one thing first . . . Okay?"

"Okay," Claudia relented. "Just *one* thing."

"It's down in the playroom." Jamie took Claudia by the hand and led her down a flight of stairs to the Newtons' playroom. He stood in the middle of the room and looked around.

"What is it?" asked Claudia.

"It's, um . . ." Jamie put his finger in his mouth. "It's this!" He darted over to a battered truck. "Look at it," he said.

"Your old truck?" asked Claudia, puzzled.

Jamie paused. "Oh, no. That wasn't it. I meant . . ." He picked up a little wooden cow that was lying next to the truck. "I meant my cow."

"Jamie," said Claudia, growing suspicious.

"No, I meant my – my Beary Bear," he said, snatching up a stuffed animal.

"That was three things, Jame-o," Claudia pointed out gently. "Time to go upstairs now."

"Can I wear my Paddington Bear pyjamas, Claudy?" asked Jamie.

"Sure," replied Claudia, glad he was actually thinking about bed.

"Good," said Jamie. "'Cause they're in the wash."

"Then I'm afraid you can't wear them." Claudia led Jamie back upstairs.

"But you just said I could."

"I didn't know they were in the wash when I said that. You can't wear them if they're dirty."

"Let's wash them," suggested Jamie.

"Sorry. That'll take too much time. We'd have to dry them, too."

"How long would it take?"

"Too long."

"How many minutes?"

"Twelve hundred and forty-nine," replied Claudia.

"Wow," said Jamie.

Claudia and Jamie tiptoed past Lucy's room and into Jamie's. Claudia pointed to his bed. "Look," she said. "Mummy laid out your farm pyjamas."

Jamie made a face. "I don't want to wear them. They're for babies. They have baby stuff all over them."

Claudia looked at them. They *were* sort of babyish. "Let's choose a different pair then." She opened his wardrobe and brought out two more pairs. "Which ones?" she asked. (She was careful not to say, "Do you want to wear any of these?" Jamie might have said "No.")

Jamie pointed to one pair.

"Great," said Claud. "Okay, off with your shirt." She waited for Jamie to raise his arms so she could slip his shirt off.

"I'll do it myself," said Jamie. "You leave."

"Leave!" exclaimed Claudia. Jamie was too young to be getting modest. "How about if I turn my back?"

Jamie considered the offer. "Okay," he said at last. "But don't peek."

Claudia sat cross-legged on Jamie's bed, facing the wall. The room grew very quiet.

Claudia studied the pattern of the wall-paper. "Jamie?" she asked after a minute or two had gone by.

No answer.

"Is it all right if I turn around to see how you're doing?"

Silence.

Very slowly, Claudia swivelled around.

Jamie was gone.

"Jamie!" Claudia cried as loudly as she dared. (She didn't want to wake Lucy.)

Claudia ran through the hallway, pausing to peek into the bathroom. No Jamie. She ran down the stairs and into the kitchen. No Jamie. She ran down the last flight of steps and into the playroom.

"Hi-hi!" said Jamie brightly, but he looked a bit sheepish. He was riding a toy car and was still fully dressed.

"James Anderson Newton. You were supposed to put your pyjamas on," said Claudia. "I'm beginning to lose my patience. Now go back to your room, please. And this time I'm not going to turn my back."

Jamie scowled, but he did as Claudia said. When he was finally in his pyjamas, Claudia tucked him in bed.

"Oops," he said. "I forgot to brush my teeth. And I ate cookies after dinner. Cookies have sugar, and sugar makes calories in your teeth."

Claudia had to smile. "Cavities," she told

him. "All right. Into the bathroom."

Jamie scampered down the hall. (Claudia had the sense to follow him.) Standing at the sink, he squeezed about a yard of toothpaste on to his brush and worked it around in his mouth, creating a great amount of foam. He rinsed and spat six times. Claudia waited patiently.

When he had finished, he dashed down the hall and leapt into his bed.

"How about a story?" asked Claudia.

"Oops," said Jamie. "I forgot to go to the bathroom." He ran down the hall again, and returned a few minutes later.

"*Now,*" said Claudia. "How about a story?"

"Oops," said Jamie. "I forgot to get a drink of water."

"I'll get it," said Claudia. "You stay right here. Don't move a muscle."

Claudia filled a paper cup with water and brought it to Jamie. He was sitting in exactly the same position as he'd been in when she'd left the room. She handed the cup to him.

Jamie didn't reach for it.

"Here you go," said Claudia.

"An I oove?" asked Jamie, barely moving his lips.

"What?"

"An I oove?"

"Can you move?"

"Yeh."

"Of course you can move."

"But you said 'don't move a muscle'."

Claudia sighed. "I just meant don't go anywhere. And you didn't. Here. Drink your water."

Jamie took the cup and drank.

"All right," said Claudia. She pulled a book off his shelf. "let's read *Harold and the Purple Crayon.*"

Claudia read the story to Jamie. When she was finished he said, "Now can we read *Make Way for Ducklings?*"

"Oh, Jame-o," said Claudia. "I'm sorry, but that one's too long."

"Please, please, please? Pretty puh-*lease* with a cherry on top."

Against her better judgment, Claudia gave in. It took nearly half an hour to read the story because Jamie kept interrupting her to ask questions.

"But," he said, as Claudia was closing the book, "why did Mr Mallard leave Mrs Mallard and the ducklings all alone?"

"He was waiting for them at their new home."

"Oh. How come Michael called all the policemen?"

"Because," replied Claudia, "the duck family needed help. Now into bed."

Jamie crawled under the covers. He asked for another drink of water . . . and another. Finally he seemed sleepy.

Claudia tiptoed downstairs and settled

herself in front of the TV. She'd been watching for about five minutes when she heard a voice behind her say, "But how come Mr Mallard just waited on the island? And can I have another drink of water?"

11th CHAPTER

"You know what I think?" asked Mary Anne dreamily.

"What?" I replied.

The two of us were lying on our backs in the hayloft in the barn. The day was stickily warm and sunny, and I could see particles of dust floating through the sunshine that streamed through the cracks in the walls. It was only the third time Mary Anne had ever been in the barn. She's such a 'fraidy cat. Just because the barn is a little rickety.

As if reading my thoughts, she went on, "I think I'm too afraid of things."

I couldn't disagree with her.

"And being afraid always makes things worse than they really are. I was afraid of boys before Stacey and I went to Sea City. I was afraid of making new friends before I met you."

"You were afraid of the barn," I pointed out.

"Yup," Mary Anne glanced through the copy of *Sixteen* magazine that was lying between us.

"Are you feeling braver now?" I asked her.

"Sure," she said absentmindedly. "Gosh, look at this kid Cam Geary. Isn't he adorable?"

"Yeah . . . How brave are you feeling?"

"Pretty brave. I wish Cam lived here in Stoneybrook."

"How'd you like to prove to me just how brave you've become?"

"Huh?" Mary Anne finally dragged her eyeballs away from Cam Geary.

"I said, 'How'd you like to prove how brave you've become?'"

"What do you mean?" asked Mary Anne suspiciously.

"I've got a great secret to show you."

"You have?"

"Yes. But you're going to have to be very, very brave. Come on!" I jumped up. "Come in the house with me and we'll get torches."

"Torches?" repeated Mary Anne. "Whatever this is – I guess it has to do with the dark?"

"Right. But you're not afraid of the dark, are you?"

"No. I'm afraid of all the things I can't

see that the dark is hiding."

"Oh, Mary *Anne*. I thought you said you were getting so brave."

"Yeah, well . . ."

I couldn't admit that I wasn't feeling particularly brave myself. What I wanted to do, of course, was show Mary Anne the secret passage. I hadn't had the nerve to go in it, let alone talk about it, since the night I'd read about Jared Mullray. I wanted someone to come with me. I also wanted someone to be able to share the amazing secret.

I got to my feet and picked up the magazine. "Let's go," I said, trying to sound enthusiastic. "You are in for the surprise of your life."

Mary Anne and I climbed out of the hayloft. We went into our house and found a couple of torches. Then I led Mary Anne to my bedroom.

I had decided to enter the passage from the house instead of the barn. For one thing, seeing my wall swing open was a lot more dramatic than shoving in the dusty old trapdoor. For another, it was a lot less scary. And if we left the wall open, it would let some light into the passage.

"Okay. Get ready," I said. I pressed the moulding and the wall began to open up. I turned around to watch Mary Anne's reaction.

It was worth it. All she was able to do was

let her mouth drop open, cover it with both hands, and stare.

"I found it," I said unnecessarily. "A secret passage."

"Oh, wow. I don't believe it." Mary Anne's voice was little more than a whisper. "How – how did you find it?"

I told her the story, but I left out all the stuff about the buckle and the nickel and Jared Mullray. I'm no fool. If Mary Anne knew those things, she'd probably never come within a mile of my house again.

"Don't you want to see it?" I asked her. I took her by the arm and edged her towards the wall.

We turned our torches on and stepped into the passage. I shoved Mary Anne ahead of me. "You go first," I said.

"Are you crazy?"

"Absolutely not. I know if I go first you won't follow. I'll find you lounging around on my bed or something. Now go. I'll be right here."

Trembling, Mary Anne led the way towards the stairs. By the time we reached them, she was fine, but I was in a panic. I didn't say anything, but I hadn't seen the Indian-head nickel. And I knew very well that I'd tossed it back in the passage after the Trip-Man had given it to me. I wasn't sure how hard I'd thrown it, but it couldn't have gone too far. Certainly not down the stairs. Where was it?

Answer: It was missing. Jared had it. He'd wanted it back. He wanted to give it to Mathias Bradford.

I tried to convince myself I was being ridiculous. As we stepped gingerly down the stairs, I swept the beam of my torch carefully from side to side, just in case.

No coin.

Mary Anne and I had almost reached the spot where Jeff and I had heard the weird noises the other night, when Mary Anne stopped dead in her tracks.

"*Shh!*" she hissed. "Did you hear that?"

"Hear what?"

"*Shh!*"

We stopped to listen. I didn't hear a sound, but I saw something at my feet. I leant over for a look. Peanut shells. They were kicked off to the side and were kind of grimy looking, but I *knew* they hadn't been in the passage before.

"Uh-oh. Oh, *no*," I moaned. I couldn't help it.

"What's wrong?" asked Mary Anne suspiciously.

"Those peanut shells weren't here the last time I was in the passage. I'm positive they weren't. Oh, it's Jared!"

"Jared?" repeated Mary Anne.

"The – the ghost."

"What ghost?" said Mary Anne in a quavery voice.

"The ghost of the secret passage." It was

too late for secrets. Besides, Mary Anne is my best friend. I *had* to tell her.

Now I know Mary Anne is timid, but I hadn't really expected her to desert me in the darkness. That's just what she did, though. Without another word, she squeezed by me, clattered along the passage, up the steps, and back to my room.

"How do you close this thing?" I could hear her yelling.

I reached the top of the stairs in time to see the patch of light at the end of the passage growing smaller. Mary Anne was shoving the wall in place.

"Don't close it, you dope!" I yelled. "I'm still in here."

"Oh, sorry," said Mary Anne. "I wasn't thinking."

I slipped through the opening and closed off the passageway.

"Now who's the crazy one?" I gasped, flopping on to my bed.

Mary Anne flopped down beside me. "Not me!" she exclaimed. "You! You brought me some place where there's a ghost!" Suddenly she stopped and looked at me. "Wait a second. A real ghost? Are you sure you haven't just been reading too many of those weird stories?"

"I'm sure," I replied, starting to get my breath back. "I'd better tell you everything, though. All right, here's the story."

"The whole story?" interrupted Mary Anne.

"Yes, the whole story. Okay. For starters, I'd been hearing a lot of weird sounds. They were coming from the direction of the passage, only I didn't know there was a passage at first. Then I discovered the passage, just like I told you. The first time I was in it – the day I found it – I came across a button, a buckle, and a key. They were all really old. Here, I'll show you." I got the things out of my desk drawer and laid them on the bed.

Mary Anne sat up. She peered at the objects. But she wouldn't touch them.

"I bet they're more than a hundred years old," I said. "Maybe more than two hundred years old."

"Wow!" whispered Mary Anne.

"And, see," I continued, "what happened is that someone once hid out in the secret passage. His name was Jared Mullray, and he 'wasn't right in the head'." I showed Mary Anne the last chapter in *A History of Stoneybrooke*. Then I added in a low, spooky voice, "And now that poor old angry ghost haunts the passage and maybe our house, too, scavenging around for food and for anything he thinks might be valuable."

"Oh, Dawn," said Mary Anne. "You don't have any proof." But she didn't sound very sure of herself.

"Well," I admitted, "not really. But Wood Acres could be our house and barn. And the secret passage would be the perfect hiding place. Anyway, listen to this. The second time I went in the passage, I was with Jeff, and he found an Indian-head nickel. You know what that is?"

Mary Anne nodded.

"I know it wasn't there before. And while we were in the passage, we heard all these weird sounds, moaning and stuff."

"You did?"

"Yes. And when we were in again just now, I looked everywhere for the nickel and it *wasn't there*."

"You didn't take it out of the passage?"

"Well, I did. I mean, someone did, but I threw it back." I told her about the Trip-Man.

"Did you put the locks on like he suggested?" Mary Anne wanted to know.

"Only on the entrance to my room," I said. "And I only lock it at night. We couldn't figure out a way to lock the trapdoor, so we just set a bale of hay on top of it."

"Anyway," I went on, "the peanut shells weren't in the passage before. They just appeared. And no living person has been in this passage except you, Jeff, and me!"

Mary Anne nodded. Then suddenly she stiffened.

"What?" I asked.

We didn't even have to keep quiet to hear it. The next sound was loud enough to wake the dead.

THUMP.

It definitely came from the secret passage.

Mary Anne started to scream, but I clapped my hand over her mouth. I didn't want Jared to hear us.

The thump was followed by another thump, then nothing.

When the passage had been quiet for ten entire minutes, I jumped up. "I'm going back in there!" I exclaimed.

"Not me," said Mary Anne. "See you later." But she must have felt guilty because a moment later she added, "I'll guard the entrance for you."

I took my torch, marched into the passage, and kept going. At the bottom of the stairs, I screamed. Lying at my feet was a book. It was called *Great Dog Tales*. It looked about a hundred years old. I had never seen it before in my life. I turned around and ran back to Mary Anne.

12th CHAPTER

Tuesday

The Pikes strike again! Today I baby-sat for Nicky, Vanessa, Claire, and Margo. Since just the four of them were there, Mrs. Pike decided she needed only one sitter. Believe me, I could have used ten or twelve more. Vanessa and Margo did something to Claire I will never, ever be able to forget. To top it off, Nicky disappeared. I didn't worry at first, but when he didn't turn up after almost an hour, I got nervous. I'm sure he breaks that two-block rule, but I can't prove it. Anyway, get a load of what the girls did.

Oh, boy. Am I glad I wasn't sitting at the Pikes' that day. As it was, I got called in to look for Nicky, but Stacey sure had her hands full with the girls, even before she knew Nicky was gone.

It started when the post arrived. Usually, the post in our neighbourhood is delivered just before lunch, but that day it was late. The post van was pulled up at the Pikes' at about three o'clock in the afternoon.

"I'll get it!" cried Vanessa. She tore out of the door with Claire and Margo at her heels. Nicky was on the sun porch, alone as usual, reading a book.

Stacey took advantage of the quiet to start in on the list of chores Mrs Pike had left her. (Sometimes, if Mr and Mrs Pike are behind with the housework, us baby-sitters pitch in with the laundry and stuff, and then we earn mother's helpers wages which are better than plain old baby-sitters wages.)

Stacey got into the rhythm of folding clean clothes and folded two basketsful. Then she moved on to the kitchen, where she unloaded the clean dishes in the dishwasher and loaded up the dirty ones.

The house was quiet. Stacey sighed contentedly. She checked on Nicky. He was still reading on the porch. She thought she remembered hearing the girls come in.

"Vanessa?" she called. "Claire? Margo?"

"We're upstairs!" Vanessa shouted back.

"Okay!"

Stacey returned to her chores.

Fifteen minutes later, things were still quiet. Quiet wasn't unusual for Nicky those days, but it was for the girls. Three girls generally make some sort of noise, but Stacey hadn't heard so much as a giggle.

She started up the stairs – and that was when the *thing* came flying down at her. It was little and shrieked and had a head of white foam. When it collided with Stacey, it left foam all over her Hawaiian shirt.

"Yikes!" cried Stacey. She backed against the wall.

The foam-thing was rubbing at its eyes. It stumbled forward and Stacey caught it before it fell down the stairs.

"Claire!" Stacey exclaimed. "Is that you?"

"Yes," wailed the foam-thing. "It's (gulp) meeeeeee!"

Stacey glanced at the top of the stairs. Margo and Vanessa were standing there solemnly, looking down at their little sister. Stacey said later that that's when she first thought something was really wrong. If the older girls had pulled some sort of prank, they would have been laughing hysterically at the sight of the foam. But they were as sombre and silent as rocks.

"Margo? Vanessa?" Stacey said. She steadied Claire and began to lead her upstairs.

"It's not our fault!" Margo cried. "Really."

"Honest," added Vanessa, wide-eyed. "Don't blame us." She was so upset, she forgot to rhyme her words.

Stacey made a huge effort to control her temper. "What happened?" she asked.

Nobody said a word.

"Claire?" Stacey peered into Claire's face, wiping away some foam.

"Shampoo?" Stacey managed to reply.

"Shampoo? Is that all?" said Stacey, suddenly feeling better. "You guys tried to give your sister a shampoo? Well, what's wrong with that? It was very thoughtful. I just wish you'd asked me first. Come on, Claire. All we have to do is wash it out."

Still the girls remained quiet. Stacey noticed that the foam was unlike any she'd seen before. It was thick, almost as thick as shaving cream, and just slightly blue in colour. But Stacey didn't pay any attention to that. She simply drew a bath for Claire, stripped off her clothes, and sat her in the tub. Then she began to rinse the soap off by pouring cupfuls of water over her head.

"Ow! Ow! Ow!" cried Claire.

"What's wrong?" asked Stacey.

"It stings."

"Keep your eyes shut, okay?"

"Okay," replied Claire, "but it still stings."

It wasn't until Stacey had poured twelve

cups of water over Claire's head that she began to feel uneasy again. The shampoo wasn't rinsing out.

Stacey dumped another cupful onto Claire. This time she rubbed Claire's hair vigorously. The foam puffed up as if it were alive. It was thicker than ever.

"Margo? Vanessa?" said Stacey.

"Yes?" they whispered. They were sitting squashed together on the toilet, their hands in their laps. They'd watched the rinsing process wordlessly.

"What shampoo did you use on Claire? The baby shampoo?"

Stacey had given Claire several shampoos when she and Mary Anne had gone to Sea City with the Pikes. She had always used Johnson's Baby Shampoo. Nothing like this had ever happened.

"Um, no," replied Vanessa. "We used . . . we used something new."

"What was it?" asked Stacey.

"I don't remember the name."

"Can you show it to me, please?"

Margo and Vanessa looked at each other. Vanessa nodded at her sister. Margo reached behind her and pulled something out of the wastebasket. She handed it to Stacey.

It was a small plastic bottle. And it was empty.

"You guys," said Stacey nervously. "I hope this wasn't your mum's. You didn't use up something of your mum's . . . did you?"

They shook their heads.

Stacey read the label on the front of the bottle. It said:

Trial Size only
Not for sale
CALLADEW'S PERFECTION SHAMPOO
Concentrated

On the back, the directions cautioned:

Concentrated shampoo — use sparingly
Pour several drops onto palm of hand.
Rub hands together vigorously to create foam.
Rub foam into hair.
Rinse twice.
Process need not be repeated.

Stacey looked up at the girls. "Where did you get this?" she asked.

"In the post," Vanessa replied. She didn't look at Stacey. "Mum and Dad always let us have the samples."

"Last week we got two sticks of chewing gum," added Margo.

"And *you* guys ate them," said Claire accusingly from under her cap of foam.

"So this came in the post today?" said Stacey.

Margo and Vanessa nodded.

"I hate to ask, but how much did you use?"

"The whole bottle," said Vanessa. "We felt bad for taking all the gum. So we gave

Claire the shampoo."

"Oh, Va*ness*a." Stacey was irritated and couldn't hide it. "You're old enough to know you're supposed to read the directions first. Didn't you look at the label?"

Vanessa hung her head. "No," she murmured.

Stacey realized she ought to see what Nicky was up to. She got to her feet. "I want you two to stay here and keep rinsing. I have to check on Nicky. I'll be right back. Be nice to your sister."

Stacey went downstairs, partly to calm down. That, of course, was when she discovered that Nicky had gone. Forty-five minutes later, Claire still had a head of foam, and Nicky still hadn't returned.

Stacey called me. I was at home alone and had been hearing one strange sound after another coming from the secret passage. I was delighted to give Stacey a hand. I couldn't wait to get out of my house.

"Oh, *thank* you for coming!" Stacey exclaimed when I reached the Pikes'. "Mrs Pike is going to be home in about fifteen minutes, and I have two disasters here. Can you look for Nicky? I better stay with the mess in the bathroom."

It was getting to be a familiar scene. I walked around our neighbourhood calling Nicky at the top of my lungs. He didn't answer. I looked behind bushes and up trees. He was a champion hider.

I had just reached the edge of my property when once again, Nicky appeared suddenly. He was dusty, and a vaguely familiar odour clung to him, but I couldn't quite place it.

"Hi," he said. "Looking for me?" He flashed me a grin, then went on chewing away at an enormous wad of gum.

"Nicky! Where have you been? Stacey was worried."

Nicky wet his hand and rubbed at a scab on his knee. Then he blew a large bubble that popped, leaving wispy pink strings all over his face. But he didn't answer me.

"You are an absolute mess," I told him. "You're filthy."

"Yeah," he said, sounding pleased.

I shook my head. "Come on. I'll walk you back to your house. Your mum'll be home any minute now."

"Okay." Unexpectedly, Nicky slipped his hand into mine as we walked along. It was dirty, sticky, and wet, but I held on to it.

When we reached his front door, I opened it and called inside to Stacey. Then I left. I didn't think it would look good for me to be there when Mrs Pike returned.

Stacey was relieved to see Nicky, but Vanessa wasn't. She was in a bad mood. Stacey had said that she would have to tell her mother what she and Margo had done.

"Why isn't Nicky in trouble, too?" she demanded.

Before Stacey could answer, Nicky broke in, "Oh, you're just jealous! You wish *you* had a dog friend who could rescue people from avalanches."

"A dog friend! What are you talking about? You don't have any dog friend," scoffed Vanessa.

"Do too!"

"Do not!"

"Stop it, you guys!" ordered Stacey.

I wasn't around to hear any of that, but if I had been, it might have helped me out. As it was, an idea was growing in my mind. Just a little one. A sprout. Just enough to make me think I wouldn't have to worry about sounds in the passage again that day.

As it turned out, I was right.

13th CHAPTER

There were no more sounds in the secret passage that afternoon. I even felt brave enough to explore it again. I propped the wall open in my room and entered, carrying a torch. I walked purposefully to the spot where I'd found the book the day Mary Anne had been over. I wished I hadn't left it there. I wanted to get a good look at it. But it was gone.

I sighed.

Then I checked out the rest of the passage. The nickel was still gone, the peanut shells were still there, and a crust of bread had turned up. I didn't feel too surprised.

At least – not until I found the key. It was similar to the one I'd found before, but smaller. And a lot older looking. It was shoved into a corner at the bottom of the steps.

It almost ruined my theory.

I left it where it was and tried not to think about it.

I wanted to test my theory, but I didn't have a chance for two whole days. They were the longest days of my life. During that time, the passage was quiet except for very late one night when we had some rain. Then I heard definite moaning coming from the passage. Even though my wall was locked, I grabbed my pillow and blanket and spent the rest of the night on the couch in the living room.

The next day, I had a sitting job at the Pikes'. Mrs Pike was taking Claire, Margo and Vanessa to get their hair cut before school started. (Claire's hair hadn't looked quite the same since her sisters had washed it with Calladew's.) Mallory and I were left in charge of Nicky and the triplets.

The afternoon got off to a good start. For once, the triplets allowed Nicky to play with them. The four boys tore around on their drive playing basketball. They'd split into teams – the triplets against Nicky – but Nicky seemed satisfied.

"What should we make for lunch?" I asked Mallory.

It was late for lunch, but Mrs Pike had had a hectic morning and hadn't got around to giving the kids lunch. She was going to feed the girls while they were out. (This probably happens a lot when you have eight children.)

"Let's do a smorgasbord," said Mallory.

"How?" I asked.

"It's simple. We take everything out of the fridge, put it on the table, and let the boys fix whatever they want."

I laughed. "It sounds messy."

"It is," agreed Mallory, "but it's fun. And Mum likes us to use up leftovers."

I looked inside the fridge. Then I looked back at Mallory. "Okay," I said. "Let's do it."

We only needed about two minutes to pull everything out of the fridge and arrange it on the kitchen table. Then we set out plates, cups, napkins, and forks, and called the boys inside.

"All *right!*" cried Jordan when he got a look at the kitchen.

"Yeah!" exclaimed Nicky. "All *right!* We're having a schmurgerbeard!"

"That's smorgasbord, stupid," said one of the triplets.

"Don't call Nicky stupid," I said.

Nobody even heard me.

Adam was glopping mayonnaise on to a piece of bread.

Byron was digging into the peanut butter with one hand, and eating a pickle with the other.

And Jordan was standing at the stove, turning the flame up under a frying pan.

"Jordan! What are you doing?" I cried.

"Making fried baloney."

"Well, let me do that."

I was beginning to think that the schmurgerbeard hadn't been such a good idea. "Does anyone else want fried baloney?" I asked.

"I want fried peanut butter and jelly," replied Byron.

"I want a fried egg," replied Adam.

"I want fried sick," replied Nicky.

"Ha, ha. So funny I forgot to laugh," said Jordan.

The triplets looked at each other, smirking.

"Hey, Nicky," said Adam, "say Mark Twain's initials and point to your head."

"Oh, simple," said Nicky. He pointed to his left ear. "M.T."

The triplets doubled over with laughter.

"M.T. Empty!" hooted Adam. "Get it? You've got nothing in your head, Nicky. Not one little brain. It's empty."

"Ha, ha. So funny I forgot to laugh," said Nicky.

I thought his comeback was pretty good, considering, but the triplets barely heard him.

"Come on now," I said. "Who wants fried what?"

After much debate, I made fried baloney for Jordan and Adam, and a fried peanut butter and jam sandwich for Byron. Nicky said he wasn't hungry, but finally fixed himself a crisp and banana sandwich. I started to say something to him about that, and then remembered that the Pike kids are allowed to eat whatever they want (within reason). Mallory made tuna sandwiches for the two of us.

We carried our lunches to the table on the sun porch. Everything was peaceful until the very end of the meal. Nicky, who had been silent since the Mark Twain incident, stood up and stacked his glass on his plate.

"Here, Nicky. You want the rest of this cupcake?" asked Adam, holding out half of a gooey chocolate concoction. He must have been having an attack of conscience.

"Sure," said Nicky, flattered. He set his plate down.

As he did so, Adam reached behind him and pulled his chair out from under him.

Nicky sat down hard on the floor.

"Adam!" I shouted. The triplets knew I was angry, but they couldn't help laughing silently, their faces turning red and their eyes filling with tears of laughter.

Nicky sat on the floor for a moment, looking surprised. Then he scrambled to his feet and ran off the porch. A second later, the front door slammed.

I counted to ten before I opened my mouth. Then I said very quietly. "You three are in major trouble."

The laughter stopped.

"You've been rotten to Nicky today. Really rotten. I'm going to have to tell your mother about this."

"Aw –" began Jordan.

"Nope!" I cried. "I don't want to hear a word about it. Right now I'm going to look for your brother. Mallory will be in charge. I want to see the porch and the kitchen sparkling by the time I get back. And if you give Mallory any trouble, your mother will hear about that, too."

I marched out of the Pikes' house. The triplets had rarely seen me angry. That's because I rarely *get* angry. Sometimes I pout or feel cross, but I don't often scold. And I had never scolded the Pikes. I felt kind of bad about it, but the triplets had really been mean to Nicky. I hoped Mallory knew I wasn't angry at her. Oh, well. I'd straighten everything out when I got back.

As I ran down the street, my anger began to turn to excitement. I realized that I was finally going to have the chance to test my theory!

I didn't bother to call for Nicky. I ran right to my own house, darted across the lawn, around to the back, and into the barn. I paused to let my eyes adjust to the dim light.

Just as I expected, the bale of hay that Mum had shoved over the trapdoor had been moved aside. In fact, the trapdoor itself was open. I drew in my breath and stepped boldly down the ladder.

"Nicky?" I called, but my voice was no higher than a whisper.

I jumped down the last two rungs.

That was when I realized I didn't even have a torch. If Nicky wasn't going to answer me, then I'd have to go after him. I ran into our kitchen, found a torch and ran back out to the barn.

"Nicky!" I called again as I lowered myself through the trapdoor.

I thought I could hear heavy breathing, but when I shone the light around I saw nothing but darkness. An awful thought struck me then: what if I was wrong? What if it wasn't Nicky in the passage? What if it was *Jared*?

The thought scared me so that I climbed all the way back up the ladder and sat down on the bale of hay.

I considered calling my mother.

I considered calling Mary Anne.

I considered calling the police.

But I didn't call any of them. I wanted to solve the mystery. I turned over the evidence and the clues I had gathered:

I had found some very old things in the secret passage. They looked like they had been there for years. I had kept them.

I had seen some things in the passage that had later disappeared.

Some other things had appeared in the passage and stayed there (like the peanut shells and the bread crust).

I had heard *tons* of strange noises coming from the passage. I'd heard a lot of them during the day, but I'd heard some of them in the dead of night.

Nicky might be in the passage now . . . and he might not. I decided to take a chance.

I eased myself through the trapdoor again and jumped on to the dirt floor. Now *there* was something that had always bothered me. Why was the dirt floor so hard-packed? Simple, I answered myself. Because it had been walked on a lot, even before I found it. Someone had been using the passage frequently – and it wasn't Jared, since ghosts don't weigh anything.

I took a deep breath and marched forward.

"Nicky!" I called. "I'm coming after you right now."

I heard footsteps then, far down the passage. With a pounding heart, I followed them.

14th CHAPTER

The footsteps began to run, and I ran after them.

The footsteps thumped up the stairs. I thumped after them.

Then I turned the corner and shone the light ahead of me to the end of the passage.

Crouched in one corner was a small figure.

"Nicky!" I exclaimed. "So it *is* you, after all."

Nicky didn't answer. I ran to him.

"Nicky?" I said again.

"Oh, *Dawn*!" he burst out. "Why'd you have to find me?"

"Is this your secret place? Is this where you go when you disappear?"

He nodded. "Well, not *right* here. Usually I stop when I get to the stairs. I mean, this is your house. I didn't want to trespass or anything . . . We are somewhere inside your house aren't we?"

"Yeah. You don't know where the passage ends up?"

"Just in this dead end, I thought."

"Nope. Not quite. I'll show you." I was pretty sure my wall was unlocked, so I released the catch.

Nicky watched wide-eyed as the wall in front of him began to move back. Through the opening, my bedspread appeared, then the dresser, the curtains, and the armchair. Nicky found himself practically in my room.

He stood up and peered inside, then looked back at me. "Whoa . . ."

"My bedroom," I said. "Come on in."

Nicky followed me inside. I showed him how the wall closed up.

"You can't even see a crack!" he exclaimed.

"I know," I said. "I looked for a secret passage in the house forever, and I never found this."

"I found the other end really easily," said Nicky in a small voice.

Nicky looked completely out of place in my bedroom. He was dirty and dusty (so was I, for that matter, but only slightly), he had chocolate cake mashed on one arm, and his cheeks were streaked with tears. Messy as he was, he was sitting on my clean white bedspread. I didn't care, though.

"You want to tell me about it, Nicky?"

He shrugged.

"How d'you find the other end?"

Nicky sighed. "One day Adam kept teasing me about this book I was reading. So I took the book – "

"Was it *Great Dog Tales?*" I interrupted.

"How did you know?"

"I saw it in the passage once. You must have left it there."

"Oh. Well, anyway, I took the book and I ran away. I didn't break the two-block rule, Dawn. I swear I didn't. The back of your barn is exactly two blocks from the front of our house. I didn't know if any of you guys were home, but I didn't think you used the barn, so I sneaked inside. It's so quiet in there."

"I know."

"And I was looking for a place to read when I found the trapdoor instead. I opened it up and climbed down the ladder. And that's how I found the passage."

"And you started coming back?" I prompted him.

"Yeah. I kept a torch buried under some hay near the trapdoor, and I could go in the passage and think of mean things to say to the triplets or read or look at my coin collection."

"Your coin collection? Oh, boy, I have about a million questions to ask you."

"You do?" Nicky looked puzzled.

"Yeah. See, I thought the secret passage had a ghost."

"A *ghost*?" Nicky shrieked. "I've been going some place where there's a ghost."

"No, silly," I said. "*You* were the ghost."

"Oh."

"I mean, I *think* you were. Do you have an Indian-head nickel in your coin collection?"

"Yeah."

"Did you lose it?"

"Yup. But I found it again.

"I found it too." I told him about the stormy night and the Trip-Man.

Nicky laughed.

"Did you ever bring snacks over here?" I asked.

"Lots of times," he replied. "Once I even brought an ice-cream cone. An ice-cream van drove by just as I got to the barn. So I bought a cone. It was called a Fancy Old-Fashioned Ice-Cream Parlour Cone and it cost a whole dollar."

"I found the end of the cone," I told him. "And some other things."

"Sorry," said Nicky. "I guess I didn't clean up too good."

"Too *well*," I corrected him, "and you cleaned up very well. I only found a couple of things. I thought the ghost had a sweet tooth."

Nicky giggled. "I was here just this morning eating peanuts. That's why I wasn't hungry for lunch," he confessed. "You know," he went on, "now that I know you used the passage, you answered a question for me."

"What's that?"

"I used to see these old things in the passage."

"A key, a buckle, and a button," I said.

"Yes. Did you take them? I couldn't figure out what happened to them."

"I took them," I said. "They're in my drawer. Where'd you get that other key, though?"

"What other key?"

"The *really* old one. The one at the bottom of the steps."

"I've never seen another key," replied Nicky. "So it can't be mine."

"Are you *sure*? I know it wasn't there a few days ago."

"It isn't mine. Honest."

"I believe you," I said, my skin crawling. If the key wasn't mine and it wasn't Nicky's, whose was it? Jared's?

"What's the matter, Dawn?" asked Nicky.

I shivered. "Nothing . . . I'm sorry I ruined your secret hiding place."

"That's okay," replied Nicky, but he didn't sound as if it were okay at all.

"I don't mind that you were coming to our passageway, Nicky," I told him. "I really don't. But you do know that it wasn't *quite* right, don't you?"

Nicky looked worried. "What?"

"Well," I said, "technically, I suppose you were trespassing, but that's not what I mean. What I mean is that, for one thing, you scared me. You made noises when you were in the passage. That was another reason I thought we had a ghost."

"I didn't mean to make any noise."

"I know you didn't. By the way, did you ever hide in the passage at night?"

"At night?" exclaimed Nicky. "No way."

"I didn't think so." I tried not to start shivering again. Who had been moaning and creaking around the passage during the night-time thunderstorms?

"I'm sorry I scared you," said Nicky.

"It's okay. Really. Let's go back to your house. Your mum's going to be home soon."

"All right." Nicky looked as if I were going to lead him into a pit of vipers.

We left my house and headed back to the Pikes'. "Another thing," I added as we walked along. "I don't know how safe the passage is. Those stairs are old. So's the trapdoor." Nicky nodded glumly.

"Last thing," I said. "When your mother made up the two-block rule for you, I don't think she meant for you to go someplace where no one could find you. That's just not a good idea. Okay?"

"Okay."

"I took Nicky's hand. "Hey," I said.

"Look at that. Your mum has beaten us home. Let's go and tell her about your adventure."

Mrs Pike had been surprised, to say the least, when she had come back and found that I wasn't there, but I explained the whole story to her, including the triplets' pranks. Mallory, luckily, had done just fine with her brothers. While I was chasing after Nicky, she had got them to clean up lunch and then had settled them into a game of Monopoly. They were extremely quiet and well-behaved when I returned. I was really impressed with Mallory.

Mrs Pike and Nicky and I had a talk before I went home.

"I *need* a hideout," Nicky said, sounding the way people do when they talk about very important things, like food or money.

"I understand that, sweetie," said Mrs Pike.

"Well," I spoke up, "I'll have to check with my mum, but it's all right with me if Nicky comes back to our passage."

"It's all right with me, too," said Mrs Pike after a moment, "as long as you tell an adult where you're going first, Nicky. And maybe someone should check the condition of the passage."

"Yippee!" cried Nicky. "I just hope the triplets don't start going there."

"Believe me, they won't," said his mother.

"How do you know?" said Nicky.

"Because I'm about to have a little talk with them."

Nicky turned to me, all smiles. "You," he said, "are my favourite baby-sitter in the whole wide world."

15th CHAPTER

"So what movie do you guys want to watch?" I asked.

"*Ghostbusters,*" said Kristy.

"*Star Wars,*" said Claudia.

"*Mary Poppins,*" said Stacey.

"*Sixteen Candles,*" said Mary Anne.

"And I want to watch *The Parent Trap,*" I said, looking woefully at the video.

It was Saturday night. The members of the Babysitters Club were crowded into my living room. We were having a pyjama party. Upstairs, sleeping bags were spread over every centimetre of the floor of my bedroom. The bathroom was a disaster area. It looked like a make-up tornado had ripped through it. (But our faces looked great. Stacey and Claudia had practised on all of us.) We had finished supper, and now we were settling in for a long night in front of the video.

"Maybe we could watch all of them," suggested Claudia.

"Well," I said, "let's see. If each one is about two hours long –"

"*Mary Poppins* is longer, I think," said Stacey.

"But *Sixteen Candles* is shorter," Mary Anne pointed out.

"An *average*," I said. "Just an *average*. What I was going to say is that that comes to about ten hours of movies. It's nine o'clock now. That would take us right up to seven in the morning."

We laughed.

"Let's pick two," I said. "We'll vote on them."

Everyone voted for the movie she had suggested plus one other. We ended up with a five-way tie. In the end, Kristy drew two of the movies out of a hat. (After all, she's the club chairman.) The winners were *Sixteen Candles* and *Ghostbusters*.

Mary Anne was jubilant. She'd brought two copies of *Sixteen* magazine with her, and there was an article about Cam Geary, the love of her life, in it. Cam Geary and *Sixteen Candles* created a really prime evening for Mary Anne.

We watched *Ghostbusters* first. Much as I like *The Parent Trap*, I have to admit that *Ghostbusters* is pretty funny. My favourite part is when that giant marshmallow guy bursts. I think it's Kristy's favourite part, too. As soon as he exploded, she said. "I'm starving! Let's toast marshmallows, Dawn. Or make s'mores."

"Kristy, we don't have stuff like that at my house. It's junk food."

Kristy and Claudia glanced at each other. "Be right back," they said, and ran upstairs.

They returned holding a bag of marshmallows, some chocolate, a box of biscuits, a bag of crisps, a supply of smarties and some nuts.

"Pig-out time!" said Kristy. "I hope you don't mind, Dawn. We can't have a pyjama party without this stuff. It isn't normal." She tossed the nuts to me. "Those are for you and Stacey," she said.

Stacey and I looked at each other. We made faces. But then we couldn't help laughing. It *was* kind of funny.

"Where'd you get all that?" I asked.

"Mary Anne and Claudia and I bought it this afternoon," said Kristy. "We thought it might be a good idea to come prepared. Don't worry, we paid for it ourselves, not out of the club treasury."

Kristy pressed the pause button the video and Bill Murray froze in action. "Quick! Let's make the s'mores before the movie comes back on!" she cried.

Kristy grabbed the marshmallows.

Mary Anne grabbed the biscuits.

Claudia grabbed the chocolate bars.

The three of them tore off, leaving Stacey

and me behind in a trail of dust (so to spea

"Boy," I said, "Just because we don't ea that junk of theirs."

"Really," agreed Stacey. "I feel like a leper."

"*I* feel like a nerd."

"We shouldn't, though," said Stacey. "They're the ones who're going to end up with spots."

I giggled. "Let's get them."

"Spots?"

"*No!* I mean, I have a plan. We'll get back at Kristy and the others. Remember our search for a secret passage?"

Stacey nodded.

"Well, I found one."

"No."

"Yup."

"Honest?"

"Cross my heart. So here's what I think we should do."

I leaned over and began to whisper to Stacey. We had just finished planning, when Kristy and Claudia and Mary Anne came back. They were eating these gooey concoctions and had chocolate all over their fingers. Every time they took a bite of their s'mores, the melted marshmallow would string out between their mouths and hands.

Stacey and I had a hard time keeping straight faces. Somehow, though, we made it through the rest of *Ghostbusters* without giving anything away.

As soon as the movie was over, Mary Anne dived for the rewind button. "Time for *Sixteen Candles,*" she said.

"Why don't we watch it later?" I suggested casually. "Wouldn't it be fun to watch it at, like, one or two this morning?"

"Yeah!" said Kristy enthusiastically. (I knew I could count on her. She loves to stay up late.)

Mary Anne looked disappointed, but she didn't want to argue with the rest of us.

"Let's go up to my room for a while," I said. "You know Cam Geary's girlfriend, Mary Anne?"

"Corrie Lalique?" she replied immediately.

"Yeah. I bet with a little more make-up I could make you look just like her."

"Really? Oh, hey, great!"

Mary Anne was the first one upstairs. The rest of us followed. After we'd worked on her for a while, I said, "Boy, am I thirsty."

"Oh, me, too," chimed in Stacey.

"So am I," said the others at once. (It figured, after all that sugar.)

"I'll go and get some lemonade," I said. "Come with me, Stace. Okay?"

"You have lemonade?" asked Claudia sceptically. "Or do you mean Perrier or sparkling, saltless mineral water from an artesian well or something?"

I tried not to sound sarcastic. "Yes, we have lemonade. Real lemonade. Mum bought it for the party. One hundred percent sugar."

"Good," said Claudia, not cracking a smile.

"Come on, Stace."

We ran downstairs. It was time to put our plan into action.

"What's your mum going to say?" asked Stacey nervously.

"Nothing," I replied. "I warned her when we went upstairs before. And Jeff's already in bed, so we don't have to worry about him. Unless the screaming gets too loud."

Stacey laughed. She and I stopped in the kitchen for torches. We turned them on, aimed the beams out the back door, and crept outside as quietly as possible. I led Stacey into the barn, shoved aside the bale of hay, and showed her the trapdoor. We lowered ourselves down the ladder.

"I don't believe it," whispered Stacey slowly. "This is great."

"Are you scared?" I asked. I hadn't told her about Jared Mullray.

"Not really. I'm not wild about the dark, but . . . let's go!"

When we'd climbed the flight of stairs and turned the corner, we paused to listen. Very faintly we could hear the voices of Mary Anne, Claudia, and Kristy.

"Now?" whispered Stacey.

"Now," I replied. "And when they've had enough, just follow me."

"Okay."

Stacey rapped lightly on a wall of the passage. I scratched on another.

We paused. The girls were still talking.

"Louder," I whispered.

We rapped and scratched more loudly. The talking stopped, then started again.

"Closer," I suggested.

We crept down the passage. Our friends' voices grew louder.

Rap, rap. Rap, rap, rap.

Scritch, scratch.

Then I distinctly heard Claudia say, "Did you guys hear something?"

Stacey and I tried not to laugh.

"Try wailing," said Stacey.

"Oooooo-eeeeee. Heeeeeelp meeeeee!" I wailed.

"Whoooooo-oooooo-eeeeee. I caaaaaannot reeeeeest!" cried Stacey. It was a brilliant choice of words.

"Aughh!" cried one of the girls in my room, but I couldn't tell which one.

"Oh, no! It's Jared! It's the ghost of the secret passage!" yelped Mary Anne.

"What?" asked Kristy. "What ghost?" (She was probably thinking of old Ben Brewer.)

"What secret passage?" added Claudia.

Rap, rap, rap. Bang, bang, bang.

I noticed a pipe, and tapped my torch on it. *Clink clink.*

"Aughh!" The shrieking in the bedroom sounded more frightened. We heard a crash.

"I think that's enough," I said. "Come on."

I dashed to the end of the passage and released the catch. The wall of my bedroom slowly opened inward.

Stacey and I were looking in on a disaster area. A chair had been knocked over. A container of eye shadow was on the rug. The sleeping bags were rumpled, as if they'd been run over by galloping horses. And Kristy, Claudia, and Mary Anne were huddled on my bed.

"I told you it was the ghost," Mary Anne was moaning.

Then Stacey and I stuck our heads in the room. When Kristy saw us, she fell off the bed.

There was a moment of silence.

"You!" shrieked Mary Anne. "It was *you*!'

"You stinkers!" Kristy exploded, rubbing one elbow. She got to her feet.

Stacey and I laughed so hard that tears ran down our faces. We couldn't speak. We dropped our torches on the bed and I closed the wall behind me.

"You found a secret passage," was all Claudia could say. "How?"

I explained. I told my friends the story – Nicky, Jared Mullray, the nickel. But I left out the parts about the small key, and the night-time noises.

"Oh, let's go inside!" exclaimed Claudia. "Please? I've never been in a true secret passage. And I've always wanted to have the chance."

"Okay," I said. "Sure. We'll all go."

I was reaching for the wall when . . .

Rap, rap, rap.

It had come from the passage. Wide-eyed, I whirled around. All four of my friends were behind me. I dashed out of my room. Mum was reading in bed. Jeff was sound asleep.

I looked at my watch. Almost one o'clock. It wasn't Nicky.

In a panic, I went to my room and fastened the lock on the wall. "Come on, you guys. Bring your sleeping bags. We'll stay in the living room tonight."

And we did. But it took us forever to fall asleep.

Did my secret passage have a ghost? I hoped I'd never find out.

The next morning dawned clear and sunny. I was wakened by the sound of a lark outside the open window. The scent of newly mown grass drifted in and mingled with the smells of toast and eggs coming from the kitchen.

I rolled over sleepily.

"Hi," whispered Kristy from her sleeping bag.

"Morning," I replied.

Stacey, Claudia, and Mary Anne were still asleep.

"You know," said Kristy, "we only have a few, and I mean a *few*, more days until school starts again."

I made a face. "I know."

"We'd better use them wisely."

"What do you mean?"

"Well, we've just had a pyjama party. While there's still time, we'd better try to cram in a few more good activities. Like swimming."

"Going to the movies," I said.

"Having a gossip-fest."

"Lying around in the sun reading magazines."

"Playing tennis."

"Swinging on the rope in the barn."

"Going to the mall," murmured Stacey, without bothering to open her eyes.

"Making s'more s'mores," mumbled Claudia.

"Having a barbecue," said Mary Anne, only her face was buried in her pillow and it sounded like she said, "Havee a fuh-fow."

"Boy," I explained, "we've got a lot to do and very little time. We'd better get going!"

I felt excited, exhilarated. With friends

like these, and so much to look forward to, who could worry about a crazy two hundred-year-old guy named Jared Mullray? Not me!